Edexcel IGCSE
Physics

Student Book

(134)

Brian Arnold, Steve Woolley, Penny Johnson

A PEARSON COMPANY

Published by Pearson Education Limited, a company incorporated in England and Wales, having its registered office at Edinburgh Gate, Harlow, Essex, CM20 2JE. Registered company number: 872828

www.pearsonschoolsandfecolleges.co.uk

Edexcel is a registered trade mark of Edexcel Limited

Text © Brian Arnold, Steve Woolley and Penny Johnson, 2009

This edition first published 2009

13 12 11

10 9 8 7

ISBN 978 0 435966 90 4

Designed by Richard Ponsford

Typeset by H L Studios

Cover design by Creative Monkey

Cover photo © Getty Images/Peter Dazeley

Printed in China (SWTC/07)

Acknowledgements

We are grateful to the following for permission to reproduce photographs:

l = left, r = right, c = centre, t = top, b = bottom

1tr & bc Getty Images; 1bl MGM/PATHE/The Kobal Collection; 1br NASA; 4l Alvey and Towers Picture Library; 4c David Brownell, photographers_direct.com; 4r Peter Gould; 12tl Getty Images; 12tr, bl & bc Alvey and Towers Picture Library; 12br Richard Stonehouse/Camera Press Ltd; 14tl, tr Getty Images; 14br 'Photos for Books'; 16tl © John Henley/Corbis, photographers_direct.com; 16tr, bl PA Photos; 16br Sporting Pictures (UK) Ltd; 18l © George B. Diebold/Corbis; 19 Science Photo Library; 23 © Peter Turnley/Corbis; 26t Peter Gould; 26b Alvey and Towers Picture Library; 28 Peter Gould; 30 Getty Images; 34 Andrew Lambert Photography – Science Photo Library; 38 © Tim Wright/Corbis; 42l Dorling Kindersley; 42r Leslie Garland Picture Library; Digital Vision; 50 NASA/ESA/STSCI/R.Beebe, New Mexico State U./Science Photo Library; 51t NASA/ JPL/ Cornell/ Texas A&M; 51c NASA / Lunar and Planetary Institute; 51br Digital Vision; 55 NASA Images / Alamy; 59t © Peter Frischmuth/Still Pictures; 59b DIY Photo Library; 60l Ecoscene/Anthony Cooper, photographers_direct.com; 60r Frank Tschakert, photographers_direct.com; 63t Education Photos/John Walmsley; 66 Keith Kent/Science Photo Library; 67 Peter Menzel/Science Photo Library; 75 Steve Woolley; 76 bl Steve Woolley; 76br Philip Harris Education; 78 The Garden Picture Library/Alamy; 84t, bl & br Steve Woolley; 91l Getty Images; 91r Alvey and Towers Picture Library; 95 NASA; 99t © Yoav Levy/Phototake/ Robert Harding Picture Library; 99b David Parker/Science Photo Library; 102t www.shoutpictures.com; 102b Action Plus; 103 Alexander Tsiaris/ Science Photo Library; 104l Getty Images; 104r © Don Mason Photography/ Corbis; 107 Western Ophthalmic Hospital/Science Photo Library; 108 Alvey and Towers Picture Library; 109 Getty Images; 114 Comstock Images; 118 © Christina Radish/Redferns; 121 © Jon Feingersh/Corbis; 123l & r Getty Images; 124t © Bob Winsett/Corbis; 124b Bruel and Kjaer; 127tl, tr, bl & br Getty Images; 133tl Getty Images; 133tr © Karen Huntt/Corbis; 133c Imagestate/Alamy; 134tl Dorling Kindersley; 134br Dorling Kindersley; 136t Dr Ray Clarke & Mervyn Goff/Science Photo Library; 136bl www.shoutpictures.com; 136bc Gail Mooney/Corbis; 136br Sheila Terry/Science Photo Library; 137l Ray Gordon/Fogstock/Alamy; 137r Steve Woolley; 139 © Farrell Grehan/Corbis; 140 Alain Torterotot/Still Pictures; 142 Science Photo Library; 145l Francois Gohier/Science Photo Library; 145r Tony & Daphne Hallas/Science Photo Library; 147 Science Photo Library; 150tl © Michael S. Yamashita/Corbis; 150bl Dorling Kindersley; 150r PA Photos; 151l Kaj R. Svensson/Science Photo Library; 151c Astrid & Hans Frieder Michler/Science Photo Library; 151r John Kaprielian/Science Photo Library; 152 Science Photo Library; 154tl Bryan Pickering/Eye Ubiquitous; 154tr Bernhard Edmaier/Science Photo Library; 154b Martin Bond/Science Photo Library; 155t Canyon Industries, Inc; 155c © Paul Thompson/Ecoscene/Corbis; 155b Allan Wright/Still Moving Picture Company; 156l NASA; 156c Peter Bowater/Alamy; 156r © Edifice/Corbis; 157 Ecoscene/Peter Hulme, photographers_direct.com; 162tl Imagestate/ Alamy; 162bl © Chris McLaughlin/Corbis; 162r © Galen Rowell/Corbis; 164l SOA Photo Agency/Meffert/Stein; 164r © Chris Anderson/IPNSTOCK, photographers_direct.com; 165 Mary Evans Picture Library; 171 By courtesy of the National Portrait Gallery; 172 Steve Woolley; 179 Alex Bartel/Science Photo Library; 184 Fredredhat @ stockxpert.com; 187 Petr Svarc/Alamy; 189t Dorling Kindersley; 189b Alvey and Towers Picture Library; 192 Peter Bowater/Alamy; 194 Matthew Nowell; 209 Jean-Loup Charmet/Science Photo Library; 216t CNRI/Science Photo Library; 216b Catherine Pouedras/ Eurelios/Science Photo Library; 217 www.mediscan.co.uk; 218 TWI Ltd, Cambridge; 223t Steve Woolley; 223b Will & Deni McIntyre/Science Photo Library; 226 Getty Images.

All other photographs by Trevor Clifford

Picture research by Anne Lyons; Sandie Huskinson-Rolfe, PHOTOSEEKERS; Sally Turner

Websites

The websites used in this book were correct and up to date at the time of publication. It is essential for tutors to preview each website before using it in class so as to ensure that the URL is still accurate, relevant and appropriate. We suggest that tutors bookmark useful websites and consider enabling students to access them through the school/college intranet.

Disclaimer

This Edexcel publication offers high-quality support for the delivery of Edexcel qualifications.

Edexcel endorsement does not mean that this material is essential to achieve any Edexcel qualification, nor does it mean that this is the only suitable material available to support any Edexcel qualification. No endorsed material will be used verbatim in setting any Edexcel examination/assessment and any resource lists produced by Edexcel shall include this and other appropriate texts.

Copies of official specifications for all Edexcel qualifications may be found on the Edexcel website, www.edexcel.com

Contents

About this **book**

This book has several features to help you with IGCSE Physics.

Introduction

Each chapter has a short introduction to help you start thinking about the topic and let you know what is in the chapter.

End of chapter checklists

These lists summarise the material in the chapter. They could also help you to make revision notes because they form a list of things that you need to revise.

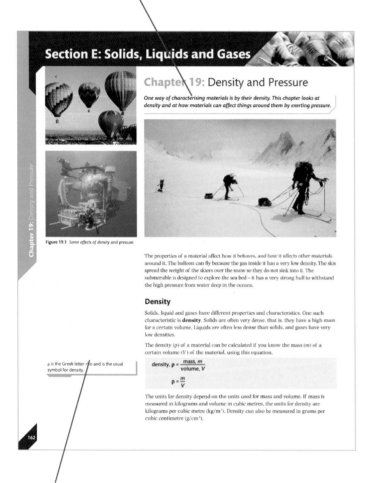

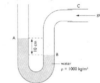

Margin boxes

The boxes in the margin give you extra help or information. They might explain something in a little more detail or guide you to linked topics in other parts of the book.

Questions

There are short questions at the end of each chapter. These help you to test your understanding of the material from the chapter. Some of them may also be research questions – you will need to use the internet and other books to answer these.

There are also questions at the end of each section. The end of section questions are written in an exam style and cover topics from all the chapters in the section.

Chapter 1: Movement and Position

It is very useful to be able to make predictions about the way moving objects behave. In this chapter you will learn about some equations of motion that can be used to calculate the speed and acceleration of objects, and the distances they travel in a certain time.

Figure 1.1 *The world is full of speeding objects.*

Speed is a term that is used a great deal in everyday life. Action films often feature high-speed chases. Speed is a cause of fatal accidents on the road. Sprinters strive for greater speed in competition with other athletes. Rockets must reach a high-enough speed to put communications satellites in orbit around the Earth. This chapter will explain how speed is defined and measured and how distance–time graphs are used to show the movement of an object as time passes. We shall then look at changing speed – acceleration and deceleration. We shall use velocity–time graphs to find the acceleration of an object. We shall also find how far an object has travelled using its velocity–time graph. You will find out about the difference between speed and velocity on page 4.

Speed

If you were told that a car travelled 100 kilometres in 2 hours you would probably have no difficulty in working out that the speed (or strictly speaking the *average* speed – see page 2) of the car was 50 km/h. You would have done a simple calculation using the following definition of speed:

$$\text{speed} = \frac{\text{distance travelled}}{\text{time taken}}$$

This is usually written using the symbol *v* for speed or velocity, *d* for distance travelled and *t* for time:

$$v = \frac{d}{t}$$

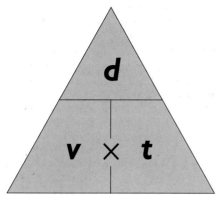

Figure 1.2 *You can use the triangle method for rearranging equations like d = v × t.*

Reminder: To use the triangle method to rearrange an equation, cover up the thing you want to find. For example, in Figure 1.2, if you wanted to work out how long (*t*) it took to travel a distance (*d*) at a given speed (*v*), covering *t* in Figure 1.2 leaves *d/v*, or distance divided by speed. If an examination question asks you to write out the formula for calculating speed, distance or time, always give the actual equation (such as *d = v × t*). You may not get the mark if you just draw the triangle.

Units of speed

Typically the distance travelled might be measured in metres and time taken in seconds, so the speed would be in metres per second (m/s). Other units can be used for speed, such as kilometres per hour (km/h), or centimetres per second (cm/s). In physics the units we use are metric, but you can measure speed in miles per hour (mph). Many cars show speed in both mph and kph (km/h). Exam questions should be in metric units, so remember that m is the abbreviation for *metres* (and *not miles*).

Rearranging the speed equation

The speed equation can be rearranged to give two other useful equations:

distance travelled, d = speed, $v \times$ time taken, t

and

time taken, $t = \dfrac{\text{distance travelled, } d}{\text{speed, } v}$

Average speed

The equation you used to work out the speed of the car, on page 1, gives you the **average speed** of the car during the journey. It is the total distance travelled, divided by the time taken for the journey. If you look at the speedometer in a car you will see that the speed of the car changes from instant to instant as the accelerator or brake is used. The speedometer therefore shows the **instantaneous speed** of the car.

Speed trap!

Suppose you want to find the speed of cars driving down your road. You may have seen the police using speed guns to check that drivers are keeping to the speed limit. Speed guns use microprocessors (computers on a "chip") to produce an instant reading of the speed of a moving vehicle, but you can conduct a very simple experiment to measure car speed.

Measure the distance between two points along a straight section of road with a tape measure or "click" wheel. Use a stopwatch to measure the time taken for a car to travel the measured distance. Figure 1.3 shows you how to operate your "speed trap".

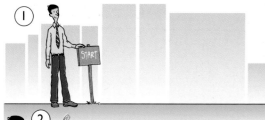
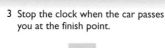

1 Measure 50 m from a start point along the side of the road.

2 Start a stop clock when your partner signals that the car is passing the start point.

3 Stop the clock when the car passes you at the finish point.

Figure 1.3 *Measuring the speed of a car.*

Using the measurements made with your speed trap, you can work out the speed of the car. Use the equation:

$$\text{speed} = \frac{\text{distance travelled}}{\text{time taken}}$$

So, if the time measured is 3.9 s, the speed of the car in this experiment is:

$$\text{speed} = \frac{50\,\text{m}}{3.9\,\text{s}} = 12.8\,\text{m/s}$$

Distance–time graphs

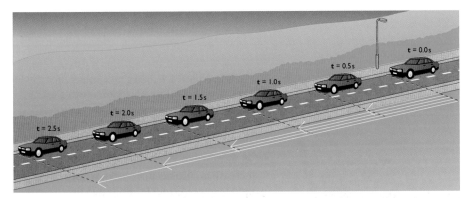

Figure 1.4 *A car travelling at constant speed.*

Figure 1.4 shows a car travelling along a road. It shows the car at 0.5 second intervals. The distances that the car has travelled from the start position after each 0.5 s time interval are marked on the picture. The picture provides a record of how far the car has travelled as time has passed. We can use the information in this sequence of pictures to plot a graph showing the distance travelled against time (Figure 1.5).

Time from start (s)	0.0	0.5	1.0	1.5	2.0	2.5
Distance travelled from start (m)	0.0	6.0	12.0	18.0	24.0	30.0

The **distance–time graph** tells us about how the car is travelling in a much more convenient form than the sequence of drawings in Figure 1.4. We can see that the car is travelling equal distances in equal time intervals – it is moving at a steady or **constant speed**. This fact is shown immediately by the fact that the graph is a *straight line*. The slope or **gradient** of the line tells us the speed of the car – the steeper the line the greater the speed of the car. So, in this example:

$$\text{speed} = \text{gradient} = \frac{\text{distance}}{\text{time}} = \frac{30\,\text{m}}{2.5\,\text{s}} = 12\,\text{m/s}$$

Speed and velocity

Some distance–time graphs look like the one shown in Figure 1.6. It is a straight line, showing that the object is moving with constant speed, but the line is sloping down to the right rather than up to the right. The gradient of such a line is negative

You can convert a speed in m/s into a speed in km/h.
If the car travels 12.8 metres in one second it will travel
    12.8 × 60 metres in 60 seconds (that is, one minute) and
    12.8 × 60 × 60 metres in 60 minutes (that is, 1 hour), which is
    46 080 metres in an hour or 46.1 km/h (to one decimal place).
We have multiplied by 3600 (60 × 60) to convert from m/s to m/h, then divided by 1000 to convert from m/h to km/h (as there are 1000 m in 1 km).
Rule: to convert m/s to km/h simply multiply by 3.6.

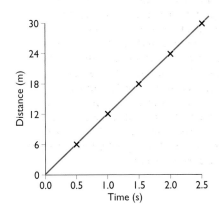

Figure 1.5 *Distance–time graph for the travelling car in Figure 1.4.*

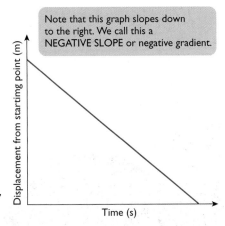

Note that this graph slopes down to the right. We call this a NEGATIVE SLOPE or negative gradient.

Figure 1.6 *In this graph distance is decreasing with time.*

A vector is a quantity that has both size *and* direction. Displacement is distance travelled in a *particular direction*.

Force is another example of a vector. The size of a force *and* the direction in which it acts are both important.

because the distance that the object is from the starting point is now *decreasing* – the object is retracing its path back towards the start. **Displacement** means "distance travelled in a particular direction" from a specified point. So if the object was originally travelling in a northerly direction, the negative gradient of the graph means that it is now travelling south. Displacement is an example of a **vector**.

Velocity is also a vector. Velocity is speed in a particular direction. If a car travels at 50 km/h around a bend its speed is constant but its velocity will be changing for as long as the direction that the car is travelling in is changing.

$$\text{velocity} = \frac{\text{increase in displacement}}{\text{time taken}}$$

Worked example

Example 1

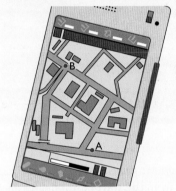

Figure 1.7 *The screen of a global positioning system (GPS). A GPS is an aid to navigation that uses orbiting satellites to locate its position on the Earth's surface.*

The GPS in Figure 1.7 shows two points on a journey. The second point is 3 km north west of the first. If a walker takes 45 minutes to travel from the first point to the second, what is the average velocity of the walker?

Write down what you know:

increase in displacement is 3 km north west
time taken is 45 min (45 min=0.75 h).

Use:

$$\text{velocity} = \frac{\text{increase in displacement}}{\text{time taken}}$$

$$\text{average velocity} = \frac{3\,\text{km}}{0.75\,\text{h}}$$

$$= 4.0 \text{ km/h north west}$$

Acceleration

Figure 1.8 shows some objects whose speed is changing. The plane must accelerate to reach take-off speed. In ice hockey, the puck decelerates only very slowly when it

Figure 1.8 *Acceleration ...*

... constant speed ...

... and deceleration.

slides across the ice. When the egg hits the ground it is forced to decelerate (decrease its speed) very rapidly. Rapid deceleration can have destructive results.

Acceleration is the rate at which objects change their velocity. It is defined as follows:

$$\text{acceleration} = \frac{\text{change in velocity}}{\text{time taken}} \quad \text{or} \quad \frac{\text{final velocity} - \text{initial velocity}}{\text{time taken}}$$

This is written as an equation:

$$a = \frac{(v - u)}{t}$$

where a = acceleration, v = final velocity, u = initial velocity and t = time. (Why u? Simply because it comes before v!)

Acceleration, like velocity, is a vector because the *direction* in which the acceleration occurs is important as well as the size of the acceleration.

Units of acceleration

Velocity is measured in m/s, so increase in velocity is also measured in m/s. Acceleration, the **rate** of increase in velocity with time, is therefore measured in m/s/s (read as "metres per second per second"). We normally write this as m/s^2 (read as "metres per second squared"). Other units may be used – for example, cm/s^2.

Worked example

Example 2

A car is travelling at 20 m/s. It accelerates steadily for 5 s, after which time it is travelling at 30 m/s. What is its acceleration?

Write down what you know:

    initial or starting velocity, u = 20 m/s

    final velocity, v = 30 m/s

    time taken, t = 5 s

Use: $a = \dfrac{v - u}{t}$

$a = \dfrac{30\,\text{m/s} - 20\,\text{m/s}}{5\,\text{s}}$

$a = \dfrac{10\,\text{m/s}}{5\,\text{s}}$

   $= 2\,\text{m/s}^2$

The car is accelerating at $2\,\text{m/s}^2$.

It is good practice to include units in equations – this will help you to supply the answer with the correct unit.

Deceleration

Deceleration means slowing down. This means that a decelerating object will have a smaller final velocity than its starting velocity. If you use the equation for finding the acceleration of an object that is slowing down, the answer will have a negative sign. A negative acceleration simply means deceleration.

Worked example

Example 3

An object strikes the ground travelling at 40 m/s. It is brought to rest in 0.02 s. What is its acceleration?

Write down what you know:

initial velocity, $u = 40$ m/s

final velocity, $v = 0$ m/s

time taken, $t = 0.02$ s

As before, use:

$$a = \frac{v - u}{t}$$

$$a = \frac{0 \text{ m/s} - 40 \text{ m/s}}{0.02 \text{ s}}$$

$$a = \frac{-40 \text{ m/s}}{0.02 \text{ s}}$$

$$= -2000 \text{ m/s}^2$$

So the acceleration is -2000 m/s^2.

In Example 3, we would say that the object is decelerating at 2000 m/s^2. This is a very large deceleration. Later, in Chapter 3, we shall discuss the consequences of such a rapid deceleration!

Measuring acceleration

When a ball is rolled down a slope it is clear that its speed increases as it rolls – that is, it accelerates. Galileo was interested in how and why objects like the ball rolling down a slope speeded up, and he devised an interesting experiment to learn more about acceleration. A version of his experiment is shown in Figure 1.9.

Galileo was an Italian scientist who was born in 1564. He developed a telescope, which he used to study the motion of the planets and other celestial bodies. He also carried out many experiments on motion.

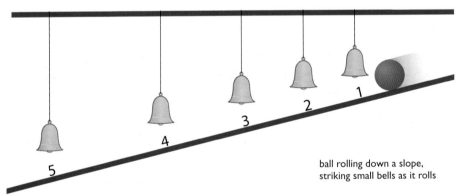

ball rolling down a slope, striking small bells as it rolls

Figure 1.9 *Galileo's experiment.*

Galileo wanted to discover how the distance travelled by a ball depends on the time it has been rolling. In this version of the experiment, a ball rolling down a slope strikes a series of small bells as it rolls. By adjusting the positions of the bells carefully it is possible to make the bells ring at equal intervals of time as the ball passes. Galileo noticed that the distances travelled in equal time intervals increased, showing that the ball was travelling faster as time passed. Galileo did not possess an accurate way of measuring time (there were no digital stopwatches in seventeenth-century Italy!) but it was possible to judge *equal* time intervals accurately simply by listening.

Though Galileo did not have a clockwork timepiece (let alone an electronic timer), he used his pulse and a type of water clock to achieve timings that were accurate enough for his experiments.

Galileo also noticed that the distance travelled by the ball increased in a predictable way. He showed that the rate of increase of speed was steady or uniform. We call this **uniform acceleration**. Most acceleration is non-uniform – that is, it changes from instant to instant – but we shall only deal with uniformly accelerated objects in this chapter.

Velocity–time graphs

The table below shows the distances between the bells in an experiment such as Galileo's.

Bell	1	2	3	4	5
Time (s)	0.5	1.0	1.5	2.0	2.5
Distance of bell from start (cm)	3	12	27	48	75

We can calculate the average speed of the ball between each bell by working out the distance travelled between each bell, and the time it took to travel this distance. For the first bell:

$$\text{velocity} = \frac{\text{distance travelled}}{\text{time taken}}$$

$$= \frac{3\,\text{cm}}{0.5\,\text{seconds}} = 6\,\text{cm/s}$$

This is the average velocity over the 0.5 second time interval, so if we plot it on a graph we should plot it in the middle of the interval, at 0.25 seconds.

Repeating the above calculation for all the results gives us the following table of results. We can use these results to draw a graph showing how the velocity of the ball is changing with time. The graph, shown in Figure 1.10, is called a **velocity–time graph**.

Time (s)	0.25	0.75	1.25	1.75	2.25
Velocity (cm/s)	6	18	30	42	54

The graph in Figure 1.10 is a straight line. This tells us that the velocity of the rolling ball is increasing by equal amounts in equal time periods. We say that the acceleration is uniform in this case.

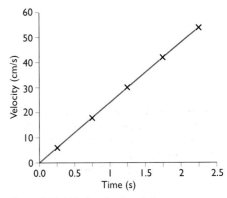

Figure 1.10 *Velocity–time graph for an experiment in which a ball is rolled down a slope. (Note that as we are plotting average velocity, the points are plotted in the middle of each successive 0.5 s time interval.)*

A modern version of Galileo's experiment

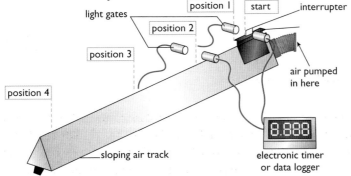

Figure 1.11 *Measuring acceleration.*

Today we can use data loggers to make accurate direct measurements that are collected and manipulated by a computer. A spreadsheet programme can be used to produce a velocity–time graph. Figure 1.11 shows a glider on a slightly sloping air-

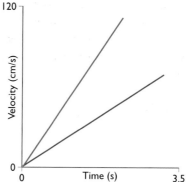

Airtrack at 1.5°		Airtrack at 3.0°	
Time (s)	Av Vel. (cm/s)	Time (s)	Av Vel. (cm/s)
0.00	0.0	0.00	0.0
0.45	11.1	0.32	15.9
1.35	33.3	0.95	47.6
2.25	55.6	1.56	79.4
3.15	77.8	2.21	111.1

Figure 1.12 *Results of two air-track experiments. (Note, once again, that because we are plotting average velocity in the velocity–time graphs, the points are plotted in the middle of each successive time interval.)*

track. The air-track reduces friction because the glider rides on a cushion of air that is pumped continuously through holes along the air-track. As the glider accelerates down the sloping track the white card mounted on it breaks a light beam, and the time that the glider takes to pass is measured electronically. If the length of the card is measured, and this is entered into the spreadsheet, the velocity of the glider can be calculated by the spreadsheet programme using $v = \frac{d}{t}$.

Figure 1.12 shows some velocity–time graphs for two experiments done using the air-track apparatus. In each experiment the track was given a different slope. The steeper the slope of the air-track the greater the glider's acceleration. This is clear from the graphs: the greater the acceleration the steeper the gradient of the graph.

> **The gradient of a velocity–time graph gives the acceleration.**

More about velocity–time graphs

Gradient

The results of the air-track experiments in Figure 1.12 show that the slope of the velocity–time graph depends on the acceleration of the glider. The slope or gradient of a velocity–time graph is found by dividing the increase in the velocity by the time taken for the increase, as shown in Figure 1.13. Increase in velocity divided by time is, you will recall, the definition of acceleration (see page 5), so we can measure the acceleration of an object by finding the slope of its velocity–time graph. The meaning of the slope or gradient of a velocity–time graph is summarised in Figure 1.14.

Area under a velocity–time graph

Tips
1 When finding the gradient of a graph, draw a **big** triangle.
2 Choose a convenient number of units for the length of the base of the triangle to make the division easier.

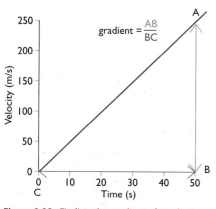

Figure 1.13 *Finding the gradient of a velocity–time graph.*

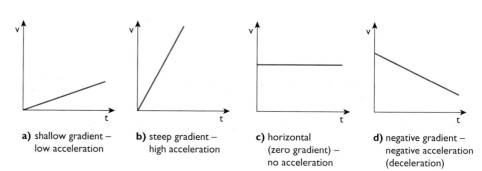

a) shallow gradient – low acceleration

b) steep gradient – high acceleration

c) horizontal (zero gradient) – no acceleration

d) negative gradient – negative acceleration (deceleration)

Figure 1.14 *The gradient of a velocity–time graph gives you information about the motion of an object at a glance.*

Figure 1.15a shows a velocity–time graph for an object that travels with a constant velocity of 5 m/s for 10 s. A simple calculation shows that in this time the object has travelled 50 m. This is equal to the shaded area under the graph. Figure 1.15b shows a velocity–time graph for an object that has accelerated at a constant rate. Its average velocity during this time is given by:

$$\text{average velocity} = \frac{\text{initial velocity} + \text{final velocity}}{2} \text{ or } \frac{u + v}{2}$$

In this example the average velocity is, therefore:

$$\text{average velocity} = \frac{0\,\text{m/s} + 10\,\text{m/s}}{2}$$

which works out to be 5 m/s. If the object travels, on average, 5 metres in each second it will have travelled 20 metres in 4 seconds. Notice that this, too, is equal to the shaded area under the graph (given by the area formula for a triangle: area = $\frac{1}{2}$ base × height).

> The area under a velocity–time graph is equal to the distance travelled by (displacement of) the object in a particular time interval.

Speed investigations using ticker tape

A ticker timer is a machine that makes a series of dots on a paper tape moving through the machine. Most ticker timers used in school physics laboratories make 50 dots each second. If the tape is pulled slowly through the machine, the dots are close together. If the tape is pulled through quickly, the dots are further apart (Figure 1.16).

Ticker tape can be used to investigate speed or acceleration. One end of the ticker tape is fastened to a trolley or air track glider, which pulls the tape through the machine as it moves. The tape can then be cut up into lengths representing equal time, and used to make speed-time graphs. As each length of tape represents 0.1 seconds, you can work out the velocity from the length of the piece of tape using the equation velocity = distance (length of tape)/time (0.1 seconds).

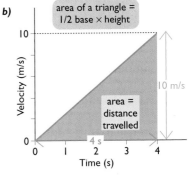

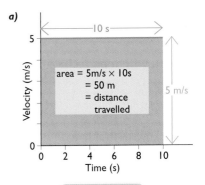

Figure 1.15 a) An object travelling at constant velocity, b) An object accelerating at a constant rate.

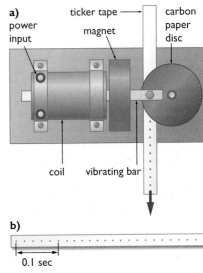

Figure 1.16 a) A ticker timer, b) A tape pulled through at a steady, slow speed. The ticker timer makes 50 dots each second, so every 5 dots show the distance moved in 0.1 second. c) A tape pulled through at a steady, faster speed. d) A tape being accelerated through the timer.

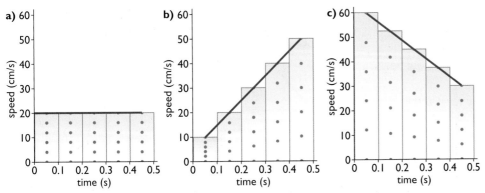

Figure 1.17 Distance-time graphs made from ticker tape. a) Constant speed, b) Accelerating, c) Decelerating.

End of Chapter Checklist

You will need to be able to do the following:

- ✓ understand and use the equation average speed, $v = \dfrac{\text{distance travelled, } d}{\text{time taken, } t}$

- ✓ recall that the units of speed are metres per second, m/s

- ✓ recall that distance–time graphs for objects moving at constant speed are straight lines

- ✓ understand that the gradient of a distance–time graph gives the speed

- ✓ recall that distance travelled in a specified direction is called displacement; displacement is a vector quantity

- ✓ understand that velocity is speed in a specified direction. It is also a vector quantity

- ✓ understand and use the equation acceleration $= \dfrac{\text{change in velocity}}{\text{time taken, } t}$ or $a = \dfrac{(v - u)}{t}$

- ✓ recall that the units of acceleration are metres per second squared, m/s²

- ✓ understand that acceleration is a vector

- ✓ understand that velocity–time graphs of objects moving with constant velocity are horizontal straight lines

- ✓ understand that the gradient of a velocity–time graph gives acceleration; a negative gradient (graph line sloping down to the right) indicates deceleration

- ✓ work out the distance travelled from the area under a velocity–time graph

- ✓ understand and use the equation average velocity $= \dfrac{\text{initial velocity} + \text{final velocity}}{2}$ or $\dfrac{u + v}{2}$

- ✓ explain how to use ticker tape to measure speed.

Questions

More questions on speed and acceleration can be found at the end of Section A on page 57.

1 A sprinter runs 100 metres in 12.5 seconds. Work out her speed in m/s.

2 A jet can travel at 350 m/s. How far will it travel at this speed in:

   a) 30 seconds

   b) 5 minutes

   c) half an hour?

3 A snail crawls at a speed of 0.0004 m/s. How long will it take to climb a garden cane 1.6 m high?

4 Look at the following sketches of distance–time graphs of moving objects.

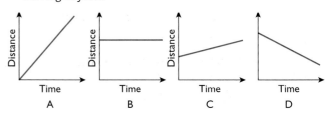

In which graph is the object:

   a) moving backwards

   b) moving slowly

   c) moving quickly

   d) not moving at all?

5 Sketch a distance–time graph to show the motion of a person walking quickly, stopping for a moment, then continuing to walk slowly in the same direction.

6 Plot a distance–time graph using the data in the following table. Draw a line of best fit and use your graph to find the speed of the object concerned.

Distance (m)	0.00	1.60	3.25	4.80	6.35	8.00	9.60
Time (s)	0.00	0.05	0.10	0.15	0.20	0.25	0.30

7 The diagram below shows a trail of oil drips made by a car as it travels along a road. The oil is dripping from the car at a steady rate of one drip every 2.5 seconds.

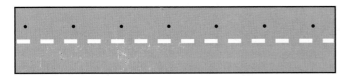

a) What can you tell about the the way the car is moving?

b) The distance between the first and the seventh drip is 135 metres. What is the average speed of the car?

8 A car is travelling at 20 m/s. It accelerates uniformly at 3 m/s² for 5 s.

a) Draw a velocity–time graph for the car during the period that it is accelerating. Include numerical detail on the axes of your graph.

b) Calculate the distance the car travels while it is accelerating.

9 Explain the difference between the following terms:

a) *average speed* and *instantaneous speed*

b) *speed* and *velocity*.

10 A sports car accelerates uniformly from rest to 24 m/s in 6 s. What is the acceleration of the car?

11 Sketch velocity–time graphs for:

a) an object moving with a constant velocity of 6 m/s

b) an object accelerating uniformly at 2 m/s² for 10 s

c) an object decelerating at 4 m/s² for 5 s.

12 A plane starting from rest accelerates at 3 m/s² for 25 s. By how much has the velocity increased after:

a) 1 s   **b)** 5 s   **c)** 25 s?

13 Look at the following sketches of velocity–time graphs of moving objects.

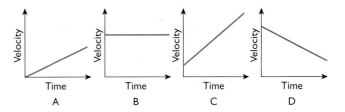

In which graph is the object:

a) not accelerating

b) accelerating from rest

c) decelerating

d) accelerating at the greatest rate?

14 Sketch a velocity–time graph to show how the velocity of a car travelling along a straight road changes if it accelerates uniformly from rest for 5 s, travels at a constant velocity for 10 s, then brakes hard to come to rest in 2 s.

15 Plot a velocity–time graph using the data in the following table.

Velocity (m/s)	0.0	2.5	5.0	7.5	10.0	10.0	10.0	10.0	10.0	10.0
Time (s)	0.0	1.0	2.0	3.0	4.0	5.0	6.0	7.0	8.0	9.0

Draw a line of best fit and use your graph to find:

a) the acceleration during the first 4 s

b) the distance travelled in

   i) the first 4 s of the motion shown

   ii) the last 5 s of the motion shown

c) the average speed during the 9 seconds of motion shown.

16 The leaky car from question 7 is still on the road! It is still dripping oil but now at a rate of one drop per second. The trail of drips is shown on the diagram below as the car travels from left to right.

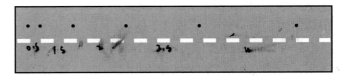

The distance between the first and second oil drip is 0.5 m. Does the spacing of the oil drips show that the car is accelerating at a steady rate? Explain how you would make and use measurements from the oil drip trail to determine this. Work out the rate of acceleration of the car.

Chapter 2: Forces and Shape

Forces are acting on us, and on objects all around us, all the time. In this chapter you will learn about different kinds of forces, how they affect the way objects move and how they can affect the shape of objects.

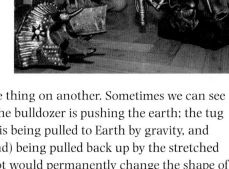

Figure 2.1 *Forces include pushing, pulling, falling and squashing.*

Forces are simply pushes and pulls of one thing on another. Sometimes we can see their effects quite clearly. In Figure 2.1, the bulldozer is pushing the earth; the tug is pulling the tanker; the bungee jumper is being pulled to Earth by gravity, and then (hopefully before meeting the ground) being pulled back up by the stretched elastic rope; the force applied by one robot would permanently change the shape of the other. In this chapter we shall discuss different types of forces and look at their effects on the way that objects move.

All sorts of forces

If you are to study forces, first you need to spot them! As we have already said, sometimes they are easy to see and their effect is obvious. Look at Figure 2.2 and try to identify any forces that you think are involved.

You will immediately see that the man is applying a force to the car – he is pushing it. But there are quite a few more forces in the picture. To make the task a little

Figure 2.2 *What forces do you think are working here?*

easier we shall confine our search to just those forces *acting on the car*. We shall also ignore forces that are very small and therefore have little effect.

The man is clearly struggling to make the car move. This is because there is a force acting on the car trying to stop it moving. This is the force of friction between the moving parts in the car engine, gearbox, wheel axles and so on. This unhelpful force opposes the motion that the man is trying to achieve. However, when the car engine is doing the work to make the car go, the friction between the tyres and the road surface is vital. On an icy road even powerful cars may not move forward because there is not enough friction between the tyres and the ice.

Another force that acts on the car is the pull of the Earth. We call this a **gravitational** force or simply **weight**. If the car were to be pushed over the edge of a cliff, the effect of the gravitational force would be very clear as the car plunged towards the sea. This leads us to realise that yet another force is acting on the car in Figure 2.2 – the road must be stopping the car from being pulled into the Earth. This force, which acts in an upward direction on the car, is called the reaction force. (A more complete name is **normal reaction** force. Here the word "normal" means acting at 90° to the road surface.) All four forces that act on the car are shown in Figure 2.3.

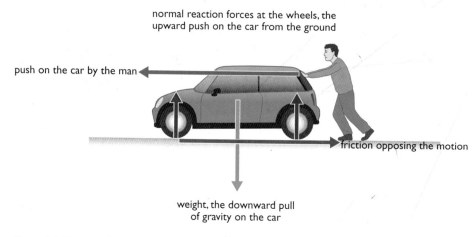

Figure 2.3 *There are four forces at work.*

You will have realised by now that it is not just the size of the force that is important – the direction in which the force is acting is important, too.

Force is another example of a **vector**.

Units of force

The unit used to measure force is the newton (N), named after Sir Isaac Newton who made a study of forces that forms the foundation of our understanding today.

> **A force of one newton will make a mass of one kilogram accelerate at one metre per second squared.**

This is explained more fully later (see Chapter 3). To give you an idea of the size of the newton, the force of gravity on a kilogram bag of sugar (its weight) is about 10 N; an average-sized apple weighs 1 N.

> Force is a **vector quantity**, because both its size and direction matter. Some quantities, such as temperature, have no direction associated with them. They are known as **scalar quantities**.

Some other examples of forces

Figure 2.4 *More forces!*

It is not always easy to spot forces acting on objects. In Figure 2.4, the parachute is causing the parachutist to descend more slowly because an upward force acts on the parachute called **air resistance** or **drag**. Air resistance is like friction – it tries to oppose movement of objects through the air. Designers of cars, high-speed trains and other fast-moving objects try to reduce the effects of this force. Objects moving through liquids also experience a drag force – fast-moving animals that live in water have streamlined shapes to reduce this force.

The hot air balloons in Figure 2.4 are carried upwards in spite of the pull of gravity on them because of a force called **upthrust**. This is the upward push of the surrounding air on the balloon. An upthrust force also acts on objects immersed in liquids.

The compass needle, which is a magnet, is affected by the **magnetic** force between it and the other magnet. Magnetic forces are used to make electric motors rotate, to hold fridge doors shut, and in many other situations.

If you comb your hair, you sometimes find that some of your hair is attracted to the comb. This happens because of an **electrostatic** force between your hair and the comb. You can see a similar effect using a Van de Graaff generator, as shown in Figure 8.5 on page 67.

More types of force, such as electric and nuclear forces, are mentioned in other chapters of this book. The rest of this chapter will look at the *effects* of forces.

More than one force

As we saw earlier, in most situations there will be more than just one force acting on an object. Look again at the man trying to push the car, shown in Figure 2.5. The force with which he is pushing on the car is the same size as the force of friction that is stopping the car moving. The two forces cancel each other out – we say that the **unbalanced force** is zero.

push on the car by the man

friction opposing the motion

Figure 2.5 *The unbalanced force is zero because the two forces have the same magnitude (size) and are acting in opposite directions.*

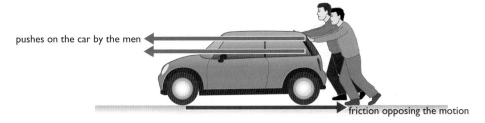

pushes on the car by the men

friction opposing the motion

Figure 2.6 *The total pushing force is the sum of the two individual forces.*

If the man gets someone to help him push the car, the forward force is bigger. Both of the forces pushing the car are acting in the same direction, so you can find the total forward force by adding the two forces together. If both people are pushing with a force of 300 N, then:

$$\text{total forward force} = 300\,\text{N} + 300\,\text{N}$$
$$= 600\,\text{N}$$

The forward force from the people pushing and the force from friction are all acting along the same line. This means we can just add all the forces together to find the unbalanced force. As force is a vector quantity, we also need to think about the directions in which the forces are acting, and we do this by deciding which direction is the positive (+) direction. In this case, we can think of the force from the people as positive and the force from friction as negative. The + and − signs just show that the forces are acting in opposite directions.

So, if the force from friction is 300 N:

$$\text{unbalanced force} = 300\,\text{N} + 300\,\text{N} - 300\,\text{N}$$
$$= 300\,\text{N}$$

Balanced and unbalanced forces

Figure 2.7 shows two situations in which forces are acting on an object. In the tug of war contest the two teams are pulling on the rope in opposite directions. For much of

Figure 2.7 *Balanced forces ... and unbalanced forces.*

the time the rope doesn't move because the two forces are **balanced**. This means that the forces are the same size but act in opposite directions along the line of the rope. There is no **unbalanced** force in one direction or the other. When the forces acting on something are balanced, the object *does not change the way it is moving*. In this case if the rope is stationary, it *remains* stationary. Eventually, one of the teams will tire and its pull will be smaller than that of the other team. When the forces acting on the rope are **unbalanced** the rope will start to move in the direction of the greater force. There will be an unbalanced force in that direction. Unbalanced forces acting on an object cause it to *change the way it is moving*. The rope was stationary and the unbalanced forces acting on it caused it to *accelerate*.

The car in Figure 2.7 is designed to have an enormous acceleration from rest. As soon as it starts to move the forces that oppose motion – friction and drag – must be overcome. The thrust of the engine is, to start with, much greater than the friction and drag forces. This means that the forces acting on the car in the horizontal direction are unbalanced and the result is a change in the way that the car is moving – it accelerates! Once the friction forces balance the thrust the car no longer accelerates – it moves at a steady speed.

Friction

Figure 2.8 *The ice skater can glide because friction is low. The cars need friction to grip the road.*

Friction is the force that causes moving objects to slow down and finally stop. The kinetic energy of the moving object is converted to heat as work is done by the friction force. For the ice skater in Figure 2.8 the force of friction is very small so she is able to glide for long distances without having to do any work. It is also the force that allows a car's wheels to grip the road and make it accelerate – very quickly in the case of the racing cars in Figure 2.8.

Scientists have worked hard for many years to develop some materials that reduce friction and others that increase friction. Reducing friction means that machines work more efficiently (wasting less energy) and do not wear out so quickly. Increasing friction can help to make tyres that grip the road better and to make more effective brakes.

Friction occurs when solid objects rub against other solid objects and also when objects move through fluids (liquids and gases). Sprint cyclists and Olympic swimmers now wear special fabrics to reduce the effects of fluid friction so they can achieve faster times in their races. Sometimes fluid friction is very desirable – for example, when someone uses a parachute after jumping from a plane!

Investigating friction

The simple apparatus shown in Figure 2.9 can be used to discover some basic facts about friction. The weight on the nylon line running over the pulley pulls the block horizontally along the track and friction opposes this force. The weight is increased until the block *just* starts to move; this happens when the pull of the weight *just* overcomes the friction force. The rig can be used to test different factors that may affect the size of the friction, such as the surfaces in contact – the bottom of the block and the surface of the track. If the track surface is replaced with a rough surface, like a sheet of sandpaper, the force required to overcome friction will be greater.

If you repeat this experiment with a model car, you will discover that changing the track surface for a rougher one will have little or no effect on the pull needed to make the model car move. This is because the tyre on the wheel does *not* slip over the surface – the tyre *grips* the surface. The car rolls because the friction force between the axles and the axle-bearings is small and it is *here* that the friction force is overcome. The distinction between the friction force between the tyres and the track surface and the friction in the bearings is a key point in understanding how cars brake.

It is important to remember friction when you are investigating forces and motion. Friction affects almost every form of motion on Earth. However, it is possible to do experiments in the science laboratory in which the friction force on a moving object is reduced to a very low value. Such an object can be set in motion with a small push and it will continue to move at a constant speed even when the force is no longer acting on it. An experiment like this is shown in Figure 2.10.

You may also have seen scientists working in space demonstrating that objects keep moving in a straight line at constant speed, once set in motion. They do this in space because the objects are weightless and the force of air resistance acting on them is very small.

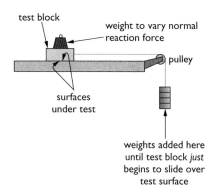

Figure 2.9 *This apparatus can be used to investigate friction.*

Objects in orbit, such as a spacecraft, are referred to as 'weightless' because they do not *appear* to have weight. However the Earth's gravity is still acting on them, and on the spacecraft. You can think of a spacecraft in orbit as 'falling around the Earth'. As the objects inside the spacecraft are also falling around the Earth at the same rate, they do not fall *relative to the spacecraft*.

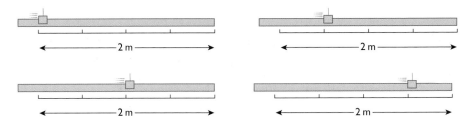

Figure 2.10 *A linear air-track reduces friction dramatically. The glider moves equal distances in equal time intervals. Its velocity is constant.*

Changing shapes

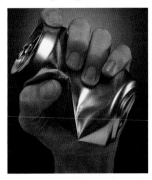

Figure 2.11 *Forces can cause changes in shape.*

We have seen that forces can make things start to move, accelerate or decelerate. The examples in Figure 2.11 show another effect that forces can have – they can change the shape of an object.

Sometimes the change of shape is temporary, as in the suspension spring in the mountain bike. Sometimes the shape of the object is permanently changed, like the crushed can or a car in collision with another object. A temporary change of shape may provide a useful way of absorbing and storing energy, as in the spring in the clockwork torch. A permanent change may mean the failure of a structure like a bridge to support a load. Next we look at temporary changes in the lengths of springs and elastic bands.

Temporary changes of shape

If you apply a force to an elastic band, its shape changes – the band stretches and gets longer. All materials will stretch a little when you put them under **tension** (that is, pull them) or shorten when you **compress** or squash them. You can stretch a rubber band quite easily, but a huge force is needed to cause a noticeable extension in a piece of steel of the same length.

Some materials, like glass, do not change shape easily and are **brittle**, breaking rather than stretching noticeably. **Resilient** or **elastic** materials do not break easily and tend to return to their original shape when the forces acting on them are removed. Other materials, like putty and plasticine, are not resilient but **plastic**, and they change shape permanently when even quite small forces are applied to them.

We shall look at resilient materials, like rubber, metal wires and metals formed into springs, in the next part of this chapter.

Springs and wires

Springs are coiled lengths of certain types of metal, which can be stretched or compressed by applying a force to them. They are used in many different situations. Sometimes they are used to absorb bumps in the road as suspension springs in a car or cycle. In beds and furniture they are used to make sleeping and sitting more comfortable. They are also used in door locks to hold bolts and catches closed and to make doors close automatically. Sometimes they are used in measuring devices like spring balances or bathroom scales.

To choose the right spring for a particular application, we must understand some important features of springs. A simple experiment with springs shows us that:

> **Springs change length when a force acts on them and return to their original length when the force is removed.**

This is true provided you do not overstretch them! If springs are stretched beyond a certain point they do not spring back to their original length.

Hooke's Law

Robert Hooke discovered another important property of springs. He used simple apparatus like that shown in Figures 2.12 and 2.13.

Hooke measured the increase in length (extension) produced by different load forces on springs. The graph he obtained by plotting force against extension looked like that in Figure 2.13b. This straight line passing through the origin shows that the extension of the spring is proportional to the force. This relationship is known as *Hooke's Law*.

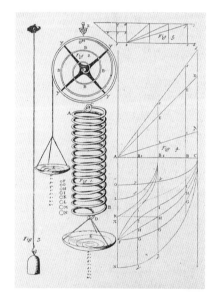

Figure 2.12 *Robert Hooke (1635–1703) was a contemporary of Sir Isaac Newton. This is a drawing of the apparatus Hooke used in his experimental work on the extension of a spring.*

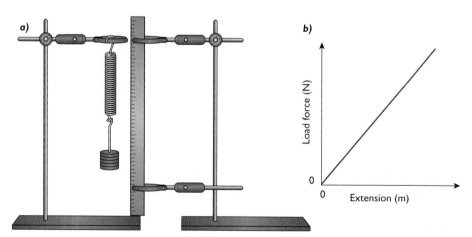

Figure 2.13 *The relationship between load and extension.*

Hooke's Law only applies if you do not stretch a spring too far. Figure 2.14 shows what happens if you stretch a spring too far. At a point called the **elastic limit** it starts to stretch more for each successive increase in the load force. Once you have stretched a spring beyond this limit it has changed shape permanently and will not return to its original length.

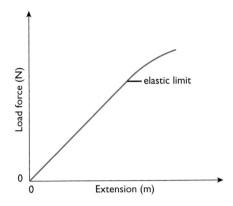

Figure 2.14 *Graph of load v extension showing spring going beyond elastic limit.*

Hooke's Law also applies to wires. If you stretch a wire, you will find that the extension is proportional to the load, until you reach the elastic limit of the wire.

Elastic bands

Elastic bands are usually made of rubber. If you stretch a rubber band with increasing load forces, you get a graph like that shown in Figure 2.15. The graph is not a straight line, showing that rubber bands do not obey Hooke's Law.

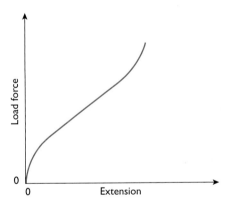

Figure 2.15 *Rubber bands do not obey Hooke's Law – the extension is not directly proportional to the force causing it.*

End of Chapter Checklist

You will need to be able to do the following:

✓ recall that forces are pushes and pulls and that they can change the way an object is moving or change the shape of an object

✓ recognise the following types of force: reaction, weight (gravitational), upthrust, friction, drag, magnetic and electrostatic

✓ recall that force is a vector and is measured in newtons (N)

✓ recall that more than one force may act on an object

✓ understand that if the forces on an object are balanced, or if no force is acting on the object, the way it is moving *will not change*

✓ recall that if the forces acting on an object are unbalanced, the way it is moving *will change*

✓ recognise that friction is a force that acts to oppose the motion of an object

✓ recognise that friction acts when an object moves through a liquid or gas

✓ explain that friction is essential in certain situations but in others it wastes energy and causes wear

✓ describe how the extension of a spring or a wire changes when you apply forces to it

✓ recall that Hooke's Law describes what happens to a spring or wire before it has been stretched to its elastic limit

✓ describe how rubber bands stretch when a force is applied to them.

Questions

More questions on forces can be found at the end of Section A on page 57.

1 Name the force that:

 a) causes objects to fall towards the Earth

 b) makes a marble rolled across level ground eventually come to rest

 c) stops a car sinking into the road surface.

2 Name two types of force that oppose motion.

3 The drawing shows two tug-of-war teams. Each person in the red team is pulling with a force of 250 N. Each person in the blue team is pulling with a force of 200 N.

a) What is the total force exerted by the blue team?

b) What is the total force exerted by the red team?

c) What is the unbalanced force on the rope?

d) Which team will win?

4 The diagram below shows a block of wood on a sloping surface. Copy the diagram and label all the forces that act on the block of wood.

block of wood on a slope

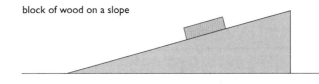

5 A car is travelling along a level road at constant velocity (that is, its speed and direction are not changing). Draw a labelled diagram to show the forces that act on the car.

6 **a)** Why is it vital that there is a friction force that opposes motion when two surfaces try to slide across one another?

b) Give two examples of things that it would be impossible to do without friction.

7 Copy the diagrams below and label the direction in which friction is acting on the objects.

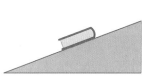 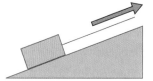

a) a book on a sloping surface   **b)** a block of wood being pulled up a slope

8 The drawing below shows a car pulling a caravan. They are travelling at constant velocity.

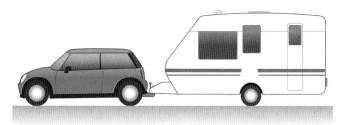

a) Copy the drawing. Label the forces that are acting on the caravan with arrows showing the direction that they act in.

b) Label the forces that act on the car.

9 The information in the following table was obtained from an experiment with a spring of original (unstretched) length 5 cm.

Load force on spring (newtons)	Length of spring (cm)	Extension of spring (cm)
0	5.0	
2	5.8	
4	6.5	
6	7.4	
8	8.3	
10	9.7	
12	12.9	

a) Copy and complete the table by calculating the extensions produced by each load.

b) Use your table to draw a graph of force (y-axis) against extension (x-axis).

c) Mark on your graph the part that shows Hooke's Law.

d) On the same axes, sketch the shape of the line you might get if you carried out the same experiment using a rubber band instead of a spring.

Chapter 3: Forces and Movement

The way an object moves depends upon its mass and the resultant force acting upon it. In this chapter you will find out how forces affect the way an object will move, particularly in the context of car safety.

Figure 3.1 *This aircraft has only a short distance to travel before taking off.*

The aircraft in Figure 3.1 must accelerate to a very high speed in a very short time. The unbalanced force on the plane causes the acceleration. The forces that act horizontally on the aircraft are the friction force between the wheels and the deck, and air resistance, when the aircraft starts to move. At the start, the forward thrust of the aircraft engines is much greater than air resistance and friction, so there is a large unbalanced force to cause the acceleration. When the aircraft lands on the carrier deck it must decelerate to a halt in a short distance. Parachutes and drag wires are used to provide a large unbalanced force acting in the opposite direction to the aircraft's movement. An unbalanced force is sometimes referred to as a **resultant** force. In this chapter we look at how acceleration is related to the force acting on an object.

Force, mass and acceleration

An object will not change its velocity (accelerate) unless there is an unbalanced force acting on it. For example, a car travelling along a motorway at a constant speed is

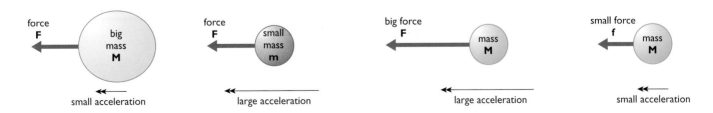

a) When the same force is applied to objects with different mass, the smaller mass will experience a greater acceleration.

b) Different-sized forces are applied to objects with the same mass. The small force produces a smaller acceleration than the large force.

Figure 3.2 *The acceleration of an object is affected by both its mass and the force applied to it.*

being pushed along by a force from its engine, but this force is needed to balance the forces of friction and air resistance acting on the car. At a constant speed, the unbalanced force on the car is zero.

If there are unbalanced forces acting on an object, the object will accelerate. The acceleration depends on the size of the unbalanced force and the mass of the object.

Investigating force, mass and acceleration

The experiment described in Figure 3.3 shows how the relationship between force, mass and acceleration can be investigated. It uses a trolley on a slightly sloping ramp. The slope of the ramp is adjusted so that the trolley just keeps moving down it if you push it gently. The slope is intended to overcome the friction in the trolley's wheels that could affect the results.

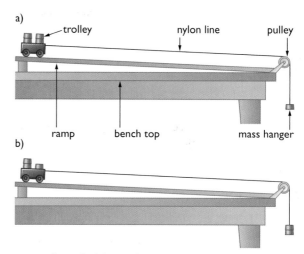

Figure 3.3 *You can use a trolley to find the acceleration caused by a particular force.*

The acceleration can be found using a video camera by measuring the distance travelled from the start for each image. Since the time between each image is known, a graph of displacement against time can be drawn. The gradient of the displacement–time graph gives the velocity at a particular instant, so data for a velocity–time graph can be obtained. The gradient of the velocity–time graph produced is the acceleration of the trolley.

The force acting on the trolley is provided by the masses on the end of the nylon line. These masses accelerate as well as the trolley, so the force is increased by transferring one of the masses from the trolley to the mass hanger, Figure 3.3b. This increases the pulling force on the trolley, while keeping the total mass of the system the same.

The acceleration of the trolley can be measured by taking a series of pictures at equal time intervals using a digital video camera. Alternatively, a pair of light gates and a data logger can be used to find the speed of the trolley near the top of the ramp and near the end. The equation on page 5 can then be used to work out the acceleration.

Figure 3.4 shows a graph of force against acceleration when the mass of the trolley and hanging masses is constant and the accelerating force is varied.

The graph is a straight line passing through the origin, which shows that:

> **force is proportional to acceleration**
> $$F \propto a$$

So doubling the force acting on an object doubles its acceleration.

In a second experiment, the accelerating force is kept constant and the mass of the trolley is varied.

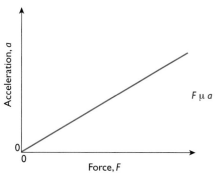

Figure 3.4 *Force is proportional to acceleration.*

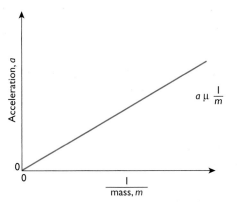

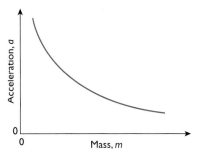

Figure 3.6 *The graph of a against m is a curve. Plotting a against 1/m gives a straight line. This makes it easier to spot the way that a is affected by m.*

Figure 3.5 *Acceleration is inversely proportional to mass.*

Figure 3.5 shows the acceleration of the trolley plotted against $1/m$. This is also a straight line passing through the origin, showing that:

> **acceleration is inversely proportional to mass**
>
> $$a \propto \frac{1}{m}$$

This means that for a given unbalanced force acting on a body, doubling the mass of the body will halve the acceleration.

Combining these results gives us:

> **force, F (in N) = mass, m (in kg) × acceleration, a (in m/s²)**
> **$F = m \times a$**

Force is measured in newtons (N), mass is measured in kilograms (kg), and acceleration is measured in metres per second squared (m/s²). From this we see that:

> **One newton is the force needed to make a mass of one kilogram accelerate at one metre per second squared.**

Deceleration in a collision

If you are designing a car for high acceleration, the equation $F = ma$ tells you that the car should have low mass and the engine must provide a high accelerating force. You must also consider the force needed to stop the car.

When a moving object is stopped, it decelerates.

> **A negative acceleration is a deceleration.**

If a large deceleration is needed then the force causing the deceleration must be large, too. Usually a car is stopped by using the brakes in a controlled way so that the deceleration is not excessive. In an accident the car may collide with another vehicle or obstacle, causing a very rapid deceleration.

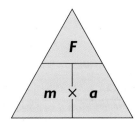

Figure 3.7 *The equation can be rearranged using the triangle method.*

If an examination question asks you to write out the formula for calculating force, mass or acceleration, always give the actual equation (such as $F = m \times a$). You may not get the mark if you just draw the triangle.

Worked example

Reminder: *v* is the final velocity, *u* is the initial velocity and *t* is the time for the change in velocity to take place.

The minus sign in Example 1 for velocity change indicates that the velocity has decreased.

Figure 3.8 *These bicycle brakes and motorcycle disc brakes each work using friction. Friction is necessary if we want things to stop.*

The "tread" of a tyre is the grooved pattern moulded into the rubber surface. It is designed to keep the rubber surface in contact with the road by throwing water away from the tyre surface.

Example 1

A car travelling at 20 m/s collides with a stationary lorry and is brought to rest in just 0.02 s. Calculate the deceleration of the car.

$$\text{acceleration} = \frac{\text{change in velocity}}{\text{time taken}} \quad \text{(see page 5)}$$

$$a = \frac{v - u}{t}$$

$$a = \frac{0 \, \text{m/s} - 20 \, \text{m/s}}{0.02 \, \text{s}}$$

$$a = \frac{-20 \, \text{m/s}}{0.02 \, \text{s}}$$

$$a = -1000 \, \text{m/s}^2$$

A person of mass 50 kg in the car would experience the same deceleration when she came into contact with a hard surface in the car. This could be the dashboard or the windscreen. Calculate the force that the person experiences.

$$F = m \times a$$

$$F = 50 \, \text{kg} \times 1000 \, \text{m/s}^2$$

$$F = 50\,000 \, \text{N}$$

This huge force would undoubtedly have unfortunate effects on the person!

In Chapter 4 you will learn about ways in which cars can be designed to reduce the forces on passengers in an accident.

Friction and braking

Brakes on cars and bicycles work by increasing the friction between the rotating wheels and the body of the vehicle, as shown in Figure 3.8.

The friction force between the tyres and the road will depend on the condition of the tyres and the surface of the road. It also depends on the weight of the vehicle. If the tyres have a good tread, are properly inflated and the road is dry, the friction force between the road and the tyres will be at its maximum.

Unfortunately, we do not always travel in ideal conditions. If the road is wet or the tyres are in bad condition the friction force will be smaller. If the brakes are applied too hard, the tyres will not grip the road surface and the car will skid. Once the car is skidding the driver no longer has control and it will take longer to stop. Skidding can be avoided by applying the brakes appropriately, so that the wheels do not lock. Most modern cars are fitted with ABS (anti-lock braking system) to reduce the chance of a skid occurring. ABS is a computer-controlled system that senses when the car is about to skid and momentarily releases the brakes.

Safe stopping distance

The Highway Code used in the United Kingdom gives stopping distances for cars travelling at various speeds. The **stopping distance** is the sum of the **thinking distance** and the **braking distance**. The faster the car is travelling the greater the stopping distance will be.

1 Thinking distance

When a driver suddenly sees an obstacle ahead, it takes time for him or her to respond to the new situation before taking any action, such as braking. This time is

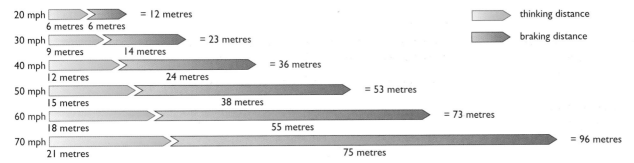
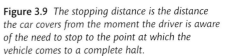

Figure 3.9 *The stopping distance is the distance the car covers from the moment the driver is aware of the need to stop to the point at which the vehicle comes to a complete halt.*

called **reaction time** and will depend on the person driving the car. It will also depend on a number of other factors including whether the driver is tired or under the influence of alcohol or other drugs that slow reaction times. Poor visibility may also make it difficult for a driver to identify a hazard and so cause him or her to take longer to respond. Clearly, the longer the driver takes to react, the further the car will travel before braking even starts – that is, the longer the thinking distance will be. Equally clear is the fact that the higher the car's speed, the further the car will travel during this "thinking time". If the distance between two cars is not at least the thinking distance then, in the event of an emergency stop by the vehicle in front, a violent collision is inevitable.

2 Braking distance

With ABS braking, in an emergency you brake as hard as you can. This means that the braking force will be a maximum and we can work out the deceleration using the equation below.

$F = m \times a$, rearranged to give:

$$a = \frac{F}{m}$$

It is worth pointing out here that vehicles with large masses, like lorries, will have smaller rates of deceleration for a given braking force – they will, therefore, travel further while braking.

Chapter 1 shows that the distance travelled by a moving object can be found from its velocity–time graph. The area under the graph gives the distance travelled. Look at the velocity–time graphs in Figures 3.10 and 3.11.

Figure 3.10 shows two cars, A and B, braking from the same velocity. Car A is braking harder than car B and comes to rest in a shorter time. Car B travels further

Reminder: The equation $F = m \times a$ can be rearranged using the triangle method (see page 25).

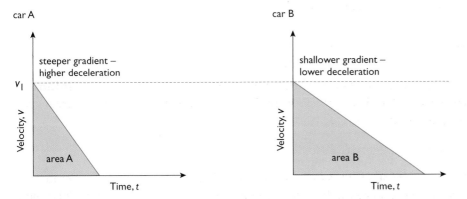

Figure 3.10 *Velocity–time graphs for two cars braking at different rates from the same speed, v_1, to rest.*

before stopping, as you can see from the larger area under the graph. Remember that the maximum rate of deceleration depends on how hard you can brake without skidding – in poor conditions the braking force will be lower.

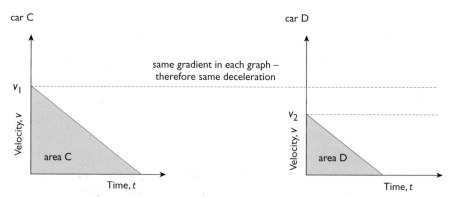

Figure 3.11 *Velocity–time graphs for two cars braking at the same rate to rest, from different speeds, v_1 and v_2.*

Figure 3.11 shows two cars, C and D, braking at the same rate, as you can see from the gradients. Car C is braking from a higher velocity and so takes longer to stop. Again, the greater area under the graph for car C shows that it travels further whilst stopping than car D.

Vehicles *cannot* stop instantly! Remember also that the chart in Figure 3.9 shows stopping distances in *ideal* conditions. If the car tyres or brakes are in poor condition, or if the road surface is wet, icy or slippery because of oil spillage, then the car will travel further before stopping.

The acceleration due to gravity

When a small object – like a steel ball-bearing or a table tennis ball – is dropped through a small distance near the Earth's surface it accelerates. Figure 3.12 shows a sequence of images of a falling table tennis ball taken with a time interval of 0.1 s between each image.

We can calculate the acceleration of the falling ball, using measurements taken from a full – scale version of an image such as Figure 3.12.

For example, we could measure the distance between two of the images of the table tennis ball – say, the second and the third. This is the distance that the ball travelled during the second interval of one tenth of a second. The average velocity during this time is found by dividing the distance travelled, 14.7 cm, by the time taken, 0.1 s. This gives an average velocity of 147 cm/s or 1.47 m/s over the interval. If we repeat the calculation for the next tenth of a second, between images 3 and 4, we find that the average velocity has increased to 2.45 m/s. We can then use the equation for acceleration:

$$\text{acceleration, } a = \frac{\text{final velocity, } v - \text{initial velocity, } u}{\text{time taken, } t}$$

We find that:

$$a = \frac{2.45 \,\text{m/s} - 1.47 \,\text{m/s}}{0.1 \,\text{s}} = 9.8 \,\text{m/s}^2$$

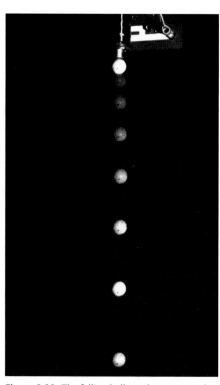

Figure 3.12 *The falling ball accelerates towards the ground.*

The result of this experiment gives us a value for the acceleration caused by the force of gravity. We use the symbol g to represent the acceleration due to gravity.

If there were no air to resist the motion of objects falling through it, *all* objects falling near the Earth's surface would accelerate at $9.8\,\text{m/s}^2$.

We often use an approximate value of $10\,\text{m/s}^2$ for the acceleration due to gravity in questions. (It makes calculations easier!)

Weight

The **weight** of an object is the force that acts on it because of gravity. We can work out the weight of an object by using the relationship between force, mass and acceleration:

> force, F (in N) = mass, m (in kg) × acceleration, a (in m/s²)
> $$F = m \times a$$

If we drop an object it accelerates at approximately $10\,\text{m/s}^2$. If the object has a mass of 0.1 kg we can work out the force that must be acting on it to cause the acceleration (its weight):

$F = m \times a$
$F = 0.1\,\text{kg} \times 10\,\text{m/s}^2$
$F = 1\,\text{N}$

The weight of the 0.1 kg mass is 1 N.

Generally, we use the equation:

> weight, W (in N) = mass of object, m (in kg) × acceleration due to gravity, g (in m/s²)
> $$W = m \times g$$

The value of g depends on how strong a planet's gravity is. For example, objects on the Moon accelerate at about $1.6\,\text{m/s}^2$. The numerical value of g is, therefore, a measure of how strong the gravitational pull on an object is. It is sometimes called **gravitational field strength** and its value is measured in N/kg, the gravitational force per unit mass.

Air resistance and terminal velocity

An object moving through air experiences a friction force which opposes the movement. This force is called **air resistance** or **drag** force. The size of the drag force acting on an object depends on its shape and its speed. Cars are designed to have a low "drag coefficient". The drag coefficient is a measure of how easily an object moves through the air. High-speed trains have a streamlined shape so that air flows more smoothly around them. Streamlined, smooth surfaces produce less drag.

It is particularly important to make fast-moving objects streamlined because the drag force increases with the speed of the object. The fact that drag increases with speed affects the way that dropped objects accelerate, because the faster they get the greater the force opposing their motion becomes.

Objects falling through the air experience two significant forces: the weight force (that is, the pull of gravity on the object) and the opposing drag force.

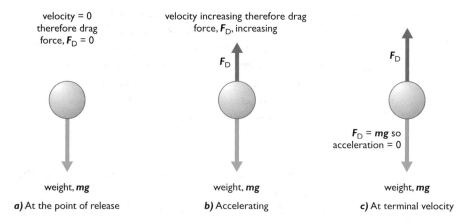

velocity = 0
therefore drag
force, F_D = 0

velocity increasing therefore drag
force, F_D, increasing

F_D

F_D

$F_D = mg$ so
acceleration = 0

weight, mg

weight, mg

weight, mg

a) At the point of release

b) Accelerating

c) At terminal velocity

Figure 3.13 *How the forces acting on a body change as its velocity changes.*

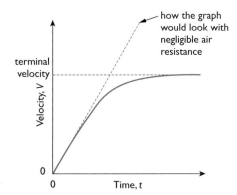

how the graph
would look with
negligible air
resistance

terminal
velocity

Velocity, V

0

0   Time, t

Figure 3.14 *The velocity–time graph for an object accelerating until it reaches terminal velocity.*

In Figure 3.13a the object has just been released and has a starting velocity of 0 m/s. This means that there is no drag. (Remember that the drag force acts on *moving* objects.) The resulting downward-acting force is just the weight force. This force makes the object accelerate towards the Earth.

Figure 3.13b shows the object now moving. Because it is moving it has a drag force, F_D, acting on it. The drag force acts *upwards* against the movement. This means that the resulting downward force on the object is ($mg - F_D$). You can see that the drag force has made the resulting downward force smaller, so the acceleration is smaller. All the time that the object is accelerating it is getting faster. The faster the object moves the bigger the drag force is.

In Figure 3.13c the drag force has increased to the point where it exactly balances the weight force – since there is now no unbalanced force on the object its acceleration is also zero. The object has reached its **terminal velocity** and although it is still falling it will not get any faster. Figure 3.14 shows a velocity–time graph for an object falling through air and reaching terminal velocity.

Parachutes

Figure 3.15 *These skydivers have just left the aeroplane. They will accelerate until they reach terminal velocity.*

When a skydiver jumps from a plane at high altitude she will accelerate for a time and eventually reach terminal velocity. Typically this will be between 150 and 200 kph. When she opens her parachute this will cause a sudden increase in the

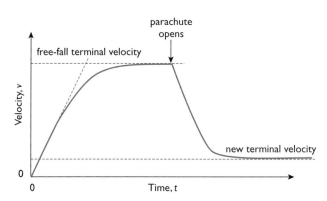

parachute
opens

free-fall terminal velocity

Velocity, v

new terminal velocity

0

0   Time, t

Figure 3.16 *Velocity–time graph for a free-fall parachutist reaching terminal velocity, then opening the parachute.*

drag force. At this velocity (around 200 kph) the drag force of the parachute is greater than the weight of the skydiver. This means that the unbalanced force acting on the parachutist acts *upwards* and, for a while, she will decelerate. As she slows down the size of the drag force decreases and, eventually, a new terminal velocity is reached. Obviously the new terminal velocity depends on the design of the parachute, but it must be slow enough to allow the parachutist to land safely. Figure 3.16 shows a velocity–time graph for a skydiver.

Modelling terminal velocity

Objects have to accelerate to quite high speeds in air to reach terminal velocity. This makes demonstrating the effect in a laboratory difficult. However, objects falling through liquids also experience a drag force that increases with speed. The sizes of drag forces in liquids are much higher than in gases. This means that objects falling through liquids have a much lower terminal velocity than objects falling through air, and can be used to model terminal velocity. You can use a tall measuring cylinder filled with water and drop small-diameter (1–2 mm) glass beads into it. Alternatively, use a much thicker liquid like glycerine or oil and use small-diameter ball-bearings. As well as demonstrating terminal velocity this presents plenty of scope for investigations. You could measure the terminal velocity using a light gate and a data logger.

End of Chapter Checklist

You will need to be able to do the following:

- ✓ recall that when an unbalanced force acts on an object along the line in which the object is moving, then the object will accelerate (or decelerate if the force acts in the opposite direction to that of the motion of the object)

- ✓ recall that for a particular object the bigger the unbalanced force acting on it the bigger the acceleration

- ✓ recall that if the *same* force is applied to objects of different mass then the more massive the object the smaller its acceleration will be

- ✓ recall and use the equation force = mass × acceleration, $F = m \times a$, rearranging it as necessary

- ✓ understand that the stopping distance for a moving vehicle is the sum of the thinking distance and the braking distance

- ✓ explain that the thinking distance is the time before the brakes are applied and that it can be affected by tiredness, drugs and poor visibility

- ✓ recall that the distance travelled while thinking depends on the speed of the vehicle

- ✓ recall that the braking distance is the distance travelled by the vehicle *after* the brakes have been applied

- ✓ explain that the braking distance (and, therefore, the stopping distance) is affected by brake and tyre condition and the condition of the road surface

- ✓ appreciate that the mass of a vehicle will also affect its braking distance

- ✓ recall and use the relationship weight = mass × acceleration due to gravity ($W = m \times g$)

- ✓ recall that all objects fall with the same acceleration *in the absence of air resistance*

- ✓ explain that objects falling through liquids and gases experience a drag force that increases with their speed

- ✓ understand that a falling object reaches terminal velocity because the drag force on the object balances its weight

- ✓ understand that the drag force also depends on the shape of the falling object; objects must be smooth or streamlined to reduce drag.

Questions

More questions on force and acceleration can be found at the end of Section A on page 57.

1 What is meant by an unbalanced force? Illustrate your answer with an example.

2 Rockets burn fuel to give them the thrust needed to accelerate. As the fuel burns the mass of the rocket gets smaller. Assuming that the rocket motors provide a constant thrust force, what will happen to the acceleration of the rocket as it burns its fuel?

3 a) What force is required to make an object of mass 500 g accelerate at 4 m/s²? (Take care with the units!)

b) An object accelerates at 0.8 m/s² when a resultant force of 200 N acts upon it. What is the mass of the object?

c) What acceleration is produced by a force of 250 N acting on a mass of 25 kg?

4 Parachutists bend their legs and roll with the fall on landing. They do this to reduce the chance of injury. Explain why this technique means that they are less likely to suffer broken bones on hitting the ground.

5 Explain the meaning of the following terms used in *The Highway Code* in the section about stopping vehicles in an emergency:

   a) thinking distance

   b) braking distance

   c) overall stopping distance.

6 What factors affect the braking distance of a vehicle?

7 The diagram below shows the velocity–time graph for a car travelling from the instant that the driver sees an obstacle in the road ahead.

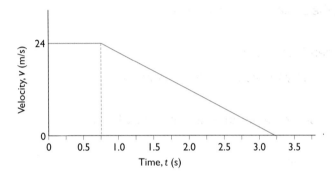

Use the graph to find out:

   a) how long the driver takes to react to seeing the obstacle (reaction time)

   b) how far the car travels in this reaction time

   c) how long it takes to bring the car to a halt once the driver starts braking

   d) the total distance the car travels before stopping.

8 Calculate the weight of an apple of mass 100 grams:

   a) on the Earth

   b) on the Moon.

9 What factors affect the drag force that acts on a high-speed train?

10 Describe an experiment to demonstrate terminal velocity. Say what measurements you need to take in your experiment to show that a falling object has reached terminal speed.

11 Look at the velocity–time graph for a free-fall parachutist shown below.

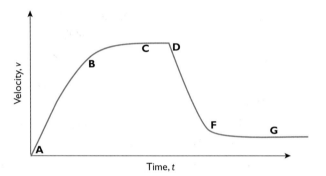

State and explain the direction and relative size of the unbalanced force acting on the parachutist at each of the points A–G labelled on the graph.

Chapter 4: Momentum

Momentum is possessed by masses in motion – it is calculated by multiplying the mass of an object by its velocity. In this chapter you will learn that, when objects speed up or slow down, the rate of change of momentum is proportional to the force causing the change. You will also see that momentum is conserved in collisions and explosions.

Do not confuse momentum, a property of moving masses, with moment, the turning effect of a force.

Figure 4.1 *Newton's cradle.*

Newton's cradle is an entertaining toy but it also demonstrates a physics conservation law. When one of the balls is drawn back a short way and released it swings and collides with the remaining group of balls. After the impact the ball at the opposite end springs away and swings out as far as the first ball was drawn back to start with. If two balls are drawn back and released then two balls will move away at the opposite end as the collision occurs. The moving ball has momentum, and momentum is conserved in collisions. This chapter is about **momentum** and what is meant by conservation of momentum.

Momentum

We talk about objects "gaining momentum" in everyday speech. When we say this we are usually trying to get across an idea of something becoming more difficult to stop. Sometimes we use the word in a way that is very close to the way it is defined in physics – for example, if a car starts rolling down a hill we might say that the car is "gaining momentum" as it speeds up.

In physics, momentum is a quantity possessed by *masses in motion*. Momentum is a measure of how difficult it is to stop something that is moving. We calculate the momentum of a moving object using the formula:

momentum, *p* (in kg m/s) = mass, *m* (in kg) × velocity, *v* (in m/s)
$$p = m \times v$$

Momentum is a **vector** quantity and is measured in kilogram metres per second (kg m/s) – provided that mass in the above equation is measured in kg and velocity in m/s.

You can see from the equation that the more mass an object has, the more momentum it will have when moving. The momentum of a moving object also increases with its speed.

Momentum and acceleration

We have already discussed the relationship $F = m \times a$ (see page 25). This relationship was first discussed by Sir Isaac Newton (1642–1727). A more precise statement of Newton's discovery would be that when a resultant force acts on an object it causes a change in the momentum of the object in the direction of the resultant force. Newton discovered that the rate of change of momentum of an object is proportional to the force applied to that object. This means that if you double the force acting on an object its momentum will change twice as quickly. Figure 4.2 shows the effect of the thrust force on the velocity of a space shuttle, and, therefore, on its momentum.

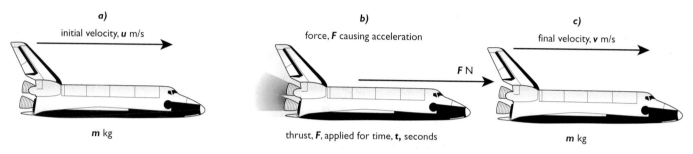

a)
initial velocity, u m/s

m kg

b)
force, F causing acceleration

F N

thrust, F, applied for time, t, seconds

c)
final velocity, v m/s

m kg

Figure 4.2 *The thrust of the rocket motor makes the velocity and, therefore, the momentum of the shuttle increase.*

initial momentum of object $= mu$
and final momentum of object $= mv$
therefore increase in momentum $= mv - mu$

so, rate of increase of momentum $= \dfrac{(mv - mu)}{t}$

As stated above, Newton identified a *proportional* relationship between the rate of increase of momentum and the force applied, but with the system of units we use the relationship appears as shown:

$$\text{force} = \frac{\text{change in momentum}}{\text{time taken}}$$

$$F = \frac{(mv - mu)}{t}$$

If you look at this equation you will notice it can be rearranged to give the more familiar equation $F = ma$:

$F = (mv - mu)/t$
$F = m(v - u)/t$
since $(v - u)/t = a$,
then $F = ma$

The rearrangement is possible because we have assumed that the mass of the object involved is constant. This will not always be the case in real situations – for example, when a space shuttle is launched the mass of the rocket changes continuously as fuel is burned and rocket stages are jettisoned. However, you will not meet problems like this at IGCSE level.

Momentum and collisions

We can express the above equation in terms of momentum change, as follows:

> **force × time = increase in momentum**

This simply says that a bigger force applied to an object for a longer time will result in a greater change in the momentum of the object.

The term **impulse** is used for the product (force × time).

Consider what happens when two balls collide, as shown in Figure 4.3.

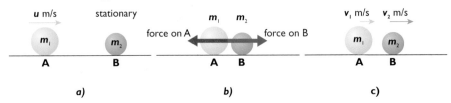

Figure 4.3 **a)** *Moving ball A, mass* **m_1**, *rolls towards stationary ball B, mass* **m_2**, **b)** *during the impact each ball exerts a force on the other – equal in size and opposite in direction,* **c)** *the balls after the collision.*

During the time the two balls are in contact each exerts a force on the other (Newton's Third Law about action and reaction, see page 39). The forces act in *opposite* directions and obviously act for the *same* amount of time. This means that $F \times t$ for each is the same size, but opposite in direction. The increase in momentum of ball B is *exactly* balanced by the decrease in momentum of ball A, so the total momentum of the two balls is unchanged before and after the collision – *momentum is conserved*.

> **momentum before the collision = momentum after the collision**

Elastic and inelastic collisions

When objects collide, some of the movement energy they possess is converted into other forms, typically heat and sound. Collisions in which *no* kinetic (movement) energy is "lost" by being transformed into other types of energy are called **elastic collisions**. Some practical collisions are close to elastic in that a very small proportion of the kinetic energy is "lost". Collisions between molecules in a gas are usually taken as perfectly elastic. (This is why the molecules in a container of air keep on moving – they don't end up in a pile at the bottom of the container.)

When a ball bounces off the ground, the collision is **partially elastic**: the ball rebounds, regaining its original shape, but loses some of its kinetic energy in the collision.

When two objects collide and stick together, the collision is said to be **inelastic**. Inelastic collisions are usually used for exam questions because they are simpler to do!

In any system, momentum is always conserved provided no external forces act on the system. This means that when two snooker balls collide the momentum of the balls is conserved if no friction forces act on them. The presence of friction means that the balls will eventually slow down and stop, thus ending up with no momentum. Although the balls have "lost" momentum something else will, inevitably, have gained an equal amount of momentum! As the balls are slowed by the friction of the snooker table they, in turn, cause a friction force to act on the table. The table gains some momentum. However, the large mass of the table means that the effect is unnoticeable.

Worked example

Example 1

A railway truck with a mass of 5000 kg rolling at 3 m/s collides with a stationary truck of mass 10 000 kg. The trucks join together. At what speed do they move after the collision?

We shall assume that friction forces are small enough to ignore, so we can apply the law of conservation of momentum:

> **momentum before the collision = momentum after the collision**

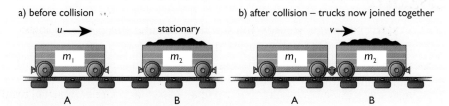

a) before collision
u→
stationary
m_1
m_2
A
B

b) after collision – trucks now joined together
v→
m_1
m_2
A
B

Figure 4.4 *Railway trucks in collision.*

so, momentum of A + momentum of B = momentum of A and B
before collision   before collision   moving together after collision

$$m_1 \times u + m_2 \times 0 = (m_1 + m_2) \times v$$

where m_1 is the mass of truck A, u is its velocity *before* the collision, m_2 is the mass of truck B (at rest before the collision so its velocity is 0), and v is the velocity of the two trucks *after* the collision.

Substituting these values gives:

$5000\,kg \times 3\,m/s + 1000\,kg \times 0\,m/s = (5000\,kg + 10\,000\,kg) \times v$

so $v = \dfrac{15\,000\,kg\,m/s}{15\,000\,kg} = 1\,m/s$

After the collision the trucks move with a velocity of 1 m/s in the same direction that the original truck was travelling.

Explosions

The conservation of momentum principle can be applied to explosions. An explosion involves a release of energy causing things to fly apart. The momentum before and after the explosion is unchanged, though there will be a huge increase in movement energy. A simple demonstration of a safe "explosion" is shown in Figure 4.5.

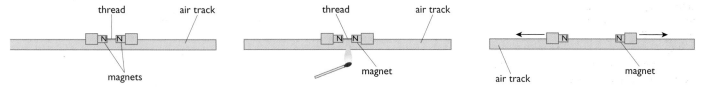

thread   air track
N N
magnets

thread   air track
N N
magnet

←
N
N
→
air track   magnet

Figure 4.5 *The momentum before and after the "explosion" is unchanged although there is an increase in movement energy.*

In this demonstration, the two gliders are fitted with magnets trying to push them apart, but they are held together by a thread. When the thread is burned through, the gliders spring apart. If the gliders have the same mass, you will notice that they move off with the same speed but in opposite directions – the gliders have gained equal amounts of momentum but in opposite directions, so there is no overall change in the momentum before and after the "explosion".

Rockets

Rocket motors use the principle of conservation of momentum to propel spacecraft through space. They produce a continuous, controlled explosion that forces large amounts of fast-moving gases (produced by the fuel burning) out of the back of the rocket. The spacecraft gains an equal amount of momentum in the opposite direction to that of the moving exhaust gases. You can see the same effect if you blow up a balloon and release it without tying up the end!

Car safety

In the worked example on page 26 you saw that the force on a person in a car crash can be very large. In that example, the force was worked out from the deceleration in a crash. You can also work out the force in a crash using the equation for momentum.

Worked example

Example 2

A car travelling at 20 m/s collides with a stationary lorry and is brought to rest in just 0.02 s. A woman in the car has a mass of 50 kg. She experiences the same deceleration when she comes into contact with a hard surface in the car (such as the dashboard or the windscreen). What force does the person experience?

$$\text{force} = \frac{\text{change in momentum}}{\text{time}}$$
$$= \frac{(50 \,\text{kg} \times 20 \,\text{m/s} - 50 \,\text{kg} \times 0)}{0.02}$$
$$= 50\,000 \,\text{N}$$

Figure 4.6 *Cars are designed to crumple.*

Cars are now designed with various safety features that increase the time over which the car's momentum changes in an accident. Figure 4.6 shows the safety features of a car being tested. The car has a rigid passenger cell or compartment with crumple zones in front and behind. The crumple zones, as the name suggests, collapse during a collision and increase the time during which the car is decelerating. For instance, if the deceleration time in Example 2 above is increased from 0.02 s to 1 s, then the impact causes a much smaller force of just 1000 N to act on the passenger, greatly increasing their chances of survival.

Crumple zones are just one of the safety features now used in modern cars to protect the passengers in an accident. They only work if the passengers are wearing seat belts so that the reduced deceleration applies to their bodies too. Without seat belts, the passengers will continue moving forward until they come into contact with some part of the car or with a passenger in front. If they hit something that does not crumple they will be brought to rest in a very short time, which – as we have seen in Example 2 – means a large deceleration and, therefore, a large force acting on them.

Many cars are now fitted with air-bags to reduce the forces acting on passengers during collisions, again by extending the time of deceleration. Air-bags are triggered by devices called accelerometers that detect the rapid deceleration that occurs during a collision.

Newton's Laws of Motion

Sir Isaac Newton lived from 1642 to 1727. He made many famous discoveries and some important observations about how forces affect the way objects move. The first observation, called Newton's 1st Law, was:

> **Things don't speed up, slow down or change direction unless you push (or pull) them.**

Newton didn't put it quite like that, of course! He said that a body would continue to move in a straight line at a steady speed unless a resultant force was acting on the body. If the forces acting on an object are balanced then a stationary object stays in one place, and a moving object continues to move in just the same way as it did before the forces were applied. You have already met this idea in Chapter 3.

Newton then asked another obvious question: how does the acceleration of an object depend on the force that you apply to it? Again Newton's formal statement of the answer (Newton's 2nd Law of Motion) sounds complicated, but the basic findings are quite simple:

> **The bigger the force acting on an object, the faster the object will speed up.**
>
> **Objects with greater mass require bigger forces than those with smaller mass to make them speed up (accelerate) at the same rate.**

The force referred to is the resultant (unbalanced) force acting on the object. This idea was also covered in Chapter 3.

Action and reaction

Another of Newton's important discoveries about forces is this:

> **When you push something it pushes back just as hard, but in the opposite direction.**

This is called Newton's 3rd Law and is usually stated as "For every action there is an equal and opposite reaction". When you sit down, your weight pushes down on the seat. The seat pushes back on you with an equal, but upward, force. An experiment to give you the idea of what this law means is shown in Figure 4.7.

In Figure 4.7, person X is clearly pushing person Y but it is not obvious that Y is pushing X back. When *both* X and Y move it is clear that X has been affected by a force pushing him to the left. The force felt by X is the reaction force.

Scientists use the word "law" very cautiously. Only when a hypothesis (idea) has been tested many times independently by careful experiment is it raised to the status of a "law". Einstein showed that in special situations Newton's Laws break down, but they are still accurate enough to predict the way objects respond to forces with a high degree of accuracy.

It can sometimes be difficult to sort out action and reaction forces from balanced forces. Balanced forces act in opposite directions on the *same object*. Action and reaction forces also act in opposite directions, but are always acting on *different* objects.

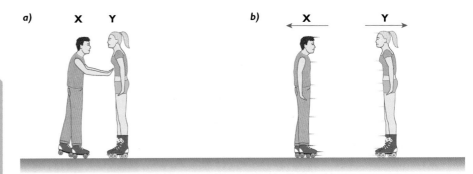

Figure 4.7 *For every action there is an equal and opposite reaction.*

Look back at Figure 2.3 on page 13. The weight of the car is pushing down on the ground. Although the weight is shown coming from the centre of gravity of the car, it acts through the wheels. The total reaction force from the ground acting through the wheels is the same as the weight of the car. It is this reaction force that stops the car sinking into the ground.

You will need to be able to do the following:

✓ recall that the momentum of a moving object is found by multiplying its mass by its velocity

✓ recall that momentum is a vector quantity – it has direction as well as size

✓ understand that when objects collide they exert equal forces on each other but in opposite directions and that this causes the momentum change for each body to be the same but opposite in direction

✓ calculate the momentum of bodies before and after collisions in a straight line

✓ understand that in collisions or explosions the total momentum of the moving objects is the same before and after the collision or explosion, provided no external forces are acting

✓ explain that kinetic energy is conserved in *perfectly elastic* collisions but normally the total kinetic energy of bodies after a collision will be less than before (because collisions are usually not perfectly elastic so kinetic energy is converted into sound, heat, and so on)

✓ recall that when colliding objects stick together the collision is described as inelastic

✓ understand that momentum conservation is used to drive spacecraft using rockets

✓ recall and use the equation force = $\dfrac{\text{change in momentum}}{\text{time taken}}$

✓ use ideas of momentum to explain some safety features in cars

✓ recall that for every force (action) there is an equal and opposite force (reaction).

Questions

More questions on momentum can be found at the end of Section A on page 57.

1 Work out, giving your answers in kg m/s, the momentum of the following moving objects:

   a) a bowling ball of mass 6 kg travelling at 8 m/s

   b) a ship of mass 50 000 kg travelling at 3 m/s

   c) a tennis ball of mass 60 g travelling at 180 km/h.

2 *a)* How does an elastic collision differ from partially elastic and inelastic collisions?

   b) Give an example of:

   i) an elastic collision

   ii) an inelastic collision.

3 An air rifle pellet of mass 2 g is fired into a block of plasticine mounted on a model railway truck. The truck and plasticine have a mass of 0.1 kg. The truck moves off after the pellet hits the plasticine with an initial velocity of 0.8 m/s. Calculate the momentum of the plasticine and truck after the collision. Hence work out the velocity of the pellet just before it hits the plasticine.

4 A rocket of mass 1200 kg is travelling at 2000 m/s. It fires its engine for 1 minute. If the forward thrust provided by the rocket engines is 10 kN (10 000 N), what is the increase in momentum of the rocket? From this, work out the increase in velocity of the rocket and its new velocity after firing the engines.

5 Crumple zones in cars are designed to reduce the forces during a collision. Explain how they do this.

Chapter 5: The Turning Effect of Forces

A force can have a turning effect – it can make an object turn around a fixed pivot point. When the anticlockwise turning effects of forces are balanced by turning forces in the clockwise direction, the object will not turn – it is in balance.

Figure 5.1 *Turning effects are used in many places.*

Forces applied to objects can make them accelerate or decelerate. In the examples in Figure 5.1, the forces acting are having a **turning effect**. They are tending to make the objects, like the see-saw, turn around a fixed point called a **pivot** or **fulcrum**. We use this turning effect of forces all the time. In our bodies the forces of our muscles make parts of our bodies turn around joints like our elbows or knees. When you turn a door handle, open a door or lever the lid off a tin of paint with a screwdriver you are using the turning effect of forces. Understanding the turning effect of forces is important. Sometimes we want things to turn or rotate – the see-saw wouldn't be much fun if it didn't. However, sometimes we want the turning effects to balance so that things don't turn – it would be disastrous if the crane did not balance!

Opening a door

a)

b)

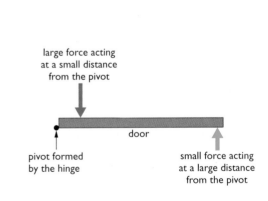

large force acting
at a small distance
from the pivot

door

pivot formed
by the hinge

small force acting
at a large distance
from the pivot

Figure 5.2 *The distance of the force from the pivot is crucial.*

Challenge a partner (perhaps one who thinks that he or she is strong!) to try to hold a door closed while you try to open it – then explain the rules! They can apply a pushing force but *no further than 20 cm* from the hinge, while you try to pull the door open by pulling on the handle. You will be able to open the door quite easily.

You will realise that you have an advantage because the turning effect of your force doesn't just depend on the *size* of the force you apply but also on the *distance* from the hinge or pivot at which you apply it. You have the advantage of greater leverage (Figure 5.2).

The moment of a force

The turning effect of a force about a hinge or pivot is called its **moment**. The moment of a force is defined like this:

moment of a force (in Nm) = force, *F* (in N) × perpendicular distance from pivot, *d* (in m)

moment = $F \times d$

The moment of a force is measured in newton metres (Nm) because force is measured in newtons and the distance to the pivot is in metres. We need to be precise about what distance we measure when calculating the moment of a force. Look at the diagrams in Figure 5.3.

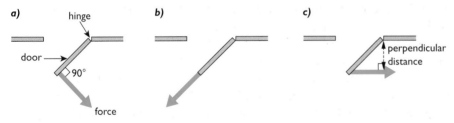

Figure 5.3 *For a force to have its biggest effect it should be at 90° to the lever.*

If you think about the simple door opening "competition" we discussed earlier you will realise that, for a force to have the biggest turning effect, it should be applied as in Figure 5.3a – that is, its line of action should be perpendicular (at 90°) to the door.

In Figure 5.3b the force has *no turning effect at all* because the line along which the force is acting passes through the pivot.

Figure 5.3c shows how the distance to the pivot must be measured to get the correct value for the moment. The distance is the *perpendicular distance from the line of action of the force to the pivot*.

In balance

An object will be in balance (that is, it will not try to turn about a pivot point) if:

sum of anticlockwise moments = sum of clockwise moments

For example, Figure 5.4 shows two children sitting on a see-saw.

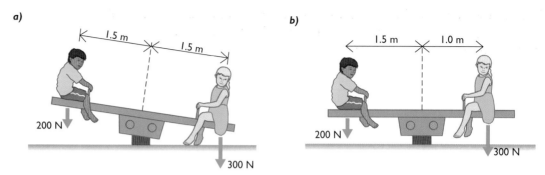

a)

b)

Figure 5.4 *The moment of the heavier child is reduced when she sits closer to the pivot, so that it balances the moment of the lighter child.*

The calculations are approximate because the forces are not acting perpendicularly to the see-saw.

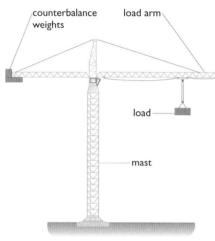

Figure 5.5 *The clockwise and anticlockwise moments on the crane must be balanced.*

In Figure 5.4a:

the anticlockwise moment = 200 N × 1.5 m = 300 Nm

the clockwise moment = 300 N × 1.5 m = 450 Nm

So the see-saw is not balanced and tips down to the right as it rotates clockwise about the pivot.

In Figure 5.4b:

the anticlockwise moment = 200 N × 1.5 m = 300 Nm

the clockwise moment = 300 N × 1.0 m = 300 Nm

So the see-saw is now balanced.

Look back at Figure 5.1 and look at Figure 5.5. The load arm is long so that the crane can reach across a construction site and move loads backwards and forwards along the length of the arm. The weight of the long load arm and the load must be counterbalanced by the large concrete blocks at the end of the short arm that projects out behind the crane controller's cabin. The **counterbalance** weights must be large because they are positioned closer to the pivot point, where the crane tower supports the crosspiece of the crane. Without careful balance the turning forces on the support tower could cause it to bend and collapse.

Centre of gravity

Try balancing a ruler on your finger, as shown in Figure 5.6.

When the ruler is balanced, the anticlockwise moment is equal to the clockwise moment, but there are no downward forces acting in this situation other than the weight of the ruler itself. We know that the weight of the ruler is due to the pull of the Earth's gravity on the mass of the ruler. The mass of the ruler is evenly spread throughout its length. It is not, therefore, surprising to find that the ruler balances at its centre point.

We say that the **centre of gravity** of the ruler is at this point – it is the point where the whole of the weight of the ruler appears to act. This means that the weight force acts at this point, so if we support the ruler at this point there is no turning moment in any direction about the point, and it balances. The centre of gravity is sometimes called the **centre of mass**.

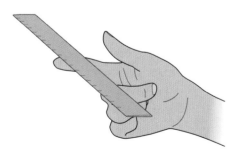

Figure 5.6 *Can you find the point at which the ruler balances?*

Finding the centre of gravity of a sheet of card

If you have a symmetrical sheet of card or any other uniform material then finding its centre of gravity is quite straight forward – it will be located where the axes of symmetry cross, as shown in Figure 5.7.

● = centre of gravity

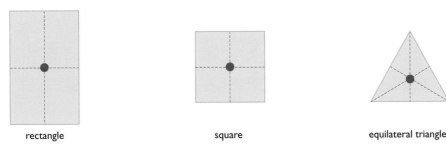

rectangle   square   equilateral triangle

Figure 5.7 *The centre of gravity for these three regular shapes is where the axes of symmetry cross. An axis of symmetry can be found using a plane mirror. If you place a plane mirror along one of the dotted lines in any of the above shapes, the reflection in the mirror looks exactly like the original.*

If the sheet of card has an irregular shape then this method clearly cannot be applied. To find the centre of gravity of an irregularly shaped sheet simply suspend it freely by a point on its edge, as shown in Figure 5.8a.

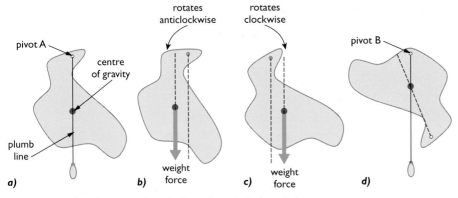

Figure 5.8 *Finding the centre of gravity for an irregularly shaped object.*

The point of suspension is a pivot point so the shape will come to rest in the balance position. The shape is in balance when there is no turning effect about the pivot. This will be when the centre of gravity of the shape is *vertically below the pivot*. If it were not, then the line of action of the weight force, passing through the centre of gravity, would not pass through the pivot and there would be a turning effect. Figures 5.8b and c show that if the centre of gravity is not directly below the pivot, there is a turning effect acting on the shape – so it rotates until the centre of gravity is below the pivot and the system is in balance.

If a plumb line (a small mass on the end of a thread) is hung from the pivot point, a line can be drawn perpendicularly down from the pivot – the centre of gravity must lie somewhere along this line. If this procedure is repeated, suspending the shape from a different pivot point as shown in Figure 5.8d, a second perpendicular line can be drawn on the sheet. The centre of gravity will lie at the point where the two lines cross.

Objects not pivoted at the centre of gravity

A simple see-saw is a uniform beam pivoted in the middle. The centre of gravity of a uniform beam is in the middle, so the see-saw is pivoted through its centre of gravity. When an object is not pivoted through its centre of gravity the weight of the object will produce a turning effect. This is shown in Figure 5.9.

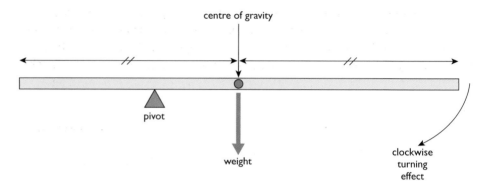

Figure 5.9 *The weight of the beam causes a clockwise turning effect about the pivot.*

Centre of gravity and stability

The position of the centre of gravity of an object will affect its stability. A **stable** object is one that is difficult to push over; when pushed and then released it will tend to return to its original position.

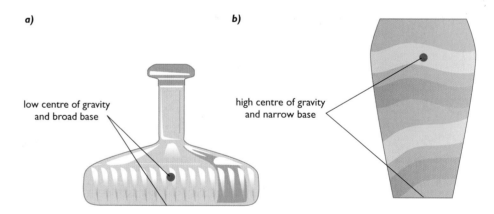

Figure 5.10 *Stable and unstable objects.*

The shape in Figure 5.10a is typical for a ship's decanter (bottle). Bottles used on ships need to be difficult to knock over for obvious reasons! It is stable because, when tipped, its low centre of gravity and wide base result in a turning moment that tries to pull it back to its original position. The object in Figure 5.10b has a higher centre of gravity and smaller base, so it is much less stable. Only a small displacement is needed to make it topple over.

Forces on a beam

Figure 5.11a shows a boy standing on a **beam** across a stream. The beam is not moving, so the upward and downward forces must be balanced. As the boy is standing in the middle of the beam, the upward forces on the ends of the beam are the same as each other. The forces are shown in Figure 5.11b – to keep things simple, we are ignoring the weight of the beam.

If he moves right to one end of the beam, as shown in Figure 5.11c, then the upward force will all be at that end of the beam. As he moves along the beam, the upward forces at the ends of the beam change. In Figure 5.11d, he is $\frac{1}{4}$ of the way along the plank. The upward force on the support nearest to him is $\frac{3}{4}$ of his weight, and the upward force on the end furthest away from him is only $\frac{1}{4}$ of his weight.

a)

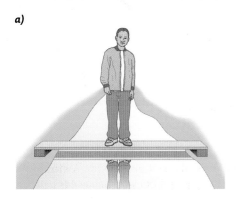

b)

Boy's weight = 400 N

200 N   200 N

c)

400 N

400 N

Figure 5.11 *The forces at the ends of a beam depend on where the load is applied.*

d)

400 N

300 N

100 N

End of Chapter Checklist

You will need to be able to do the following:

✓ understand that forces can have a turning effect or moment on a body

✓ recall that the moment of a force is given by force × perpendicular distance from force to pivot

✓ understand and apply the condition for balance to an object: sum of anticlockwise acting moments = sum of clockwise acting moments

✓ explain what is meant by centre of gravity

✓ find the centre of gravity of regularly and irregularly shaped sheets of material by simple experiment

✓ appreciate that stable objects have low centres of gravity and wide bases

✓ understand that when a heavy object is resting on a beam, the upward forces at the ends of the beam depend on the position of the object.

Questions

More questions on the turning effect of forces can be found at the end of Section A on page 57.

1 Look at the diagram below. It shows various forces acting on objects about pivots. Which one has the largest moment? Put the diagrams in order starting with the largest moment.

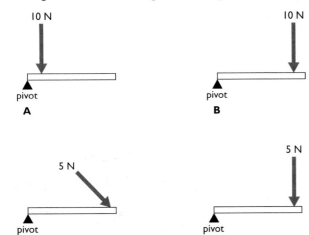

2 **a)** Which see-saw in the diagram below is balanced?

   b) In which direction will the unbalanced see-saws tip?

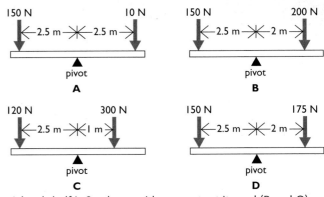

3 A bookshelf is 2 m long, with supports at its end (P and Q).

   a) Draw a sketch of the shelf, showing the supports.

   b) A book weighing 10 N is placed in the middle of the shelf. What are the upward forces at P and Q?

   c) The book is moved so that it is 50 cm from Q. What are the forces at P and Q now?

   d) The first book is still 50 cm from Q. Another book with a weight of 5 N is put in the middle of the shelf. What are the forces at P and Q? (You can work out the forces at P and Q due to the two books separately, then add them together.)

   e) The bookshelf weighs 10 N. Repeat parts **b)** and **c)** taking into account the weight of the shelf as well as the weight of the book.

Chapter 6: Astronomy

Our Solar System is held together by gravitational forces acting between bodies. These forces hold planets, asteroids and comets in orbit around the Sun, and keep moons and satellites in orbit around planets. In this chapter you will read about the planets and how the orbital speed of a planet or moon depends on its distance from the centre of its orbit.

Many years ago travellers, and in particular sailors, believed that the Earth was flat and if they travelled too far, they would fall over the edge. Figure 6.1 is a photograph that was taken from a Lunar Orbiter 1 orbiting the Moon in 1966. It clearly shows that the ancient travellers had incorrect ideas about the shape of the Earth.

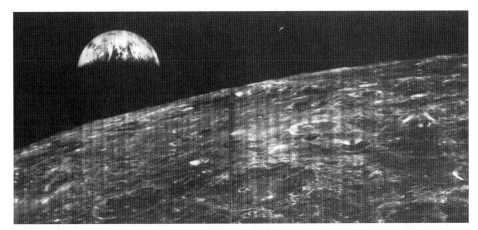

Figure 6. 1 *The world's first view of the Earth. This photograph was taken by Lunar Orbiter 1 orbiting the Earth in 1966.*

Our explanations of the behaviour of astronomical bodies, such as moons, planets and stars are based upon the evidence we have before us today. In the future new evidence may be found, which may cause us to change our present-day ideas and models.

The Solar System

Figure 6.2 *Our Solar System.*

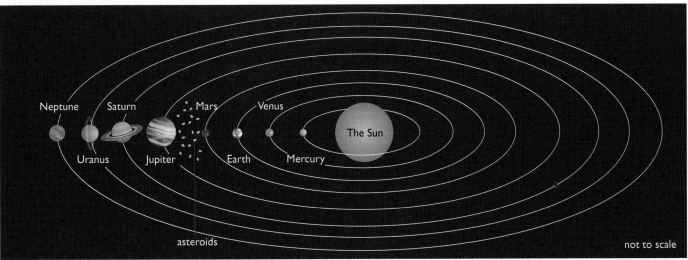

The Earth is one of eight planets that orbit the Sun. The orbits of the planets are **elliptical** (like squashed circles) with the Sun close to the centre.

The table gives some information about the planets, compared to Earth.

Planet	Average distance from Sun compared with the Earth	Time for one orbit of the Sun in Earth years	Diameter compared with the Earth	Average surface temperature (°C)	Gravitational field strength (N/kg)
Mercury	0.4	0.2	0.4	+350	4
Venus	0.7	0.6	0.9	+470	9
Earth	1.0	1.0	1.0	+15	10
Mars	1.5	1.9	0.5	−30	4
Jupiter	5.0	12	11	−150	23
Saturn	9.5	30	9	−180	9
Uranus	19	84	4	−210	9
Neptune	30	165	4	−220	11

The strength of gravity on a planet or moon is called its **gravitational field strength**, and given the symbol g. In Chapter 3 you saw that the gravitational field strength on the Earth is approximately 10 N/kg, and on the Moon it is approximately 1.6 N/kg.

Planets are **non-luminous** objects – they do not emit light. We see them because they *reflect* light from the Sun. The five planets closest to the Sun (not including the Earth) are all visible to us with the naked eye. The last two planets – Uranus and Neptune – are so far away that they were only discovered after the invention of the telescope.

HST · WFPC2
December 1, 1994

Figure 6.3 *We can see Saturn because it reflects light from the Sun, but does not emit light itself.*

Planets are held in orbit by the **gravitational pull** of the Sun. The gravitational pull on Mercury is quite large compared with that exerted on Neptune. This is the reason Mercury follows a much more tightly curved path than Neptune.

Planets and stars can look very similar in the night sky. But if you watch them over a period of several nights the planets will change their positions against the background of the distant stars. The word "planet" comes from the ancient Greek word meaning *wanderer*.

Figure 6.4 *These photographs, taken over several days, show how the planet Mars moves across the background of stars, the Pleiades. The position in the sky in which we see a planet depends upon where it and the Earth are in their orbits.*

Moons

Moons are natural objects that orbit a planet. Their motions, like those of the planets, are determined by gravitational forces. Moons are non-luminous objects. We see them because they reflect light from the Sun.

The Earth has just one moon. It is approximately 400 000 km from the Earth and has a mass and surface gravity just one sixth that of the Earth. The Moon has no atmosphere and has a surface that is covered with craters caused by the impact of meteorites.

It takes the Moon 29.5 days (1 **lunar month**) to orbit the Earth. The Moon, like the Earth, spins on its axis, but much more slowly than the Earth turns. It completes one full rotation every 29.5 days. Because the time it takes to complete one orbit around the Earth is the same as the time for one rotation, the Moon always keeps the same part of its surface facing the Earth.

Some planets have no moons and some have more than one. For instance, Mars has two moons, Jupiter has over 60 moons and Uranus has 27 moons. Some moons are very small and not easily seen from the Earth and more are being discovered orbiting the outer planets.

Figure 6.5 *Gibbous moon. There are many craters on the surface of the Moon.*

Comets

Comets orbit the Sun. They are approximately 1–30 km in diameter and made of dust and ice. Their orbits are very elongated. At times they are very close to the Sun, while at other times they are found at the outer reaches of the Solar System.

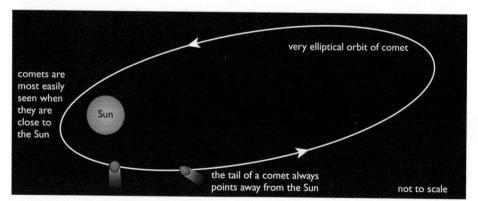

Figure 6.6 *As a comet gets closer to the Sun, the gravitational forces acting upon it increase and it speeds up. At the opposite end of its orbit, a long way from the Sun, the gravitational forces are smaller, so the comet travels at its slowest speed.*

Figure 6.7 *Halley's comet could be last viewed from Earth in 1986.*

Close to the Sun, some of a comet's frozen gases evaporate, forming a long tail that shines in the sunlight. These tails can be millions of kilometres in length. Perhaps the most famous of the comets is Halley's Comet, which visits our part of the Solar System every 76 years. It was last visible from the Earth in 1986.

Asteroids

Asteroids are minor planets or rocks that orbit the Sun. There is a belt of asteroids between the orbits of Mars and Jupiter. They vary greatly in size from just a few metres to several hundreds of kilometres across. The first asteroid to be discovered was called Ceres. It has a diameter of 933 km. It is believed that asteroids were formed at the same time as the rest of the Solar System and possibly are the rocky remains of a planet that broke apart or failed to form.

Satellites

Satellites are objects that orbit a planet. They are held in orbit by gravitational forces. Moons are examples of **natural satellites**. Some objects that orbit the planets are manufactured objects. They are **artificial satellites**.

Gravitational forces

The movements of all astronomical bodies – for example, planets, comets and asteroids – are determined by gravitational forces. It was careful observation and measurement of the movements of planets that led to developments in the theory of gravity.

Astronomical models

Initially, it was thought that the Earth was at the centre of the Universe and other astronomical bodies moved around it. This was known as the Ptolemaic System, after the Egyptian astronomer Ptolemy who published a detailed model of this idea in approximately 150 AD. Later, however, careful observation of the movements of the stars and planets led to this model being abandoned and new models with the Sun at the centre of the Solar System (heliocentric systems) were suggested.

Figure 6.8 *The Hubble Space Telescope being launched from the cargo bay of the Space Shuttle. The HST is an artificial satellite.*

The Earth-centred model of the Solar System.

In 1530 Nicolai Copernicus suggested this Sun-centred model of the Solar System.

Johannes Kepler suggested that the orbits of planets are elliptical and not circular. The new model agreed closely with the observations and measurements of astronomers.

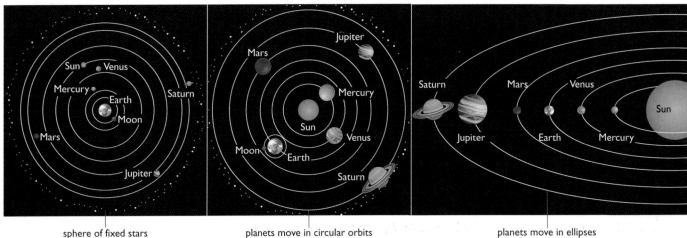

sphere of fixed stars

planets move in circular orbits around the Sun

planets move in ellipses

Figure 6.9 *The development of astronomical models.*

In 1687, Isaac Newton put forward a theory of gravity. This theory not only explained the movements of the planets in the Solar System but also eventually provided an explanation of how the stars and the Solar System were formed.

Newton's Laws of Gravity

Newton suggested that between any two objects there is a force of attraction. This attraction is due to the masses of the objects. He called this force **gravitational force**. The size of this force depends upon:

1 the masses of the two objects

2 the distance between the masses.

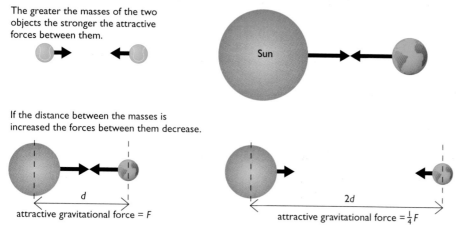

The greater the masses of the two objects the stronger the attractive forces between them.

Sun

If the distance between the masses is increased the forces between them decrease.

d

attractive gravitational force = F

$2d$

attractive gravitational force = $\frac{1}{4}F$

Figure 6.10 *Gravitational forces obey an inverse square law – that is, if the distance between the masses is doubled, the forces between them are quartered; if the distance between them is trebled, the forces become one ninth of what they were.*

The gravitational attraction between two objects with small masses is extremely small. Only when one or both of the objects has a very large mass – for example, a moon or a planet – is the force of attraction noticeable.

Moving in a circle

The model aircraft in Figure 6.11 flies in a circle because a force is being applied to it through the wire. If the wire breaks the aircraft will fly away in a straight line.

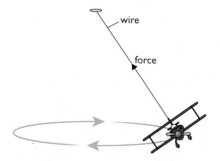

wire

force

Figure 6.11 *If an object is to travel in a circle, a force must be applied to it.*

Planets travel in orbits around the Sun. They must have a force applied to them. This force is the gravitational attraction between two masses. Our Sun contains over 99% of the mass of the Solar System. It is the gravitational attraction between this mass and each of the planets that holds the Solar System together and causes the planets to follow their curved paths.

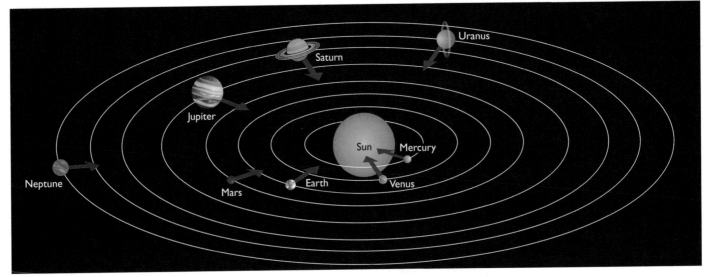

Figure 6.12 *Gravitational forces make the planets follow curved paths.*

Orbital speeds of satellites

The speeds of satellites vary greatly depending on the tasks they are performing. For example, communication satellites are put in high orbits and travel at approximately 3 km/s, while those monitoring the whole surface of the Earth are put into low polar orbits with speeds of about 8 km/s.

> The orbital period of a communications satellite is 24 hours, so that it remains above the same part of the Earth's surface. It is said to be 'geostationary'.

We can calculate the speed of a satellite using the equation:

$$\text{speed} = \frac{\text{distance}}{\text{time period}}$$

In orbital terms, the distance travelled is the circumference of the circular orbit:

$$\text{distance} = 2 \times \pi \times \text{radius of orbit}$$

The time period is the time for one complete orbit (**T**). So:

> Remember to be consistent with your units. Distances are likely to be given in kilometres and so must be converted into metres. In the example, you must multiply both 8.2 km and 6600 km by 1000. Times given in hours and minutes need to be conveerted into seconds.

$$\text{orbital speed} = \frac{2 \times \pi \times \text{orbital radius}}{\text{time period}}$$

$$\text{orbital speed} = \frac{2\pi r}{T}$$

The same equation can be used to calculate the speeds of the planets, where r is the average distance from the Sun.

Worked example

Example 1

Calculate the speed of a satellite that is orbiting 200 km above the Earth's surface and completes one orbit in 1 h 24 min. The radius of the Earth is 6400 km.

Orbital period = $1.4 \times 60 \times 60$ seconds
= 5040 seconds

Using orbital speed = $2\pi \times \dfrac{r}{T}$

orbital speed = $2\pi \times \dfrac{6600 \text{ km}}{5040 \text{ s}}$ or   = $2\pi \times \dfrac{6\,600\,000 \text{ m}}{5040 \text{ s}}$

= 8.2 km/s   = 8200 m/s

The Milky Way

Our nearest star is the Sun. It is approximately 150 million kilometres from the Earth. Its surface temperature is approximately 6000 °C whilst temperatures within its core are about 15 000 000 °C. Gravitational forces between stars cause them to cluster together in enormous groups called **galaxies**. Galaxies consist of billions of stars. Our galaxy is a **spiral galaxy** called the **Milky Way**. We are approximately two thirds of the way out from the centre of our galaxy along one of the arms of the spiral.

The Universe is mainly empty space within which are scattered large numbers of galaxies – astronomers believe that there are billions of galaxies in the Universe. The distances between galaxies are millions of times greater than the distances between stars within a galaxy. The distances between the stars in a galaxy are millions of times greater than the distances between planets and the Sun.

Figure 6.13 *A spiral-shaped galaxy, something like our own.*

You will need to be able to do the following:

✓ recall that the Earth is one of eight planets in the Solar System, and that the Earth and some of the other planets have moons orbiting them

✓ explain what gravitational field strength means, and recall that it is different on other planets and moons

✓ explain that gravitational force causes the planets and comets to orbit the Sun, and causes moons and artificial satellites to orbit planets

✓ describe how the orbit of a comet is different to the orbit of a planet

✓ recall and use the equation for orbital speed: orbital speed $= \dfrac{2\pi r}{T}$

✓ recall that the Solar System is part of the Milky Way galaxy, and that the Universe is a large collection of billions of galaxies.

Questions

More questions on the Solar System and gravity can be found at the end of Section A on page 57.

1 a) What is an asteroid?

   b) What is a comet?

   c) Describe two differences between an asteroid and a comet.

   d) In which direction does the tail of a comet point?

   e) Describe how the speed of a comet changes as it orbits the Sun.

2 What is the Milky Way?

3 A satellite is in an orbit 35,786 km above the surface of the Earth. The radius of the Earth is approximately 6400 km. The satellite is moving at 3.07 km/s.

   a) How long does the satellite take to orbit the Earth once?

   b) What do you notice about the period of this satellite? (Hint: convert the period into hours.)

4 Work out the speed at which the following planets are moving around the Sun. The information you need is in the table on page 50.

   a) Earth

   b) Jupiter

1 Copy and complete the following passage about forces, filling in the spaces.

Forces are _____ quantities that can change the _____ or motion of bodies. The _____ caused by a force depends on the size of the force and on the _____ of the body. Falling objects are acted on by their _____ and by air resistance. A falling object reaches its _____ velocity when the weight and drag forces are _____ .

Objects that must balance, such as cranes, must have equal _____ in each direction. The moment of a force depends on the size of the force and on the _____ distance between the force and the _____ .

Total 10 marks

2 The diagram shows a displacement–time graph for a person taking a walk.

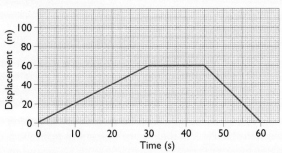

a) How fast is the person walking during the first 30 seconds of the walk? Show how you obtained your answer.
(3 marks)

b) Describe what the person is doing during the next 15 seconds.
(1 mark)

c) What is the person doing during the last 15 seconds of the walk?
(3 marks)

d) What is the average velocity of the person during the first 45 seconds of the walk?
(2 marks)

Total 9 marks

3 The diagram shows a velocity–time graph for a space shuttle during the early part of a flight.

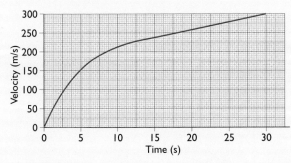

a) Calculate the acceleration during the first 5 seconds of the flight. Show all steps in your working.
(3 marks)

b) Estimate the distance travelled during the first 30 seconds of the flight. Explain your method.
(4 marks)

c) What is the average velocity of the shuttle during the 30-second period shown on the graph?
(3 marks)

Total 10 marks

4 A parachutist jumps from a plane flying at a height of 5000 metres. She falls for 30 seconds before opening her parachute. Take the acceleration due to gravity as 9.8 m/s^2.

a) If we ignore the effect of air resistance, how fast will the parachutist be falling after 30 seconds?
(2 marks)

b) In practice, we cannot ignore air resistance. Use a sketch graph to show how the velocity of the parachutist will *actually* change as she falls. Explain the shape of your sketch graph.
(4 marks)

Total 6 marks

5 A car travelling at 40 m/s brakes and decelerates uniformly to rest. The car has a mass of 700 kg. The car takes 10 s to come to rest.

a) Work out the deceleration of the car.
(3 marks)

b) What is the average braking force acting on the car?
(2 marks)

Total 5 marks

6 Copy this diagram of a wooden float tethered to the seabed so that it is completely submerged.

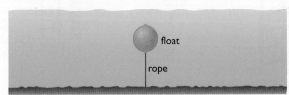

a) Label all the forces that act on the float, the rope and the sea bed. Indicate the direction in which each force acts.
(4 marks)

b) The float is not moving. What does this tell us about the forces acting on it?
(2 marks)

c) The rope securing the float to the seabed breaks. Describe what happens to the float.
(2 marks)

Total 8 marks

7 The diagram below shows the hand on a swimming pool clock. The hand is balanced so that the turning effect of the weight of each side of the hand is the same. This makes it easier for the low-power electric motor to keep the hand moving round at a steady rate. The hand measures 80 cm from tip to tip.

a) Define the *moment* or turning effect of a force.   *(2 marks)*

b) A clock of this type is checked and the hands are found to be unbalanced. The result is that there is a clockwise moment of 0.05 Nm. You are provided with a number of small self-adhesive weights, each weighing 0.1 N. Show how you would use these to re-balance the hand, so that the turning moment about the centre spindle is zero. You should use a diagram to illustrate your answer.   *(5 marks)*

Total 7 marks

8 The drawing shows part of a climbing frame in a playground.

The girl weighs 300 N and the boy weighs 350 N.

a) What are the upward forces at A and B if the girl is hanging in the centre of the climbing frame?   *(2 marks)*

b) Both children hang from the frame at a point 1 m from A. What are the upward forces at A and B? Show all your working.   *(4 marks)*

c) Where would both children have to be so that the upward force at B was at its minimum?   *(1 mark)*

Total 7 marks

9 a) Define *momentum*.   *(2 marks)*

b) A cannon, of mass 200 kg, fires a cannon ball with a mass of 10 kg. The cannon ball leaves the barrel of the cannon with a velocity of 60 m/s. Using the law of conservation of momentum, explain what happens to the cannon when the cannon ball is fired. Your answer should include a calculation.   *(6 marks)*

Total 8 marks

10 The table below contains information about some of the planets in our Solar System.

Planet	Surface gravity compared with the Earth	Distance from Sun compared with the Earth	Period in Earth years
Mercury	0.4	0.4	0.2
Venus	0.9	0.7	0.6
Mars	0.4	1.5	1.9
Jupiter	2.6	5.0	12
Saturn	1.1	9.5	30

a) Name three planets that have a weaker gravitational pull on their surface than there is on Earth.   *(1 mark)*

b) How long is a year on Saturn?   *(1 mark)*

c) If the distance from the Earth to the Sun is 150 million kilometres, calculate the distance of Saturn from the Sun.   *(2 marks)*

d) Assuming that the orbital path for Saturn is circular, calculate its orbital speed in km/s. (Hint: circumference of a circle = 2πr.)   *(3 marks)*

Total 7 marks

11 a) Draw a diagram to show the shape of the orbit of a comet around the Sun.   *(2 marks)*

b) Describe and explain how the speed of a comet changes as it travels around its orbit.   *(4 marks)*

Total 6 marks

Chapter 7: Mains Electricity

We use mains electricity, supplied by power stations, for all kinds of appliances in our homes, so it is very important to know how to use it safely. In this chapter you will learn how mains electricity is brought into our homes and supplied to appliances. You also will read about devices that protect users from electric shocks.

Using electricity

Figure 7.1 *We use a huge amount of electricity every day for heating and lighting.*

When you turn on your computer, television and most other appliances in your home the electricity you use is almost certainly going to come from the **mains supply**. This electrical energy usually enters our homes through an underground cable. The cable is connected to an **electricity meter**, which measures the amount of electrical energy used. From here, the cable is connected to a **consumer unit** or a **fuse box**, which contains fuses or circuit breakers for the various circuits in your home. Fuses and circuit breakers are safety devices which shut off the electricity in a circuit if the current in them becomes too large (see page 61).

Most of the wires that leave the fuse box are connected to **ring main circuits** that are hidden in the walls or floors around each room. Individual pieces of electrical equipment are connected to these circuits using plugs.

Ring circuits usually consist of three wires – the live wire, the neutral wire and the earth wire.

The **live wire** provides the path along which the electrical energy from the power station travels. This wire is alternately positive and negative causing **alternating current** (**ac**) to flow along it.

The **neutral wire** completes the circuit.

Figure 7.2 *Consumer unit in a house.*

Ring main circuits provide a way of allowing several appliances in different parts of the same room to be connected to the mains using the minimum amount of wiring. Imagine how much wire would be needed if there was just one mains socket in each room.

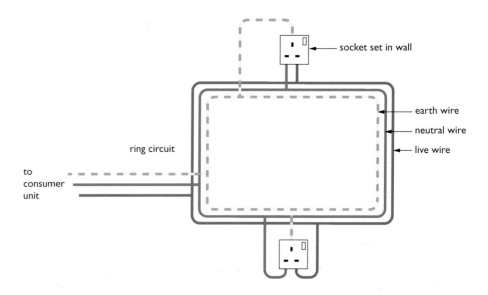

Figure 7.3 *Ring mains help to cut down on the amount of wiring needed in a house.*

The **earth wire** usually has no current flowing through it. It is there to protect you if an appliance develops a fault.

Plugs and sockets in different countries look different, but the principles of electrical wiring are similar.

Figure 7.4 *Plug sockets in the UK and in Portugal.*

Mains electricity is supplied to homes in the UK at about 230 V. This is a much higher voltage than the cells and batteries used in portable electrical appliances. If you come into direct contact with mains electricity you could receive a severe electric shock, which might even be fatal. The outer part of a plug, called the casing, is therefore made from plastic, which is a good insulator. Connections to the circuits are made via three brass pins, as brass is an excellent conductor of electricity. Figure 7.5b shows some common mistakes made when wiring a plug. This figure shows the inside of a 3-pin plug used in the UK, but similar principles apply to all kinds of plug.

Using electricity safely

Electricity is very useful, but it can be dangerous if it is not used safely. There are safety devices built into houses and electrical appliances that you will learn about later, but there are things we can do to keep ourselves safe as well.

a)

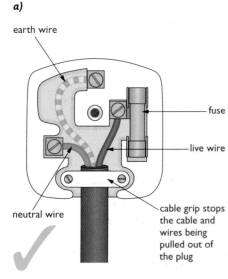

earth wire

fuse

live wire

neutral wire

cable grip stops the cable and wires being pulled out of the plug

b)

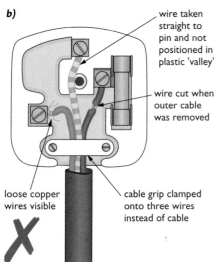

wire taken straight to pin and not positioned in plastic 'valley'

wire cut when outer cable was removed

loose copper wires visible

cable grip clamped onto three wires instead of cable

Figure 7.5 a) *A correctly wired UK plug.*
b) *How not to wire a plug!*

a)

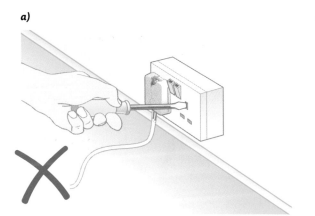

b)

Figure 7.6 *Some electrical hazards.*

Figure 7.6 shows some of the following hazards of electricity that can easily be avoided. Broken plugs and frayed wires can expose the metal wires or parts of the plug that are carrying the electricity. Anyone touching these would get an electric shock, so they should be replaced as soon as the damage occurs. Anyone poking a metal object into a socket will also get an electric shock. Cables to electrical appliances should be kept as short as possible to prevent them causing spills. Water can conduct electricity at high voltages, so spilling water onto electrical equipment can be dangerous. Water should also be kept away from sockets and you must never use electrical equipment with wet hands.

Safety devices

Fuses

Many plugs contain a fuse. The fuse is usually in the form of a cylinder or cartridge, which contains a thin piece of wire made from a metal that has a low melting point. If too large a current flows in the circuit the fuse wire becomes very hot and melts. The fuse "blows", shutting the circuit off. This prevents you getting a shock and reduces the possibility of an electrical fire. Once the fault causing the surge of current has been corrected, the blown fuse must be replaced with a new one of the same size before the appliance can be used again.

There are several sizes of fuses. The most common for domestic appliances are 3 A, 5 A and 13 A. The correct fuse for a circuit is the one that allows the correct current to flow but blows if the current is a little larger. If the correct current in a circuit is 2 A then it should be protected with a 3 A fuse. If the correct current is 4 A then a 5 A fuse should be used. It is possible to calculate the correct size of fuse for an appliance but nowadays manufacturers provide appliances fitted with the correct size of fuse.

Modern safety devices such as those you might find in your consumer unit are often in the form of **trip switches** or **circuit breakers**. If too large a current flows in a circuit a switch opens making the circuit incomplete. Once the fault in the circuit has been corrected, the switch is reset, usually by pressing a reset button. There is no need for the switch or circuit breaker to be replaced, as there is when fuses are used. The consumer unit shown in Figure 7.2 uses circuit breakers.

circuit symbol for a fuse

Figure 7.7 *Fuses are important safety devices in electrical appliances.*

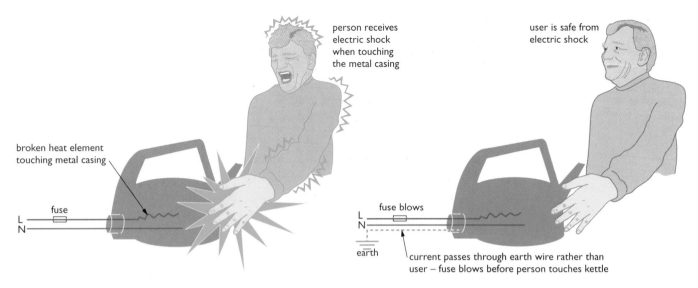

person receives
electric shock
when touching
the metal casing

user is safe from
electric shock

broken heat element
touching metal casing

fuse

L
N

fuse blows

L
N

earth

current passes through earth wire rather than
user – fuse blows before person touches kettle

Figure 7.8 *The earth wire provides protection when electrical appliances develop a fault.*

Earth wires and double insulation

Many appliances have a metal casing. This should be connected to the earth wire so that if the live wire becomes frayed or breaks and comes into contact with the casing the earth wire provides a low-resistance path for the current. This current is likely to be large enough to blow the fuse and turn the circuit off. Without the earth wire anyone touching the casing of the faulty appliance would receive a severe electric shock as current passed through them to earth (Figure 7.8).

Some modern appliances now use casings made from an insulator such as plastic rather than from metal. If all the electrical parts of an appliance are insulated in this way, so that they cannot be touched by the user, the appliance is said to have **double insulation**. Appliances that have double insulation use a two-wire flex. There is no need for an earth wire.

Switches

Switches in mains circuits should always be included in the live wire so that when the switch is open no electrical energy can reach an appliance. If the switch is included in the neutral wire, electrical energy can still enter an appliance, and could possibly cause an electric shock (Figure 7.10).

Figure 7.9 *This plastic kettle has double insulation which means that there is no need for an earth wire.*

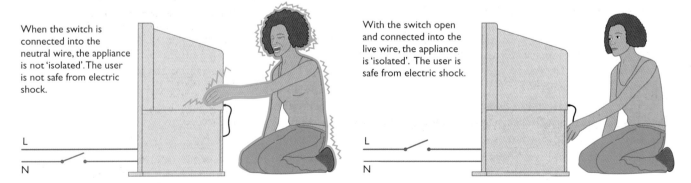

When the switch is
connected into the
neutral wire, the appliance
is not 'isolated'. The user
is not safe from electric
shock.

With the switch open
and connected into the
live wire, the appliance
is 'isolated'. The user is
safe from electric shock.

L
N

L
N

Figure 7.10 *The switch in a circuit should be in the live wire.*

The heating effect of current

The wiring in a house is designed to let current pass through it easily, and we say that it has a low **resistance**. However things such as the heating elements in kettles or toasters (Figure 7.11) are designed to have a high resistance. As the current passes through the element, energy is transferred and the element heats up. We use the heating effect of current in many different ways in our homes. You will learn more about resistance in Chapter 10.

In the kitchen shown in Figure 7.12 the heating effect of electricity is used in the toaster, kettle, dishwasher, cooker and washing machine. It is also used in the lights – normal light bulbs have a very thin filament which gets so hot when current passes through it that it glows white. The heating effect of electricity is also used in electric fires and fan heaters, hair dryers and so on.

Figure 7.11 *The wires inside a toaster have a high resistance and heat up when a current passes through them*

Figure 7.12 *Uses of electricity in a kitchen.*

Electrical power

Figure 7.13 shows two light bulbs connected to a supply of electricity. Both bulbs are converting electrical energy into heat and light. The brighter 100 W bulb is converting 100 J of electrical energy into 100 J of heat and light energy every second. The dimmer 60 W bulb is converting 60 J of electrical energy into 60 J of heat and light energy every second. The 100 W bulb has a higher **power** rating.

Power is measured in joules per second or **watts** (W).

The power (*P*) of an appliance is related to the voltage (*V*) across it and the current (*I*) flowing through it. You will learn more about voltage and current in Chapters 9 and 10.

The equation is:

> **power, *P* (in watts) = current, *I* (in amps) × voltage, *V* (in volts)**
> $$P = I \times V$$

Figure 7.13 *The 100 W bulb converts more electrical energy into heat and light energy every second.*

Figure 7.14 *You can use the triangle method for rearranging equations like P = I × V.*

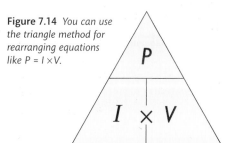

Worked example

If an examination question asks for the formula for calculating power, voltage or current, always give the actual equation (such as $P = I \times V$).
You may not be awarded a mark if you just draw the triangle.

Example 1

If a 230 V television takes a current of 3 A, calculate its power.

$P = I \times V$

$P = 3\,A \times 230\,V$

$P = 690\,W$

Worked example

Example 2

Calculate the correct fuse that should be used for a 230 V, 1 kW electric hair dryer (1 kW = 1000 W).

$P = I \times V$

$I = \dfrac{P}{V}$

$I = \dfrac{1000\,W}{230\,V}$

$I = 4.3\,A$

The correct fuse for this hair dryer is therefore a 5 A fuse.

Calculating the total energy converted by an appliance

The power of an appliance (*P*) tells you how much energy it converts each second. This means that the total energy (*E*) converted by an appliance is equal to its power multiplied by the length of time (in seconds) the appliance is being used.

> **energy, *E* (in joules) = power, *P* (in watts) × time, *t* (in seconds)**
> $$E = P \times t$$
>
> since $P = I \times V$
> $$E = I \times V \times t$$

Worked example

Example 3

Calculate the energy converted by a 60 W bulb that is turned on for **a)** 20 s, and **b)** 5 min.

a) $E = P \times t$

$E = 60\,W \times 20\,s$

$E = 1200\,J$ or $1.2\,kJ$

b) $E = P \times t$

$E = 60\,W \times 5 \times 60\,s$

$E = 18\,000\,J$ or $18\,kJ$

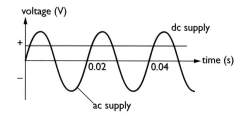

Figure 7.15 *How the voltage of an ac supply compares with that of a dc supply.*

Alternating current and direct current

The mains electricity supply provides alternating current (ac), which means that the flow of electricity is constantly changing direction. This is because of the way that electricity generators work – you will find out more about this in Chapter 22. Cells and batteries provide direct current (dc), where the current is always in the same direction. Figure 7.15 shows how the voltage of an ac supply compares with a dc supply.

You will need to be able to do the following:

✓ realise the dangers of using mains electricity incorrectly

✓ understand the steps taken to protect users from electric shocks – for example, use of insulators, earthing, fuses, circuit breakers and double insulation

✓ understand that a current can cause an energy transfer and give some examples of domestic uses of the heating effect

✓ understand the phrase "power rating" when applied to an electrical appliance and be able to use the equation $P = I \times V$ to determine the correct fuse to use with an appliance

✓ use the equation $E = I \times V \times t$ to calculate the total energy transferred by an appliance

✓ recall and explain the difference between alternating current (ac) and direct current (dc).

Questions

More questions on domestic electricity can be found at the end of Section B on page 89.

1   a) A current of 0.25 A flows through a bulb when a voltage of 12 V is applied across it. Calculate the power of the bulb.

   b) Calculate the voltage that is being applied across a 10 W bulb if a current of 0.2 A flows through it.

   c) Calculate the current that flows through a 60 W bulb if the voltage across it is 230 V.

   d) How much energy is transferred if a 100 W bulb is left on for 5 hours?

2   An electric kettle is marked "230 V, 1.5 kW".

   a) Explain what these figures mean.

   b) Calculate the correct fuse that should be used.

   c) Explain why a 230 V, 100 W bulb glows more brightly than a 230 V, 60 W bulb when both are connected to the mains supply.

3   a) Give one advantage of using a circuit breaker rather than a wire or cartridge fuse.

   b) Why is the switch for an appliance always placed in the live wire?

   c) What is meant by the sentence "The hair dryer has double insulation."?

Section B: Electricity

Chapter 8: Electric Charge

Static electricity is the result of an imbalance of charge. It can be very useful, but it can also be extremely hazardous. In this chapter, you will learn about some of the uses and problems associated with static electricity.

Figure 8.1 *Thunderclouds discharge their static electricity as lightning.*

The photograph in Figure 8.1 shows a spectacular example of **static electricity**. Bolts of lightning are seen when thunderclouds discharge their electricity. The discharging currents that flow can be as large as 20 000A and typically take place in just 0.1 s. The flow of such a large current causes the air to heat up to temperatures of approximately 30 000 °C. At such high temperatures, the air immediately around the bolt of lightning expands at supersonic speeds, causing thunder. As the sound waves travel outwards, they slow down and interact with the air and ground along their paths. The results of these interactions are the prolonged claps and rumbles we normally associate with thunder.

Charges within an atom

All atoms contain small particles called **protons**, **neutrons** and **electrons**. The protons are found in the centre or **nucleus** of the atom and carry a relative charge of +1. The neutrons are also in the nucleus of the atom but carry no charge. The electrons travel around the nucleus in orbits. The electrons carry a relative charge of −1.

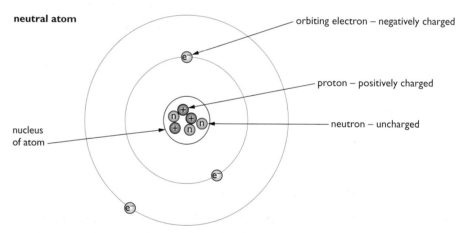

Figure 8.2 *A neutral atom has the same number of negative electrons and positive protons (not to scale).*

Normally the number of protons in the nucleus is equal to the number of orbiting electrons. The atom therefore has no overall charge. It is **neutral**. If an atom gains extra electrons, it is then negatively charged. If an atom loses electrons, it becomes positively charged. An atom that becomes charged by gaining or losing electrons is called an **ion**.

Charging materials by friction

Some materials are good electrical conductors, such as metals. Other materials do not allow electricity to flow through them easily, and are known as electrical insulators.

Electrical insulators include materials such as plastic, rubber, glass, wood, and so on. Insulating materials can be given an electric charge by rubbing them.

If an uncharged plastic rod is rubbed with an uncharged cloth, it is possible for both of them to become charged. This is sometimes called charging by friction. During the rubbing, electrons from the atoms of the rod may move onto the cloth. There is now an imbalance of charge in both objects. The rod is short of electrons and so is positively charged. The cloth has excess electrons and so is negatively charged.

It is important to remember that the rubbing action does not produce or create charge. It simply separates charge – that is, it transfers some electrons from one object to another.

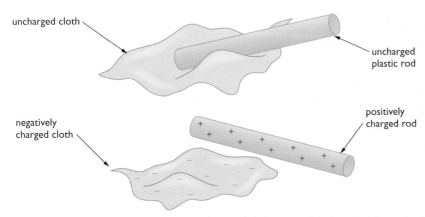

Figure 8.3 *Rubbing a neutral rod with a neutral piece of cloth can result in them both becoming charged.*

Forces between charges

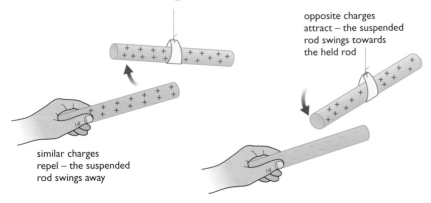

Figure 8.4 *Similar charges repel and opposite charges attract.*

Charged objects can exert forces on other charged objects without being in contact with them. If the charges are similar, the objects repel each other. If the charges are dissimilar (opposite), the objects attract each other.

The photograph in Figure 8.5 shows what can happen if a person is charged with static electricity. The girl has her hands on a Van de Graaff generator. When it is turned on, charges flow onto the large metal dome. Some of the charges flow over her hands and onto all parts of her body including her hair. Each strand of hair has the same type of charge as its neighbour, so there are repulsive forces between the strands. These forces cause her hair to stand on end.

For this demonstration to work, the girl must stand on an insulator to prevent any of the charges she is receiving from the generator from escaping into the floor. At the end of the demonstration the girl steps off the insulator – the charges can now escape and her hair falls. When a path is provided for charges to escape it is called **earthing**.

Figure 8.5 *A build-up of static electricity means that each hair on the girl's head has the same charge, and they repel each other.*

Forces between charged and uncharged objects

It is possible for a charged object to attract something that is uncharged.

The balloon experiment

If you charge a balloon by rubbing it against your jumper or your hair and then hold the balloon against a wall you will probably find that the balloon sticks to the wall. There is an attraction between the charged balloon and the uncharged wall.

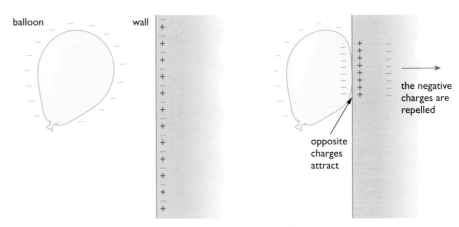

Figure 8.6 *The balloon is negatively charged and induces a positive charge in the wall.*

After the balloon has been charged with static electricity, but before it is brought close to the wall, the charges will be distributed as shown in Figure 8.6. The balloon is charged (we have assumed negatively charged) and the wall is uncharged – that is, it has equal numbers of positive and negative charges.

As the negatively charged balloon is brought closer to the wall some of the negative electrons are repelled from the surface of the wall. This gives the surface of the wall a slight positive charge that attracts the negatively charged balloon.

You can try a similar experiment using a plastic comb and some small pieces of paper. Immediately after combing your hair, the comb is likely to be charged, as shown in Figure 8.7. (In this example, we have assumed that the comb has become positively charged.) As the comb is brought close to the uncharged pieces of paper some of their electrons are attracted to the edges of the paper closest to the comb. There is attraction between these negative parts of the paper and the comb and repulsive forces between the comb and the positive parts of the pieces of paper. The attractive forces are stronger than the repulsive forces because the opposite charges are closer. The paper therefore moves towards the comb.

For you to try

Take a plastic ruler or rod and rub it against a jumper to charge it with static electricity. Turn on a water tap so that the water flows from the tap as slowly as possible but as a continuous flow (not as a series of drops). Hold the charged rod or ruler close to the stream of water but not in it. What happens to the water? Can you explain what is happening?

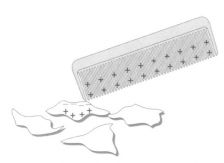

Figure 8.7 *The comb induces a charge in the paper, and the two attract.*

The charges that appear on the pieces of paper are called **induced charges**. When the comb is removed the charges redistribute themselves so that the pieces of paper are once again uncharged.

The gold leaf electroscope

The electroscope is an instrument for detecting electric charge. It was invented by Jean Antoine Nollet (1700–1770). Figure 8.8 shows a modern version. The metal plate at the top is connected to the metal rod inside the instrument, but insulated from the rest of the apparatus. The metal rod has a sheet of very thin metal (called a 'leaf') attached to it. This is usually made of gold, as gold can be beaten into extremely thin sheets. If an electrically charged object is brought close to the plate at the top, the gold leaf moves (Figure 8.9a and 8.9b).

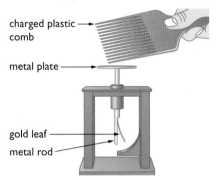

Figure 8.8 *A modern gold leaf electroscope.*

An electroscope can be used to investigate the charges on different objects. Figure 8.9 shows how this can be done. The electroscope is charged by bringing a positively charged rod close to it (Figure 8.9b). This attracts negative charges towards the metal plate, leaving a positive charge on the metal rod and the gold leaf. These like charges repel each other, so the leaf rises. The bigger the charge on the rod, the greater the deflection of the gold leaf.

If you touch the top of the electroscope briefly (Figure 8.9c) negative charges are attracted to it from earth. The electrons move from earth, through your finger and onto the electroscope. If you remove your finger and then take the charged rod away, the gold leaf is still deflected because the electroscope now has an overall negative charge (Figure 8.9d). Now if you bring a positively charged object close to the electroscope it will attract some of the negative charges from the leaf so there will be less repulsion and the leaf will fall (Figure 8.9e). If you hold a negatively charged rod close to the plate, it will repel more negative charges from the plate onto the leaf and the leaf will rise.

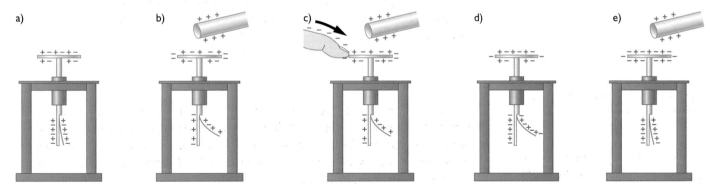

Figure 8.9 *Using an electroscope to investigate charge.* **a)** *An uncharged electroscope,* **b)** *A positively charged rod is brought close to the metal plate.* **c)** *The electroscope is earthed by touching the plate,* **d)** *The electroscope is left with a negative charge.* **e)** *A positively charged rod reduces the deflection of the gold leaf.*

Uses of static electricity

Electrostatic paint spraying

Painting an awkwardly shaped object such as a bicycle frame with a spray gun can be very time consuming and very wasteful of paint. Using electrostatic spraying can make the process much more efficient.

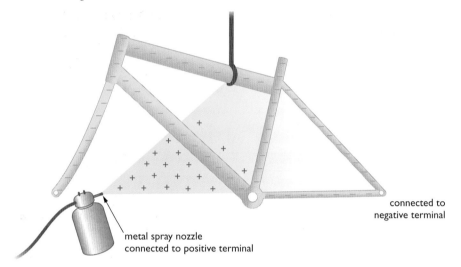

connected to
negative terminal

metal spray nozzle
connected to positive terminal

Figure 8.10 *The positive paint is attracted to all parts of the negatively charged object.*

As the droplets of paint emerge from the spray gun, they are charged. As the droplets all carry the same charge they repel and spread out forming a fine spray. The metal bicycle frame has a wire attached to an electrical supply giving the frame the opposite charge. The paint droplets are therefore attracted to the surface of the frame. There is the added benefit that paint is attracted into places, such as tight corners, that might otherwise not receive such a good coating.

Inkjet printers

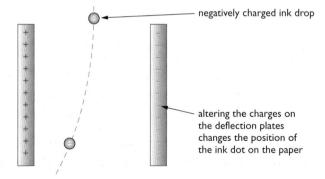

negatively charged ink drop

altering the charges on
the deflection plates
changes the position of
the ink dot on the paper

Figure 8.11 *The charged ink droplets are deflected into the correct position on the paper.*

Many modern printers use inkjets to direct a fine jet of ink drops onto paper. Each spot of ink is given a charge so that as it falls between a pair of deflecting plates, electrostatic forces direct it to the correct position. The charges on the plates change hundreds of times each second so that each drop falls in a different position, forming pictures and words on the paper as required.

Photocopiers

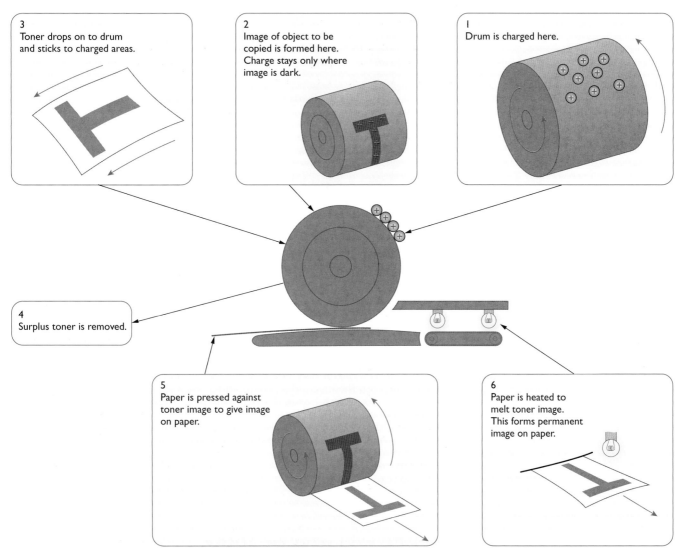

3
Toner drops on to drum and sticks to charged areas.

2
Image of object to be copied is formed here. Charge stays only where image is dark.

I
Drum is charged here.

4
Surplus toner is removed.

5
Paper is pressed against toner image to give image on paper.

6
Paper is heated to melt toner image. This forms permanent image on paper.

Figure 8.12 *Static electricity is used in photocopiers.*

Positive charges are sprayed onto a rotating drum whose surface is coated with a metal called selenium. A bright light is shone onto the sheet of paper to be copied. The white parts of the paper reflect light onto the drum; the dark or printed parts do not. In those places where light is reflected onto the drum the selenium loses its charge but where no light is reflected onto the drum the charge remains. A fine negatively charged carbon powder called toner is blown across the drum and sticks to just those parts of the drum that are charged. A sheet of paper is now pressed against the drum and picks up the pattern of the carbon powder. The powder is then fixed in place by a heater.

Electrostatic precipitators

Many heavy industrial plants, such as steel-making furnaces and coal-fired power stations, produce large quantities of smoke. This smoke carries small particles of ash and dust into the environment, causing health problems and damage to buildings. One way of removing these pollutants from the smoke is to use electrostatic precipitators.

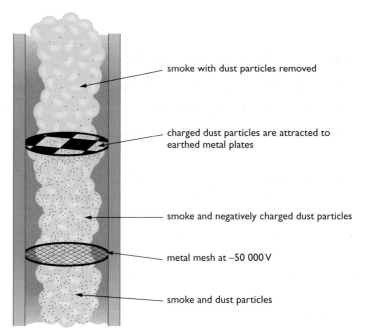

smoke with dust particles removed

charged dust particles are attracted to earthed metal plates

smoke and negatively charged dust particles

metal mesh at −50 000 V

smoke and dust particles

Figure 8.13 *Electrostatic precipitators help to cut down the amount of pollution released into the atmosphere.*

As the smoke initially rises up the chimney it passes through a mesh of wires that are highly charged. (The wires are at a voltage of approximately −50 000 V.) As they pass through the mesh, the ash and dust particles become negatively charged. Higher up the chimney these charged particles are attracted by and stick to large metal earthed plates. The cleaner smoke is then released into the atmosphere. When the earthed plates are completely covered with dust and ash, they are given a sharp rap. The dust and ash fall into collection boxes, which are later emptied.

In a large coal-fired power station, 50–60 tonnes of dust and ash may be removed from smoke each hour!

Problems with static electricity

In some situations the presence of static electricity can be a disadvantage.

- As aircraft fly through the air, they can become charged with static electricity. As the charge on an aircraft increases, so too does the potential difference between it and earth. With high potential differences there is the possibility of charges escaping to earth as a spark during refuelling, which could cause an explosion. The solution to this problem is to earth the plane with a conductor as soon as it lands and before refuelling commences. Fuel tankers that transport fuel on roads must also be earthed before any fuel is transferred, to prevent sparks causing a fire or explosion.

- Television screens and computer monitors become charged with static electricity as they are used. These charges attract light uncharged particles – that is, dust.

- Our clothing can, under certain circumstances, become charged with static electricity. When we remove the clothes there is the possibility of receiving a small electric shock as the charges escape to earth.

You will need to be able to do the following:

✓ identify some materials that are electrical conductors and some that are electrical insulators

✓ recall that there are two types of electrical charge – positive and negative

✓ understand that objects that are uncharged contain equal numbers of positive and negative charges

✓ understand how the transfer of electrons between objects can cause them to become charged; objects that gain electrons become negatively charged; objects that lose electrons become positively charged

✓ recall that opposite charges attract and similar charges repel, and use these ideas to explain how an electroscope works

✓ recall how electrostatic charge can cause explosions when fuelling aircraft and tankers, and how this problem can be avoided

✓ recall some uses of static electricity including electrostatic paint spraying, inkjets, photocopiers and electrostatic smoke precipitators.

Questions

More questions on static electricity can be found at the end of Section B on page 89.

1 **a)** What charge is carried by each of these particles?

    i) a proton

    ii) an electron

    iii) a neutron

  b) Where inside an atom are each of the three particles mentioned in **a)** found?

  c) How many protons are there in a neutral atom compared to the number of electrons?

  d) What do we call an atom that has become charged by gaining or losing electrons?

  e) Describe with diagrams how two objects can be charged by friction (rubbing).

2 Explain the following.

  a) A crackling sound can sometimes be heard when removing a shirt or blouse.

  b) Sometimes after a journey in a car you can get a mild electric shock when you touch the handle of the door.

  c) A plastic comb is able to attract small pieces of paper immediately after it has been used.

  d) Dust always collects on the screens of televisions and computer monitors.

3 **a)** In a photocopier, why does toner powder stick to some places on the selenium-coated drum but not to others?

  b) Explain why ash and dust particles are attracted towards the earthed metal plates of an electrostatic precipitator after they have passed through a highly negatively charged mesh of wires. (Hint: Read again about the balloon experiment.)

4 Lightning is caused by clouds discharging their static electricity.

  a) Find out:

    i) how the clouds become charged

    ii) how a lightning conductor works.

  b) Suggest two places where it might be i) unsafe, and ii) safe during a thunderstorm.

5 Computer chips can be damaged by static electricity. Find out how workers who build and repair computers avoid this problem.

Section B: Electricity

Chapter 9: Current and Voltage in Circuits

We rely on electricity in many areas of our lives. This chapter looks at what electric current is and what makes it flow. You will learn what happens to electric current in different circuits, and what effects it has as it flows.

Look around the room you are in. If you are at home, you will probably be able to see a television, a radio or a computer. If you are in a science laboratory, you may be able to see a calculator or power supply. These and many other everyday objects need electric currents if they are to work. But what are electric currents? How are they produced and what do they do when they flow?

Conductors, insulators and electric current

An electric current is a flow of **charge**. In metal wires the charges are carried by very small particles called **electrons**. Electrons flow easily through all metals. We therefore describe metals as being good **conductors** of electricity. Electrons do not flow easily through most plastics – they are poor conductors of electricity. A very poor conductor is known as an **insulator** and is often used in situations where we want to prevent the flow of charge – for example, in the casing of a plug.

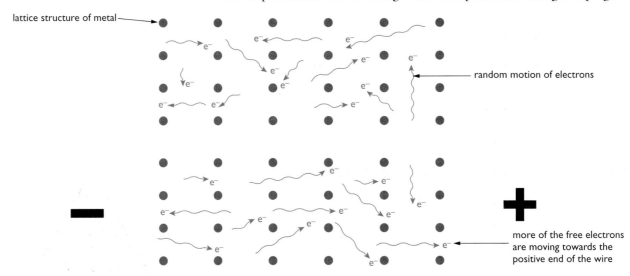

Figure 9.1 *Some electrons in a metal will flow when a voltage is applied.*

When scientists first experimented with charges flowing through wires they assumed that it was positive charges that were moving and that current therefore passes from the positive to the negative. We now know that this is incorrect and that when an electric current passes through a wire it is the negative charges or electrons that move. Nevertheless when dealing with topics such as circuits and motors it is still considered that current flows from positive to negative. This is **conventional current**.

In conductors some electrons are free to drift between the atoms. Under normal circumstances this drifting is random – that is, the number of electrons flowing in any one direction is roughly equal to the number flowing in the opposite direction. There is therefore no overall flow of charge. If, however, a cell or battery is connected across the conductor, more of the electrons now flow in the direction away from the negative terminal and towards the positive terminal than in the opposite direction – that is, there is now a net flow of charge. This flow of charge is an **electric current**.

In insulators all the electrons are held tightly in position and are unable to move from atom to atom. Charges are therefore unable to pass through insulators.

Measuring current

We measure the size of the current flowing in a circuit using an **ammeter**. The ammeter is connected in series with the part of the circuit being investigated.

The size of an electric current indicates the rate at which charge flows.

We measure electric charge (Q) in units called coulombs (C). One coulomb of charge is the equivalent of the charge carried by approximately six million, million, million (6×10^{18}) electrons.

We measure electric current (I) in amperes or amps (A). If 1 C of charge flows along a wire every second the current passing through the wire is 1 A.

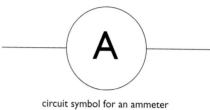

circuit symbol for an ammeter

Figure 9.2 *An ammeter is used to measure current in a circuit.*

$$1 \text{ C/s} \quad = \quad 1 \text{ A}$$

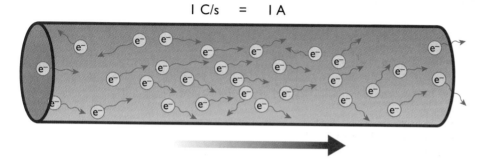

Figure 9.3 *One coulomb of charge flowing each second is one amp.*

We can calculate the charge passing along a wire using the equation:

> charge, *Q* (in coulombs) = current, *I* (in amps) × time, *t* (in seconds)
> $Q = I \times t$

Worked example

Example 1

Calculate the charge flowing through a wire in 5 s if the current is 3 A.

$Q = I \times t$

$Q = 3\,\text{A} \times 5\,\text{s}$

$Q = 15\,\text{C}$

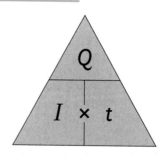

Figure 9.4 *You can use the triangle method for rearranging equations like this* $I = \frac{Q}{t}$

Voltage

We often use cells or batteries to move charges around circuits. We can imagine them as being "electron pumps". They transfer energy to the charges. The amount of energy given to the charges by a cell or battery is measured in volts (V) and is usually indicated on the side of the battery or cell.

If we connect a 1.5 V cell into a circuit and current flows, 1.5 J of energy is given to each coulomb of charge that passes through the cell.

If two 1.5 V cells are connected in series so that they are pumping in the same direction each coulomb of charge will receive 3 J of energy.

If an examination question asks you to write out the formula for calculating charge, current or time, always give the actual equation (such as $Q = I \times t$). You may not get the mark if you just draw the triangle.

When several cells are connected together it is called a **battery**.

Cells and batteries provide current flowing in one direction. This is known as **direct current** (dc).

Figure 9.5 *When one coulomb of charge passes through this cell it gains 1.5 J of energy.*

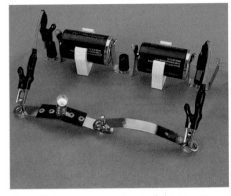

Figure 9.6 *When one coulomb of charge passes through both these cells in turn it gains 3 J of energy.*

As the charges flow around a circuit the energy they carry is converted into other forms of energy by the components they pass through. The **voltage** across each component tells us how much energy it is converting. If the voltage across a component is 1 V this means that the component is changing 1 J of electrical energy into a different kind of energy each time 1 C of charge passes through it.

Measuring voltages

Figure 9.7 *A voltmeter measures voltages across a component.*

bulb

circuit symbol for a voltmeter

A voltmeter has a very high resistance, so very little current flows through it.

We measure voltages using a **voltmeter**. This is connected *across* (in parallel with) the component we are investigating. A voltmeter connected across a cell or battery will measure the energy given to each coulomb of charge that passes through it. A voltmeter connected across a component will measure the electrical energy converted into other forms when each coulomb of charge passes through it.

Electrical circuits

When the button on the torch shown in Figure 9.8 (opposite) is pressed the circuit is *complete* – that is, there are no gaps. Charges are able to flow around the circuit and the torch bulb glows. When the button is released the circuit becomes *incomplete*. Charges cease to flow and the bulb goes out.

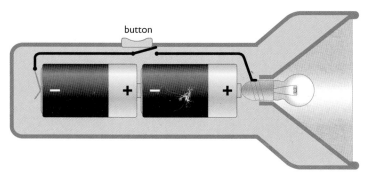

Figure 9.8 *A torch contains a simple electrical circuit – a series circuit.*

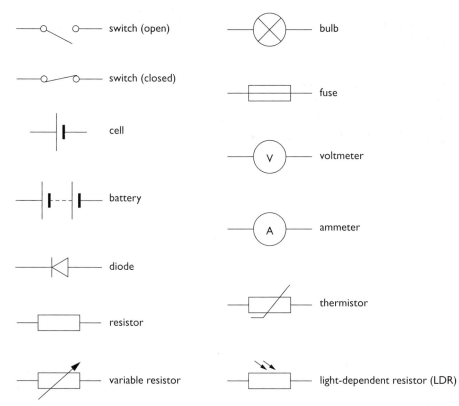

Figure 9.9 *Circuit symbols.*

Drawing diagrams of the actual components in a circuit is a very time-consuming and skilful task. It is much easier to use symbols for each of the components. Diagrams drawn in this way are called **circuit diagrams**. Here is a table of common circuit components and their symbols. You should know the common symbols but you will find a full list in Appendix B. Do not waste time memorising some of the less common ones as these will be given to you in the exam if you need them.

If a lamp (bulb) in a circuit is lit, it shows that current is flowing in the circuit. Many appliances such as TVs or DVD players have a small **light emitting diode** (LED) fitted to show when the appliance is switched on or on standby. An LED glows when current is flowing through it.

Series and parallel circuits

In the torch circuit in Figure 9.8 there is only one path for the charges to flow along. There are no branches or junctions. This simple "single loop" type of circuit is called a **series circuit**.

Circuits that have branches or junctions are called **parallel circuits**. There is more than one path that current can flow along.

Switches turn circuits on and off by making them complete or incomplete. In a series circuit the whole circuit is turned on and off by one switch.

In parallel circuits it is possible to turn different parts of the circuit on and off using switches.

Series and parallel circuits have different characteristics that make them suitable for different applications.

In a series circuit:

- one switch can turn all the components on and off together

- if one bulb (or other component) breaks, it causes a gap in the circuit and all of the other bulbs will go off

- the voltage supplied by the cell or mains supply is "shared" between all the components, so the more bulbs you add to a series circuit the dimmer they all become. The larger the resistance of the component, the bigger its 'share' of the voltage.

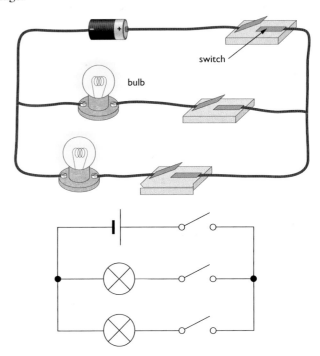

Figure 9.10 *A parallel circuit.*

In a parallel circuit:

- switches can be placed in different parts of the circuit to switch each bulb on and off individually, or all together

- if one bulb (or other component) breaks, only the bulbs on the same branch of the circuit will be affected

- each branch of the circuit receives the same voltage, so if more bulbs are added to a circuit in parallel they all stay bright.

Decorative lights are usually wired in series. Each bulb only needs a low voltage, so even when the voltage from the mains supply is "shared" out between them all each bulb still gets enough energy to produce light. If one of the bulbs is not in its holder properly, the circuit is not complete and none of the bulbs will be on. In the past, if the filament in one of the bulbs broke all of the other bulbs would go out. Today, many bulbs used in decorative lights are provided with a 'shunt' which allows current to continue to flow through the bulb even after the filament has broken.

Figure 9.11 *Decorative lights are usually wired in series.*

The lights in your home are wired in parallel. Each bulb can be switched on and off separately, and the brightness of the bulbs does not change when other bulbs are on or off. If one bulb breaks or is removed, you can still use the other lights.

Current in a series circuit

In a series circuit the current is the same in all parts. Current is not used up as it passes around a circuit.

The size of the current in a series circuit depends on the voltage supplied to it, and the number and nature of the other components in the circuit. In the circuit in Figure 9.12, the current will double if another cell is added in series, as more energy is being given to the electrons. The extra energy allows more charge to flow per second.

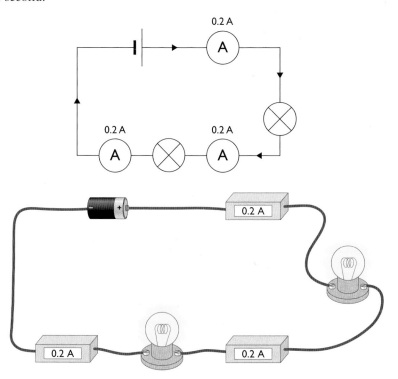

Figure 9.12 *In a series circuit the current does not vary.*

If more bulbs are added to the circuit the current will get less. This is because bulbs have resistance and the more bulbs there are, the greater the resistance of the whole circuit. When the resistance is higher, less current can flow. You will find out more about resistance in Chapter 10.

End of Chapter Checklist

You will need to be able to do the following:

✓ understand how the proportion of free electrons in a material determines whether a material is a conductor or an insulator

✓ recall that current is a flow of charge

✓ understand and use the equation $Q = I \times t$

✓ recall that the voltage between two points is the number of joules of energy converted when 1 C of charge flows between them

✓ recall that in series circuits **a)** there is only one path for the current to follow, **b)** the current is the same everywhere, **c)** the current depends on the applied voltage and on the number and nature of other components

✓ recall the different characteristics of series and parallel circuits, and explain why they are suitable for different applications.

Questions

More questions on electrical circuits can be found at the end of Section B on page 89.

1 Current is a flow of charge.

a) What are the charge carriers in metals?

b) Explain why charges are able to flow through metals but not through a plastic.

c) If the current flowing through a heater is 3 A, calculate the charge that flows through it in *i)* 1 s, *ii)* 10 min and *iii)* 1 hour.

2 Currents flow around circuits.

a) Explain the differences between:

i) a complete circuit and an incomplete circuit

ii) a series circuit and a parallel circuit.

b) Look carefully at the circuits shown. Assuming that all switches are initially closed, decide which of the bulbs go out when each of the switches in turn is opened.

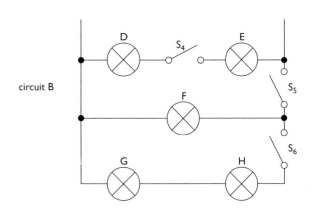
circuit B

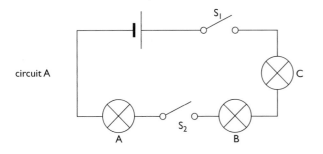
circuit A

c) In circuit A, which bulb(s) glow the brightest when all the switches in all the circuits are closed?

d) Explain your answer to **c)**.

3 The voltage between two points in a circuit is measured using a voltmeter.

a) Draw a circuit diagram to show how a voltmeter should be connected to measure *i)* the voltage across a bulb, and *ii)* the voltage of a cell.

b) Explain in your own words the phrase "a cell has a voltage of 1.5 V".

4 The diagram below shows a circuit containing two two-way switches.

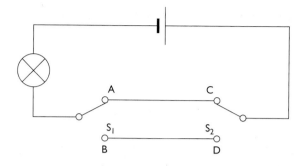

a) Explain in your own words what happens when each of the switches is moved to a new position.

b) Suggest one important application of this circuit in the home.

5 Decorative lights in your home are wired in series. Your town decorates the main street and uses 60 W light bulbs to decorate it. These bulbs are similar to light bulbs you may have at home for lighting a room.

Should the lights for the main street be wired in series or parallel? Explain your answer.

Chapter 10: Electrical Resistance

In this chapter you will learn what resistance is, and how it can be useful in electrical appliances. You will learn what factors affect resistance, and how to work out the resistance of a component by measuring the current flowing in it and the voltage across it (Ohm's law). You will also read about some special resistors, and their uses.

Figure 10.1 *You can control electrical appliances such as stereos by adjusting the resistance of the circuits.*

It is likely that almost every day of your life you will make some adjustments to at least one electrical appliance. You may turn up the volume of your radio or adjust the colour on your television. In each of these examples your adjustments are changing the currents and the voltages in the circuits of your appliance. You are achieving the results you require by altering the **resistance** of the circuits. This chapter will help you understand the meaning and importance of resistance and how we make use of it.

Resistance

All components in a circuit offer some resistance to the flow of charge. Some (for example, connecting wires) allow charges to pass through very easily losing very little of their energy. We describe connecting wires as having very **low resistance**. The flow of current through some components is not so easy and a significant amount of energy is used to move the charges through them. This energy is converted into other forms, usually heat. Components like this are said to have a **high resistance**.

We normally assume that connecting wires have zero resistance.

We measure the resistance (R) of a component by comparing the size of the current (I) that flows through that component and the voltage (V) applied across its ends. Voltage, current and resistance are related as follows.

> **voltage, *V* (in volts) = current, *I* (in amps) × resistance, *R* (in ohms)**
> $$V = I \times R$$

We measure resistance in units called ohms (Ω).

Example 1

When a voltage of 12 V is applied across a buzzer a current of 0.1 A flows. Calculate the resistance of the buzzer.

$$V = I \times R$$

Rearrange the equation.

$$R = \frac{V}{I}$$

$$R = \frac{12\,V}{0.1\,A}$$

$$R = 120\,\Omega$$

Using resistance

Fixed resistors

In many circuits you will find components similar to those shown in Figure 10.3. They are called **fixed resistors**. They are included in circuits in order to control the sizes of currents and voltages. The resistor in the circuit in Figure 10.4 is included so that the correct voltage is applied across the bulb and the correct current flows through it. Without the resistor the voltage across the bulb may cause too large a current to flow through it and the bulb may "blow".

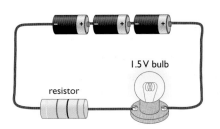
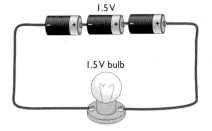

Figure 10.4 *Resistors can be used to protect components such as bulbs.*

Variable resistors

Figure 10.5 shows examples of a different kind of resistor. They are called **variable resistors** as it is possible to alter their resistance. When you alter the volume of your television or your radio you are using a variable resistor to do this.

In the circuit in Figure 10.6 a variable resistor is being used to control the size of the current flowing through a bulb. If the resistance is decreased a larger current flows and the bulb glows more brightly. If the resistance is increased a smaller current flows and the bulb will glow less brightly or not at all. The variable resistor is behaving in this circuit as a dimmer switch. In circuits containing electric motors variable resistors can be used to control the speed of the motor.

Worked example

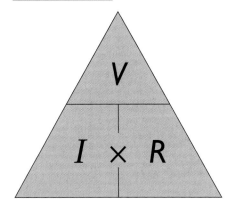

Figure 10.2 *You can use the triangle method for rearranging equations like $V = I \times R$*

If an examination question asks you to write out the formula for calculating resistance, current or voltage, always give the actual equation (such as $V = I \times R$). You may not get the mark if you just draw the triangle.

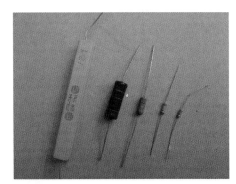

Figure 10.3 *A selection of resistors.*

Figure 10.5 *Variable resistors.*

circuit symbol for a
variable resistor

Special resistors

Thermistors

A **thermistor** is a resistor whose resistance changes quite dramatically with temperature. It is made from a semiconducting material such as silicon or germanium. At room temperature the number of free electrons is small and so the resistance of a thermistor is large. If however if it is warmed the number of free electrons increases and its resistance decreases. Thermistors are often used in temperature-sensitive circuits in devices such as fire alarms and thermostats.

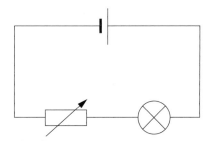

Figure 10.6 *Circuit with a variable resistor being used as a dimmer switch.*

Thermistors are also available that increase their resistance when the temperature increases. However, for your IGCSE Physics exam you only need to know about thermistors whose resistance decreases with increasing temperature.

Figure 10.7 *Some thermistors. The resistance of a thermistor decreases as the temperature rises.*

circuit symbol
for a thermistor

Light-dependent resistors (LDRs)

In dark conditions **light-dependent resistors (LDRs)** contain few free electrons and so have a high resistance. If however light is shone onto an LDR more electrons are freed and the resistance decreases. LDRs are often used in light-sensitive circuits in devices such as photographic equipment, automatic lighting controls and burglar alarms.

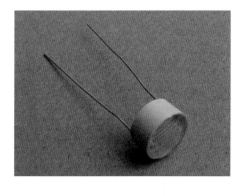

cicuit symbol for an LDR

Figure 10.8 *Light-dependent resistors have a lower resistance when it is light.*

Diodes

Diodes are very special resistors that behave like one-way valves or one-way streets. When current flows through them in one direction it can do so quite easily as the diode has a low resistance. But if current tries to flow in the opposite direction the diode has a very high resistance and very little current can now flow. Diodes are often used in circuits where it is important that current flows only in one direction – for example, in rectifier circuits that convert alternating current into direct current. **Light emitting diodes** (**LEDs**) are diodes that glow when a current is flowing through them.

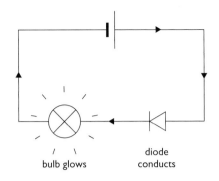

bulb glows   diode conducts

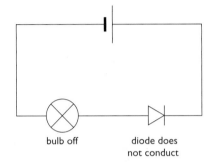

bulb off   diode does not conduct

Figure 10.9 *Diodes will only let current flow one way.*

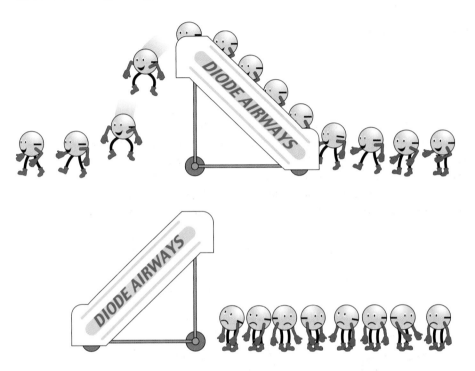

You can imagine a diode as behaving like a set of aeroplane steps, which the charges have to climb over. If the charges are moving towards the right side of the steps they can "flow through it". If however they try to flow the opposite way there are no steps for them to climb so the flow in this direction is almost zero.

Figure 10.10 *Diodes are like aeroplane steps – from the ground, you can only climb them in one direction. In a diode the current can only flow in one direction.*

Measuring resistance – Ohm's Law

We have already seen that the resistance (R) of a component is related to the current (I) through it and the voltage (V) across it by the equation $V = I \times R$. If we wish to find the resistance of a component, this equation can be rearranged to give $R = V/I$. The circuit in Figure 10.11 can be used to investigate this relationship for a piece of resistance wire.

When the switch S is closed the readings on the ammeter and voltmeter are noted. The value of the variable resistor is then altered and a new pair of readings taken from the meters. The whole process is repeated at least six times, the results are placed into a table and a graph of current (I) against voltage (V) is drawn.

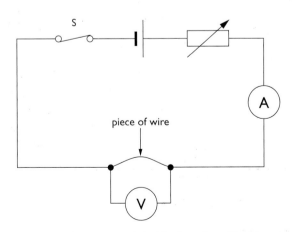

Figure 10.11 *This circuit can be used to investigate Ohm's Law.*

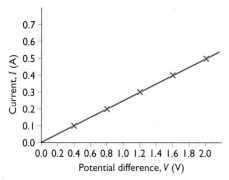

Figure 10.12 *The graph shows that current and voltage increase proportionally.*

Current, *I* (A)	Voltage, *V* (V)
0.0	0.0
0.1	0.4
0.2	0.8
0.3	1.2
0.4	1.6
0.5	2.0

Table 10.1 *Typical results for an investigation of Ohm's Law.*

The graph in Figure 10.12 is a straight line graph passing through the origin. This tells us that the current flowing through the wire is *directly proportional* to the voltage applied across its ends – that is, if the voltage across the wire is doubled the current flowing through it doubles.

The relationship between the voltage across a component and the current that flows through it is described by **Ohm's Law**, which states:

> **The current that flows through a conductor is directly proportional to the potential difference across its ends, provided its temperature remains constant.**

The resistance of the wire can be found by selecting any value of voltage (*V*), reading from the graph the current (*I*) that flows when this voltage is applied to the wire and calculating a value for the ratio *V*/*I*.

In this case the resistance of the wire is

$$\frac{1.2 \, \text{V}}{0.3 \, \text{A}} = 4 \, \Omega.$$

If we extend the range of readings in the above experiment, such that the currents flowing cause the wire to become warm, the shape of the *I*/*V* graph changes.

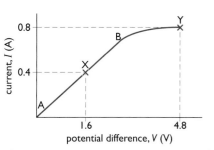

Figure 10.13 *Resistance in a wire increases as the current increases.*

Between A and B, in Figure 10.13, the relationship between current and voltage is still a direct proportionality and the wire has a constant resistance. Beyond B the current flowing through the wire is large enough to change its temperature and the resistance of the wire increases. This happens because at higher temperatures the atoms in the wire vibrate more vigorously, impeding the flow of electrons.

At point X the graph shows a current of 0.4A is flowing through the wire so the resistance of the wire is

$$\frac{V}{I} = \frac{1.6 \, \text{V}}{0.4 \, \text{A}} = 4 \, \Omega.$$

At point Y the graph shows a current of 0.8A is flowing through the wire so its resistance now is

$$\frac{V}{I} = \frac{4.8 \, \text{V}}{0.8 \, \text{A}} = 6 \, \Omega.$$

The current in a resistor varies with voltage in a similar way to the variation in a wire.

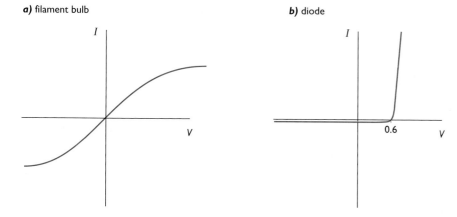

a) filament bulb
b) diode

Figure 10.14 *The current/voltage graphs for a filament bulb and a diode.*

The current/voltage graph in Figure 10.14a shows that when a filament bulb is first turned on its resistance is quite low but as the filament becomes hot its resistance increases. It does not matter which way the voltage is applied – the effect is the same.

The graph for a diode, in Figure 10.14b, shows that a small voltage of approximately 0.6 V must be applied to the diode before it will conduct. Further increases in voltage then result in increases in current. If the voltage is applied in the opposite direction almost no current flows.

End of Chapter Checklist

You will need to be able to do the following:

✓ describe qualitatively the effect of changing resistance on the current flowing in a circuit

✓ understand that the size of the current that passes through a component depends upon the voltage across the component and its resistance, and use the equation $V = I \times R$

✓ recall the special properties of thermistors, light-dependent resistors and diodes

✓ describe an experiment to obtain voltage and current measurements for a number of components, construct I–V graphs and then interpret the shapes of these graphs.

Questions

More questions on electrical resistance can be found at the end of Section B on page 89.

1 *a)* State Ohm's Law.

b) Draw a diagram of the circuit you would use to confirm Ohm's Law for a piece of wire.

c) Describe how you would use the apparatus and what readings you would take.

d) Draw an I–V graph for

   i) a piece of wire at room temperature

   ii) a filament bulb

   iii) a diode.

   Explain the main features of each of these graphs.

2 *a)* A current of 5 A flows when a voltage of 20 V is applied across a resistor. Calculate the resistance of the resistor.

b) Calculate the current that flows when a voltage of 12 V is applied across a piece of wire of resistance 50 Ω.

c) Calculate the voltage that must be applied across a wire of resistance 10 Ω if a current of 3 A is to flow.

> Remember when doing calculations like these to show all your working out and include units with your answer.

3 *a)* Explain how the resistance of:

   i) a thermistor

   ii) a light-dependent resistor

   can be increased.

b) Describe in detail one practical application for each of these resistors.

1 Copy and complete the following passage about electricity, filling in the spaces.

An electric current is a flow of _____ A current of 1 amp is 1 _____ of charge flowing each second. The voltage is the _____ transferred per coulomb of charge.

The current flowing in a component depends on the voltage and the _____; the higher the resistance, the _____ the current.

Total 5 marks

2 Bill set up the circuit shown below to investigate how the resistance of a bulb changes as the current flowing through it changes.

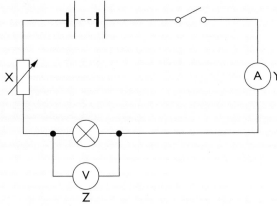

a) What are the names of the instruments labelled Y and Z? (2 marks)

b) What is the name of the component labelled X? (1 mark)

c) What is the purpose of X in this circuit? (1 mark)

Bill takes a series of readings. He measures the voltage across the bulb and the current passing through it. He then plots the graph shown below.

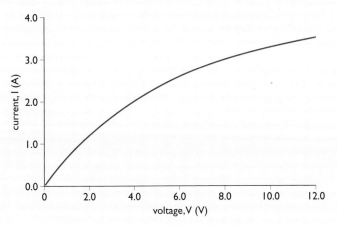

d) What current passes through the bulb when a voltage of 6V is applied across it? (1 mark)

e) What voltage is applied across the bulb when a current of 2.0 A passes through it? (1 mark)

f) Calculate the resistance of the bulb when a current of 2.0 A passes through it. (2 marks)

g) What happens to the resistance of the bulb as the current passing through it increases? (1 mark)

Total 9 marks

3 A simple series circuit containing a 12 V battery and a 10 Ω resistor was constructed as shown below.

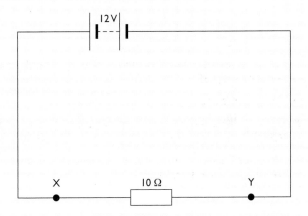

a) Calculate the current that flows between points X and Y. (2 marks)

b) Calculate the total charge that flows between X and Y in 5 s. (2 marks)

c) Calculate the energy transferred in the resistor in 1 minute. (2 marks)

Total 6 marks

4 An electric kettle is rated at 2 kW when connected to a 230 V electrical supply.

a) Calculate the current that will flow when the kettle is turned on. (3 marks)

b) What value fuse should be included in the circuit of the kettle? Assume that the fuses available are 3 A, 5 A and 13 A. (1 mark)

c) Modern kettles often have double insulation. Explain what this means and how it provides extra safety for the user. (2 marks)

d) Calculate the resistance of the heating element of the kettle. (3 marks)

Total 9 marks

5 **a)** Explain in detail how insulating materials can be charged by friction. *(4 marks)*

b) When an aircraft lands it is important that it is earthed before it is refuelled.

i) Explain why the aircraft should be earthed. *(3 marks)*

ii) Suggest one way in which the aircraft could be earthed. *(1 mark)*

c) Explain why electrostatic painting of objects such as bicycle frames makes good economic sense. *(3 marks)*

d) Describe briefly how an inkjet makes use of some of the properties of static electricity. *(3 marks)*

Total 14 marks

6 **a)** Describe four uses of the heating effect of electricity in the home. *(1 mark)*

b) Write down four safety rules to be followed in the home to prevent accidents with electricity, and explain why each rule is necessary. *(2 marks)*

c) Explain why a double-insulated hair dryer does not need an earth wire in its cable. *(2 marks)*

Total 5 marks

Chapter 11: Properties of Waves

Waves, such as sound waves and light waves, affect all aspects of our lives. We also use many types of waves to our advantage, particularly in the field of communication. In this chapter, you will learn about some basic features and properties of waves.

Speaking to someone on the other side of the Earth using a mobile phone may only be a matter of being able to dial the correct number, but the technology that had to be developed for this to happen was based on a thorough understanding of the properties of waves. In this section we will be looking at the basic properties of waves and seeing how these properties can be used to our advantage.

What are waves?

Waves are a means of transferring energy from place to place. They can also be used to transfer information. These transfers take place with no matter being transferred.

Figure 11.1 *Mobile phones rely on waves.*

Figure 11.2 *Waves are produced if you drop a large stone into a pond. The waves spread out from the point of impact, carrying energy to all parts of the pond. But the water in the pond does not move from the centre to the edges.*

Transverse waves

Waves can be produced in ropes and springs. If you waggle one end of a slinky spring from side to side you will see waves travelling through it. The energy carried by these waves moves along the slinky from one end to the other, but if you look

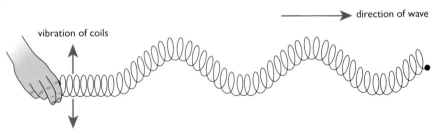

direction of wave

vibration of coils

Figure 11.3 *A transverse wave vibrates at right angles to the direction in which the wave is moving.*

closely you can see that the coils of the slinky are vibrating *across* the direction in which the energy is moving. This is an example of a **transverse wave**.

A transverse wave is one that vibrates, or **oscillates**, at right angles to the direction in which the energy or wave is moving. Examples of transverse waves include light waves and waves travelling on the surface of water.

Longitudinal waves

If you push and pull the end of a slinky in a direction parallel to its axis, you can again see energy travelling along it. This time however the coils of the slinky are vibrating in directions that are *along its length*. This is an example of a **longitudinal wave**.

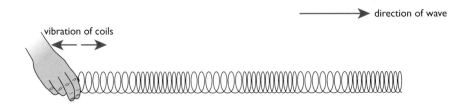

Figure 11.4 *A longitudinal wave vibrates along the direction in which the wave is travelling.*

A longitudinal wave is one in which the vibrations, or oscillations, are along the direction in which the energy or wave is moving. Examples of longitudinal waves include sound waves.

Describing waves

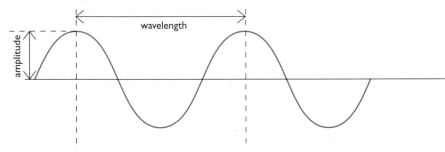

Figure 11.5 *A wave has amplitude and wavelength.*

When a wave moves through a substance, it causes the particles in the substance to move from their equilibrium or resting position. The maximum movement of particles *from their resting position* caused by a wave is called its **amplitude (A)**.

The distance between a particular point on a wave and the same point on the next wave (for example, from crest to crest) is called the **wavelength** (λ).

If the source that is creating a wave vibrates quickly it will produce a large number of waves each second. If it vibrates more slowly it will produce fewer waves each second. The number of waves produced each second by a source, or the number passing a particular point each second, is called the **frequency** of the wave (*f*). Frequency is measured in hertz (Hz). A wave source that produces five complete waves each second has a frequency of 5 Hz.

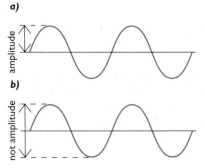

Figure 11.6 *The amplitude of a wave is as shown in a), and not as in b).*

λ is the Greek letter lambda and is the usual symbol for wavelength.

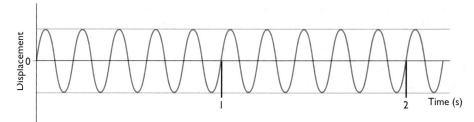

Figure 11.7 *This graph shows a wave with a frequency of 5 Hz.*

The time it takes for a source to produce one wave is called the **period** of the wave
(T). It is related to the frequency (f) of a wave by the equation:

frequency, f (in hertz) $= \dfrac{1}{\text{time period, } T \text{ (in seconds)}}$

$$f = \frac{1}{T}$$

This equation can also be written as $T = \dfrac{1}{f}$

Example 1

Calculate the period of a wave with a frequency of 200 Hz.

$T = 1/f$

$T = 1/200$

$\quad = 0.005$ or $5\,\text{ms}$ $\qquad$ $(1000\,\text{ms} = 1\,\text{s})$

Worked example

The wave equation

There is a relationship between the wavelength (λ), the frequency (f) and the wave
speed (v) that is true for all waves:

wave speed, v (in metres per second) = frequency, f (in hertz)
$\times$ wavelength, λ (in metres)

$$v = f \times \lambda$$

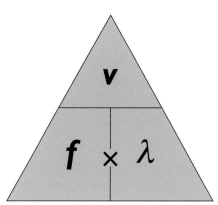

Figure 11.8 *You can use the triangle method for rearranging equations like $v = f \times \lambda$.*

If an examination question asks you to write
out the formula for calculating wave speed,
wavelength or frequency, always give the
actual equation (such as $v = f \times \lambda$). You may
not be awarded a mark if you just draw the
triangle.

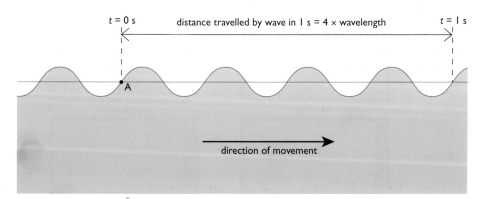

$t = 0\,\text{s}$ $\qquad$ distance travelled by wave in 1 s = 4 × wavelength $\qquad$ $t = 1\,\text{s}$

A

direction of movement

Figure 11.9 *A wave with a frequency of 4 Hz.*

Imagine that you have created water waves with a frequency of 4 Hz. This means that four waves will pass a particular point each second. If the wavelength of the waves is 3 m, then the waves travel 12 m each second. The speed of the waves is therefore 12 m/s:

$$v = f \times \lambda$$

$$v = 4\,\text{Hz} \times 3\,\text{m}$$

$$v = 12\,\text{m/s}$$

Worked example

Example 2

A tuning fork creates sound waves with a frequency of 170 Hz. If the speed of sound in air is 340 m/s, calculate the wavelength of the sound waves.

$$v = f \times \lambda$$
$$\text{So } \lambda = v/f$$
$$\lambda = \frac{340\,\text{m/s}}{170\,\text{Hz}}$$
$$\lambda = 2\,\text{m}$$

The ripple tank

We can study the behaviour of water waves using a ripple tank.

When the motor is turned on the wooden bar vibrates creating a series of ripples on the surface of the water. A light placed above the tank creates patterns of the water waves on the floor. By observing the patterns we can see how the water waves are behaving.

Wavelength and frequency

The motor can be adjusted to produce a small number of waves each second. The frequency of the waves is small and the pattern shows that the waves have a long wavelength.

At higher frequencies, the water waves have shorter wavelengths. The speed of the waves does not change.

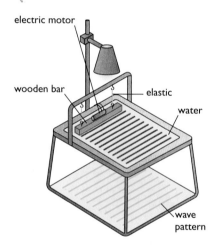

Figure 11.10 *The light shines through the water and we can see the patterns of the waves.*

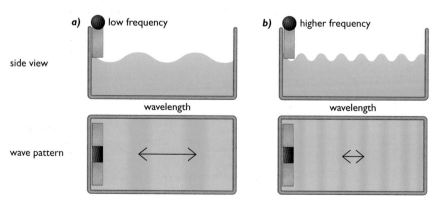

Figure 11.11 *When the frequency of the waves is low, the wavelength is long. When the frequency is higher, the wavelength is shorter.*

Reflection

When waves strike a straight or flat barrier, the angle at which they leave the barrier surface is equal to the angle at which they meet the surface. That is, the waves are reflected from the barrier at the same angle as they struck it.

The angle of incidence is equal to the angle of reflection.

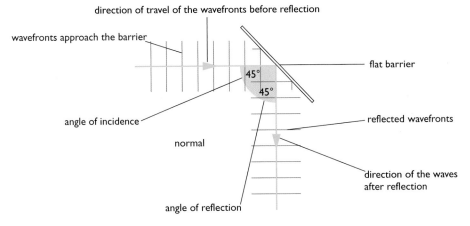

A normal is a line drawn at right angles to a surface.

Figure 11.12 *Waves striking a flat barrier are reflected. The angle at which they strike the barrier is the same as the angle at which they are reflected.*

When the waves strike a concave barrier, they become curved and are made to converge.

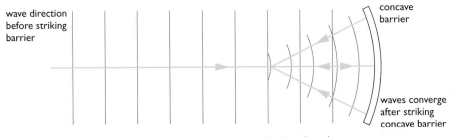

Figure 11.13 *Waves striking a concave barrier are reflected backwards and converge.*

When the waves strike a convex barrier, they are made to diverge (spread out).

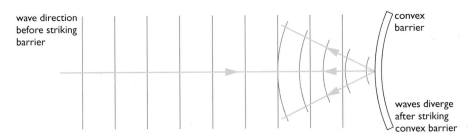

Figure 11.15 *Waves striking a convex barrier are reflected backwards and spread out.*

Figure 11.14 *Radio telescope dishes have a concave shape so that the signals they receive are made to converge onto a detector.*

Refraction

If a small glass plate is placed in the centre of the ripple tank, the depth of the water here is reduced. As waves enter this region we can see that their wavelength becomes shorter. The frequency of the waves is unaltered. It follows therefore, from the formula $v = f\lambda$, that the waves are travelling more slowly in the shallower water. As the waves enter the deeper water again their wavelength increases, indicating that their speed has increased.

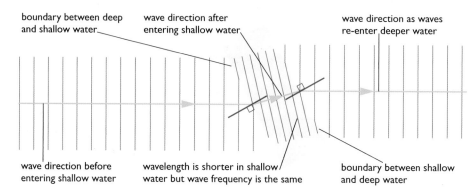

Figure 11.16 *As waves enter shallow water their wavelength becomes shorter. If the boundary between the deep and shallow water is at an angle, the waves are refracted.*

If the boundary between the shallow water and the deep water is at an angle to the direction in which the waves are moving, the direction of the waves changes. We say the waves have been **refracted** or have undergone **refraction**. The waves bend towards the normal as they enter the shallow water and are slowed down. The waves bend away from the normal as they leave the shallow water and enter the deeper water.

Diffraction

If a barrier with a large gap is placed in the path of the waves, the majority of the waves passing through the gap continue through in a straight line. There are regions to the left and right of the gap where there are no waves.

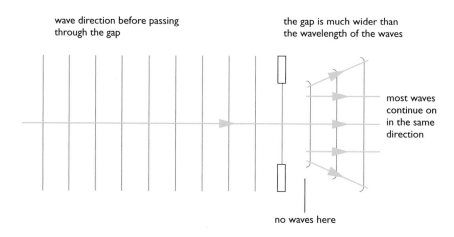

Figure 11.17 *Most waves passing through a large gap in a barrier continue in a straight line.*

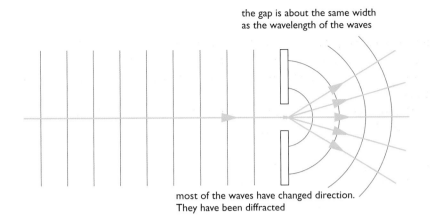

the gap is about the same width
as the wavelength of the waves

most of the waves have changed direction.
They have been diffracted

Figure 11.18 *If the gap in the barrier is the same size as the wavelength, then the waves spread out.*

If the size of the gap is adjusted so that it is equal to the wavelength of the water waves, the wave pattern shows that there are waves to the left and the right of the gap where previously they had been absent. The waves have spread out from the "straight-on" direction.

This spreading out is called **diffraction**. Diffraction is a property that is demonstrated by all waves. The effect is most noticeable when the wavelength of the waves is approximately equal to the size of the aperture (hole) through which they are moving. Examples of diffraction include sound waves that diffract as they pass through doorways.

Diffraction also happens when waves pass a single edge. You can think of an edge as just one side of a very large gap. Examples of diffraction around an edge include radio waves that are diffracted as they pass over hills.

End of Chapter Checklist

You will need to be able to do the following:

- ✓ recall that waves carry energy and information from place to place, but not matter
- ✓ describe the difference between transverse and longitudinal waves
- ✓ recall examples of transverse and longitudinal waves
- ✓ recall the meaning of amplitude, wavelength, frequency and period of a wave
- ✓ use the relationship $f = \dfrac{1}{T}$
- ✓ use the relationship $v = f \times \lambda$
- ✓ recall that all waves can be reflected, refracted and diffracted
- ✓ explain that diffraction of a wave is most pronounced when the wavelength of the wave and the size of the gap through which it is travelling are the same.

Questions

More questions on wave properties can be found at the end of Section C on page 126.

1 **a)** Explain the difference between a transverse wave and a longitudinal wave.

   b) Give one example of each.

   c) Draw a diagram of a transverse wave. On your diagram, mark the wavelength and amplitude of the wave.

2 Plane water waves in a ripple tank pass through a narrow gap in a barrier.

   a) Draw the appearance of the waves when the gap is much larger than the wavelength of the water waves.

   b) Draw the appearance of the waves when the gap is the same size as the wavelength of the water waves.

   c) Explain why designers must choose the size of a harbour entrance carefully if boats moored there are to be in calm water.

3 The diagram below shows the displacement of water as a wave travels through it.

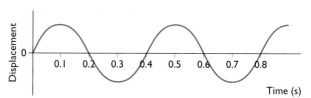

From the diagram calculate:

   a) the period of the wave

   b) the frequency of the wave.

4 The speed of sound in water is approximately 1500 m/s.

   a) What is the frequency of a sound wave with a wavelength of 1.5 m?

   b) What is the period of this wave?

Chapter 12: Using Waves

The electromagnetic spectrum is a family of waves, varying in wavelength and frequency. Although it is continuous, it is helpful to consider groups of waves within the entire spectrum that have a smaller range of wavelengths and frequencies. Each group has distinct properties and therefore can be used in different ways. In this chapter, you will learn about many ways in which we use electromagnetic waves, from cooking to communication.

Figure 12.1 *Lasers are a source of concentrated light waves. They can be used to carry large amounts of energy and coded information over long distances.*

In this chapter, we shall be looking at the ways in which we make use of waves.

The electromagnetic spectrum

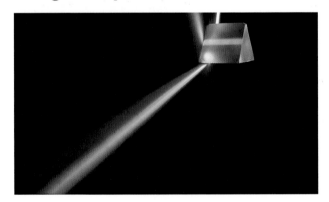

Figure 12.2 *The visible part of the electromagnetic spectrum.*

The **electromagnetic spectrum** (EM spectrum) is a continuous spectrum of waves, which includes the visible spectrum. At one end of the spectrum the waves are of very long wavelength (low frequency), while at the other end the waves have a very short wavelength (high frequency). All the waves have the following properties:

1 they all transfer energy

2 they are all transverse waves

3 they all travel at the speed of light in a vacuum (300 000 000 m/s)

4 they can all be reflected, refracted and diffracted.

Worked example

Example 1

Yellow light has a wavelength of 5.7×10^{-7} m. What is the frequency and period of yellow light waves.

$v = f \times \lambda$

So $f = \dfrac{v}{\lambda}$

$= \dfrac{3 \times 10^8 \, \text{m/s}}{5.7 \times 10^{-7} \, \text{m}}$

$= 5.26 \times 10^{14} \, \text{Hz}$

$T = \dfrac{1}{f}$

$= \dfrac{1}{5.26 \times 10^{14} \, \text{Hz}}$

$= 1.9 \times 10^{-15} \, \text{s}$

Although the spectrum is continuous – that is, the wavelengths vary gradually and smoothly from one end to the other – it is easier to study if we divide it into groups. Different groups of waves have different properties because they have different frequencies and wavelengths. The following table shows the different groups of waves in order, and gives some of their uses.

	Typical frequency (Hz)	Typical wavelength (m)	Sources	Detectors	Uses
Radio waves	10^5–10^{10}	10^3–10^{-2}	radio transmitters, TV transmitters	radio and TV aerials	long-, medium- and short-wave radio, TV (UHF)
Microwaves	10^{10}–10^{11}	10^{-2}–10^{-3}	microwave transmitters and ovens	microwave receivers	mobile phone and satellite communication, cooking
Infra-red (IR)	10^{11}–10^{14}	10^{-3}–10^{-6}	hot objects	skin, blackened thermometer, special photographic film	infra-red cookers and heaters, TV and stereo remote controls, night vision
Visible light	10^{14}–10^{15}	10^{-6}–10^{-7}	luminous objects	the eye, photographic film, light-dependent resistors	seeing, communication (optical fibres), photography
Ultraviolet (UV)	10^{15}–10^{16}	10^{-7}–10^{-8}	UV lamps and the Sun	skin, photographic film and some fluorescent chemicals	fluorescent tubes and UV tanning lamps
X-rays	10^{16}–10^{18}	10^{-8}–10^{-10}	X-ray tubes	photographic film	X-radiography to observe the internal structure of objects, including human bodies
Gamma rays	10^{18}–10^{21}	10^{-10}–10^{-14}	radioactive materials	Geiger–Müller tube	sterilising equipment and food, radiotherapy

Radio waves

Radio waves have the longest wavelengths in the electromagnetic spectrum. They are used mainly for communication.

radio waves emitted by the transmitter
transmitter
aerial detects radio waves
radio changes radio waves into sound waves
signal to be transmitted

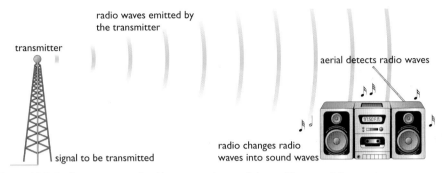

Figure 12.3 *Radio waves are emitted by a transmitter and detected by an aerial.*

Radio waves are given out (emitted) by a transmitter. As they cross an aerial, they are detected and the information they carry can be received. Television and FM radio use radio waves with the shorter wavelengths to carry their signals.

Microwaves

Microwaves are used for cooking foods, communications and radar.

microwaves are reflected from metal casing
special electric circuits produce microwaves
metal guides direct microwaves towards rotating reflector
reflector sends microwaves in all directions
food absorbs microwaves and becomes hot
DEFROST

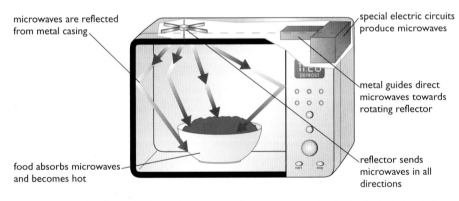

Figure 12.5 *Food cooks quickly in a microwave oven because water molecules in the food absorb the microwaves.*

Food placed in a microwave oven cooks more quickly than in a normal oven. This is because water molecules in the food absorb the microwaves and become very hot. The food therefore cooks throughout rather than just from the outside.

Microwaves are used in communications. The waves pass easily through the Earth's atmosphere and so are used to carry signals to orbiting satellites. From here, the signals are passed on to their destination or to other orbiting satellites. Messages sent to and from mobile phones are also carried by microwaves. The fact that we are able to use mobile phones almost anywhere in the home and at work confirms that microwaves can pass through glass, brick and so on.

Microwave ovens have metal screens that reflect microwaves and keep them inside the oven. This is necessary because if microwaves can cook food, they can also heat human body tissue! The microwaves used by mobile phones transmit much less energy than those used in a microwave oven, so they do not cook your brain when you use the phone. However there is still some speculation that using mobile phones may eventually cause some harm to the brain.

You do not need to remember the values of frequency and wavelength given in the table but you do need to know the order of the groups and which has the highest frequency or longest wavelengths. Most importantly, you need to realise that it is these differences in wavelength and frequency that give the groups their different properties – for example, gamma rays have the shortest wavelengths and highest frequencies, and carry the most energy.

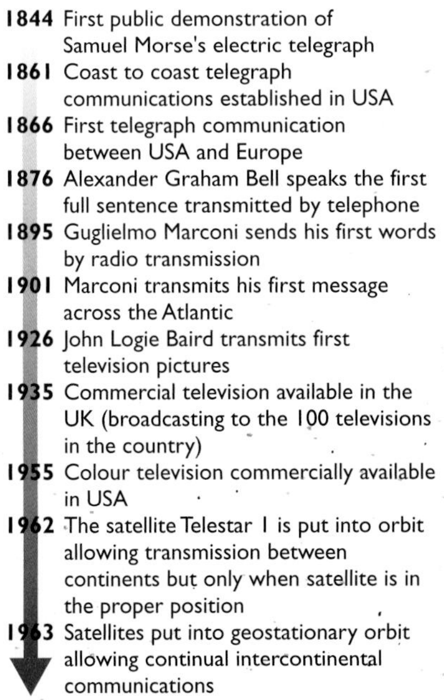

1844 First public demonstration of Samuel Morse's electric telegraph
1861 Coast to coast telegraph communications established in USA
1866 First telegraph communication between USA and Europe
1876 Alexander Graham Bell speaks the first full sentence transmitted by telephone
1895 Guglielmo Marconi sends his first words by radio transmission
1901 Marconi transmits his first message across the Atlantic
1926 John Logie Baird transmits first television pictures
1935 Commercial television available in the UK (broadcasting to the 100 televisions in the country)
1955 Colour television commercially available in USA
1962 The satellite Telestar I is put into orbit allowing transmission between continents but only when satellite is in the proper position
1963 Satellites put into geostationary orbit allowing continual intercontinental communications

The BBC (www.bbc.co.uk) website contains lots of information on the history of communication.

Figure 12.4 *Timeline of telecommunications.*

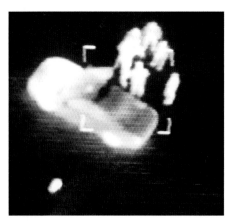

Figure 12.6 *This picture was taken using the infra-red waves being emitted by the people and the car.*

Infra-red

All objects, including your body, emit infra-red (IR) radiation. The hotter an object is, the more energy it will emit as infra-red. Energy is transferred by infra-red radiation to toast in a toaster or food under a grill. Electric fires also transfer heat energy by infra-red.

Special cameras designed to detect infra-red waves can be used to create images even in the absence of visible light. These cameras have many uses, including searching for people trapped in collapsed buildings, tracking criminals and checking for heat loss from buildings.

Infra-red radiation is also used in remote controls for televisions, videos and stereo systems. It is very convenient for this purpose because the waves are not harmful, they have a low penetrating power and will therefore operate only over small distances, so they are unlikely to interfere with other signals or waves.

The human body can be harmed by too much exposure to infra-red radiation, which can cause skin burns.

Visible light

This is the part of the electromagnetic spectrum that is visible to the human eye. We use it to see. Visible light from lasers is used to read compact discs and barcodes. It can also be sent along optical fibres, so it can be used for communication or for looking into inaccessible places such as inside the body of a patient. Visible light can be detected by the sensors in digital cameras, and used to take still photographs or videos.

When talking about light and colour, we often refer to the seven colours in the visible spectrum. These colours are red, orange, yellow, green, blue, indigo and violet; red light has the longest wavelength and lowest frequency. If you look back at Figure 12.2, you may only be able to make out six colours – most people have difficulty separating indigo and violet. Sir Isaac Newton (1642–1727) discovered that 'white' light can be split up into different colours. He believed that the number 7 had mystical significance, and so he decided there were seven colours in the spectrum!

Ultraviolet light

Part of the light emitted by the Sun is ultraviolet (UV) light. UV radiation is harmful to human eyes and can cause damage to the skin.

UV light causes the skin to tan, but overexposure will lead to sunburn and blistering. Ultraviolet radiation can also cause skin cancer and blindness. Protective goggles or glasses and skin creams can block the UV rays and will reduce the harmful effects of this radiation.

Ozone in the Earth's atmosphere absorbs large quantities of the Sun's UV radiation. There is real concern at present that the amount of ozone in the atmosphere is decreasing due to pollution. This may lead to increased numbers of skin cancers in the future.

Some chemicals glow, or fluoresce, when exposed to UV light. This property of UV light is used in security markers. The special ink is invisible in normal light but becomes visible in UV light.

Figure 12.7 *UV light can cause sunburn so we need to protect our skin.*

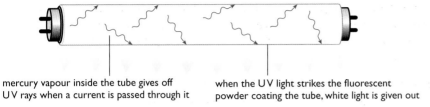

mercury vapour inside the tube gives off UV rays when a current is passed through it

when the UV light strikes the fluorescent powder coating the tube, white light is given out

Figure 12.8 *Fluorescent tubes glow when UV light hits the fluorescent coating in the tube.*

Fluorescent tubes glow because the UV light they produce strikes a special coating on the inside of the tube, which then emits visible light.

X-rays

X-rays pass easily through soft body tissue but cannot pass through bones. As a result, radiographs or X-ray pictures can be taken to check a patient's bones.

Overexposure to X-rays can cause cancer. Workers such as radiographers who are at risk of overexposure therefore stand behind lead screens or wear protective clothing.

X-rays are also used in industry to check the internal structures of objects – for example, to look for cracks and faults in buildings or machinery – and at airports as part of the security checking procedure.

Gamma rays

Gamma rays, like X-rays, are highly penetrating rays and can cause damage to living cells. The damage can cause mutations in genes and can lead to cancer. They are used to sterilise medical instruments, to kill micro-organisms so that food will keep for longer and to treat cancer using radiotherapy. Gamma rays can both cause and cure cancer: a small dose of gamma rays may be enough to cause changes to a cell, known as mutations, and make it become cancerous. However, large doses of gamma rays targeted directly at the cancerous growth can be used to kill the cancer cells completely.

Figure 12.9 *X-rays were used to see what was in this suitcase.*

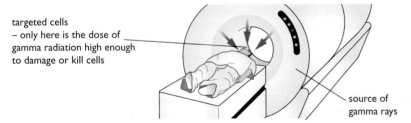

targeted cells – only here is the dose of gamma radiation high enough to damage or kill cells

source of gamma rays

Figure 12.10 *The gamma rays are aimed carefully so that they cross at the exact location of the cancerous cells.*

Communicating using waves

When we talk to the person next to us, we use sound waves. If we want to communicate with someone who is further away we might use light waves – for example, semaphore (signalling with flags) or beacons. With modern radio and other telecommunication systems, we can use waves to communicate with each other over large distances and very quickly.

Morse code can be transmitted using light, sound, electricity or radio waves. It uses combinations of long and short signals to represent letters and numbers. The sequence ● ● ● − − − ● ● ● represents the letters "SOS", which is the international distress signal.

Figure 12.11 *Semaphore being used to communicate over distance.*

Figure 12.12 *These machines all allow us to communicate through a telephone line.*

Telephones, fax machines and Internet-linked computers can all be used to transmit information. All three use the telephone system but before their information can travel down the telephone lines, it must be converted into a stream of electrical pulses or light pulses. These pulses may carry the information as **digital signals** or **analogue signals**.

Digital signals

To send a message using a digital signal, the information is converted into a sequence of numbers called a **binary code**. The code uses just two digits (0 and 1) rather than the ten digits we normally use. These numbers are then converted into a series of electrical pulses that are sent down the telephone lines.

Analogue signals

In the analogue method, the information is converted into electrical voltages or currents that vary continuously.

Figure 12.14 shows that a microphone converts sound waves into continuous electrical signals. These signals are then amplified (made stronger) and fed into a loudspeaker.

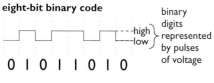

eight-bit binary code

binary digits represented by pulses of voltage

0 1 0 1 1 0 1 0

0 0 0 0 0 0 0 0	=	0
0 0 0 0 0 0 0 1	=	1
0 0 0 0 0 0 1 0	=	2
0 0 0 0 0 0 1 1	=	3
0 0 0 0 0 1 0 0	=	4
0 0 0 0 0 1 0 1	=	5
0 0 0 0 0 1 1 0	=	6
0 0 0 0 0 1 1 1	=	7
0 0 0 0 1 0 0 0	=	8
0 0 0 0 1 0 0 1	=	9

Figure 12.13 *An eight-bit pattern of 1s and 0s can be used to represent numbers 0 to 255.*

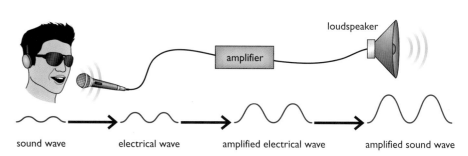

sound wave   electrical wave   amplified electrical wave   amplified sound wave

Figure 12.14 *An analogue signal follows the actual pattern of the original information.*

Advantages of using digital signals

There are several advantages in transmitting information in a digital form rather than as analogue signals.

All signals become weaker during transmission and need to be amplified or regenerated. Regeneration of digital signals creates a clean, accurate copy of the original signal. But when analogue signals are amplified, any accompanying noise is also amplified. Eventually the level of noise may "drown out" the original signal or introduce errors in the information being carried.

Digital systems are generally easier to design and build than analogue systems. They also deal with data that is easy to process.

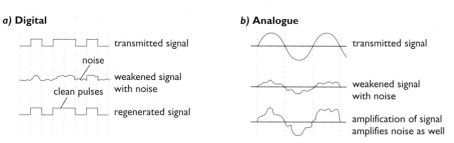

Figure 12.15 *Digital signals are easy to regenerate, analogue signals are easily distorted.*

We normally think of noise as being unwanted sounds but in this context noise is stray unwanted voltages or currents that distort the waveform of the signal.

TV and radio signals used to be broadcast using analogue signals. The frequency of a radio wave would be changed to carry the analogue signals. Today in the UK most TV programmes and radio channels are also broadcast digitally. Eventually there will be no more analogue broadcasts of TV or radio programmes. It takes a wider range of frequencies to broadcast an analogue signal than a digital one. Using digital signals only means that more programmes can be broadcast over the same frequencies.

End of Chapter Checklist

You will need to be able to do the following:

✓ understand that the electromagnetic spectrum is a family of waves, which includes radio waves, microwaves, infra-red waves, visible light, ultraviolet waves, X-rays and gamma rays

✓ recall those properties that are common to all waves in the spectrum

✓ recall the order in which these waves appear in the spectrum and relate this to their wavelengths and frequencies

✓ recall some of the uses of these waves

✓ recall some of the dangers associated with exposure to certain types of radiation

✓ recall that waves can be used to carry information

✓ understand the difference between analogue and digital signals

✓ describe the advantages of using digital signals rather than analogue signals.

Questions

More questions on using waves can be found at the end of Section C on page 126.

1 *a)* Name four wave properties that are common to all members of the electromagnetic spectrum.

   b) Name three types of wave that can be used for communicating.

   c) Name two types of wave that can be used for cooking.

   d) Name one type of wave that is used to treat cancer.

   e) Name one type of wave that might be used to "see" people in the dark.

   f) Name one type of wave that is used for radar.

2 Explain why:

   a) microwave ovens cook food much more quickly than normal ovens

   b) X-rays are used to check for broken bones

   c) it is important not to damage the ozone layer around the Earth

   d) food stays fresher for longer after it has been exposed to gamma radiation.

3 *a)* Explain the difference between analogue signals and digital signals.

   b) Explain the advantages of sending messages in digital form.

Chapter 13: Light Waves

We see objects because they emit or reflect light. In this chapter you will learn how light behaves when it reflects from different surfaces, and what happens when light travels from one transparent material to another.

Seeing the light

The patient shown in Figure 13.1 has a cataract. The front of one of his eyes has become so cloudy that he is unable to see. Nowadays it is possible to remove this damaged part of the eye and replace it with a clear plastic that will again allow light to enter the eye.

There are many sources of light, including the Sun, the stars, fires, light bulbs and so on. Objects such as these that emit their own light are called **luminous** objects. When the emitted light enters our eyes we see the object. Most objects, however, are **non-luminous**. They do not emit light. We see these non-luminous objects because of the light they **reflect**.

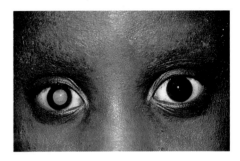

Figure 13.1 *Cataracts mean that light cannot enter the eye correctly.*

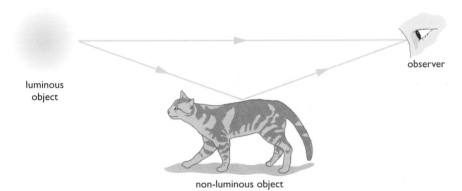

Figure 13.2 *Luminous objects, such as the Sun, give out light. Non-luminous objects only reflect light.*

Light waves are transverse waves and, like all waves, can be reflected, refracted and diffracted.

Reflection

When a ray of light strikes a plane (flat) mirror, it is reflected so that the **angle of incidence** is equal to the **angle of reflection**.

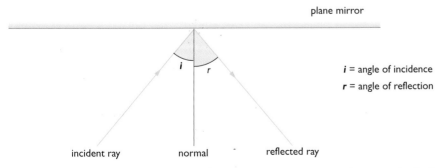

i = angle of incidence

r = angle of reflection

Figure 13.3 *Light is reflected from a plane mirror. The angle of incidence is equal to the angle of reflection. The normal is a line at right angles to the mirror.*

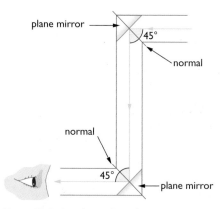

Figure 13.4 *A periscope is used to see over or around objects.*

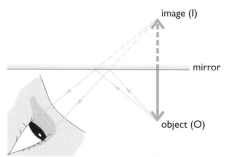

Figure 13.5 *Virtual images look like they are behind the surface of the mirror.*

If you can produce an image on a screen, it is real.

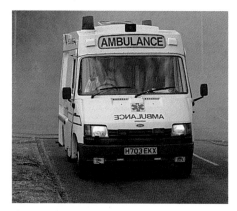

Figure 13.7 *Some emergency vehicles have mirror writing on their bonnets so that drivers in front can read the name when they look in their mirrors.*

Mirrors are often used to change the direction of a ray of light. One example of this is the simple periscope, which uses two mirrors to change the direction of rays of light.

Rays from the object strike the first mirror at an angle of 45° to the normal. The rays are reflected at 45° to the normal and so are turned through an angle of 90° by the mirror. At the second mirror the rays are again turned through 90°. Changing the direction of rays of light in this way allows an observer to use a periscope to see over or around objects.

Images created by a plane mirror

When you look into a plane mirror, you see images of the room that appear to be behind the mirror. These images are created by rays of light from objects inside the room striking the mirror and being reflected into your eyes. Figure 13.5 shows how these images are created.

Because rays of light normally travel in straight lines, your brain interprets the rays as having come from **I** (that is, an image of the object is seen at **I**). Images like these, through which rays of light do not actually pass, are called **virtual images**. Images created with rays of light actually passing through them (for example, on a cinema screen) are called **real images**.

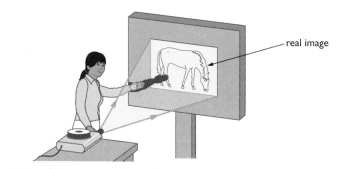

Figure 13.6 *Real images are produced when light passes through them.*

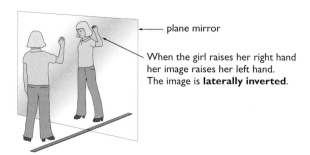

Figure 13.8 *The image in a mirror is the same size as the object, is laterally inverted and is virtual. The image also appears to be the same distance from the mirror as the object.*

Properties of an image in a plane mirror

- The image is as far behind the mirror as the object is in front.
- The image is the same size as the object.
- The image is virtual – that is, it cannot be produced on a screen.
- The image is **laterally inverted** – that is, the left side and right side of the image appear to be interchanged.

Refraction

Figure 13.9 *This rainbow is caused by refraction.*

Rays of light can travel through many different transparent media, including air, water and glass. Light can also travel through a vacuum. In a vacuum and in air, light travels at a speed of 300 000 000 m/s. In other media it travels more slowly. For example, the speed of light in water is approximately 200 000 000 m/s. When a ray of light travels from air into glass or water it slows down as it crosses the boundary between the two media. The change in speed may cause the ray to change direction. This change in direction of a ray is called **refraction**.

> A **medium** is a material – such as glass or water, through which light can travel. The plural of medium is media.

> Light does travel more slowly in air than in a vacuum but the difference is negligible.

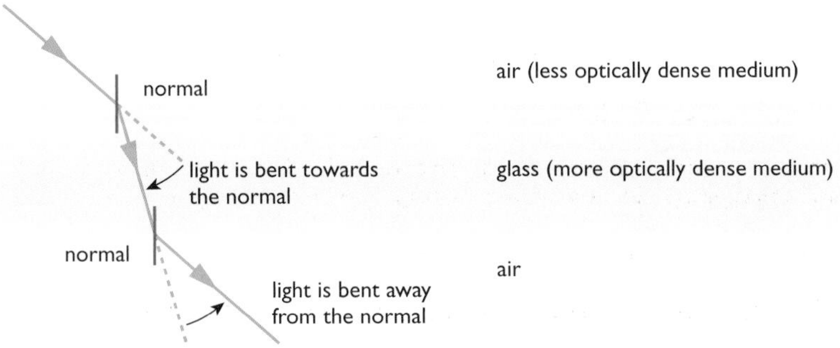

normal

air (less optically dense medium)

light is bent towards the normal

glass (more optically dense medium)

normal

light is bent away from the normal

air

Figure 13.10 *Light rays bend as they travel from air into glass and out again. This is called refraction.*

As a ray enters a glass block, it slows down and is refracted towards the normal. As the ray leaves the block it speeds up and is refracted away from the normal.

If the ray strikes the boundary between the two media at 90°, the ray continues without change of direction (Figure 13.11).

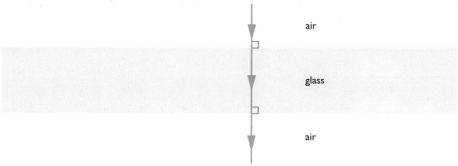

air

glass

air

Figure 13.11 *If the light hits the boundary at 90° the ray does not bend.*

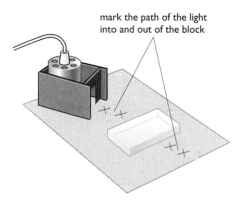

mark the path of the light into and out of the block

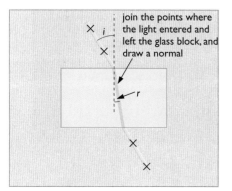

join the points where the light entered and left the glass block, and draw a normal

Figure 13.12 *How to investigate refraction using a rectangular glass block.*

Refractive index

You can investigate refraction in glass using a rectangular glass block. By tracing the rays of light on a piece of paper, you can measure the angles of incidence (i) and refraction (r).

If you carry out the procedure shown in Figure 13.12 for a range of different angles of incidence, you would find that the ratio between the sine of the angle of incidence and the sine of the angle of refraction is constant. This ratio is called the **refractive index** of the material, and is given the letter n. As it is a ratio, it has no units.

The angles of incidence and refraction and the refractive index are related by the following equation:

$$n = \frac{\sin i}{\sin r}$$

Worked example

Example 1

In an experiment similar to the one shown in Figure 13.12, the angle of incidence was measured as 30° and the angle of refraction as 19°. Calculate the refractive index of the glass block.

$$n = \frac{\sin i}{\sin r}$$

$$n = \frac{\sin 30}{\sin 19.5}$$

$$n = \frac{0.5}{0.33}$$

$$n = 1.51$$

Total internal reflection

When a ray of light passes from an optically more dense medium into an optically less dense medium – for example, from glass into air – the majority of the light is refracted away from the normal but there is a small amount that is reflected from the boundary.

'Optical density' describes how much light slows down when it enters a material. It is not the same as density (mass per unit volume; see page 162).

You can investigate total internal reflection in the laboratory using a semi-circular glass block. As shown in Figure 13.13, a ray of light is directed at the centre of the straight side of the block, through the curved side. The incident ray always hits the edge of the glass block at 90°, so there are no refraction effects to take into account as the light goes into the block.

Figure 13.13 *A semi-circular glass block used to demonstrate total internal reflection.*

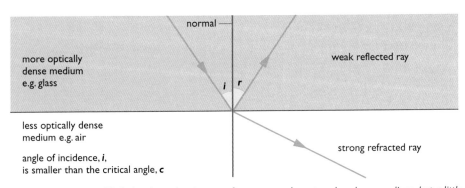

Figure 13.14 *A ray of light is refracted as it passes from a more dense to a less dense medium, but a little ray of light is reflected.*

As the angle of incidence in the more dense medium increases the angle of refraction also increases until, at a special angle called the **critical angle**, the angle of refraction is 90°.

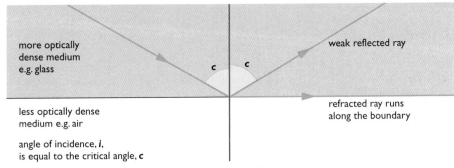

Figure 13.15 *At the critical angle the light is refracted at 90° to the normal.*

If the angle of incidence in the glass is further increased, *all* of the light is reflected from the boundary. The ray is said to have undergone **total internal reflection.**

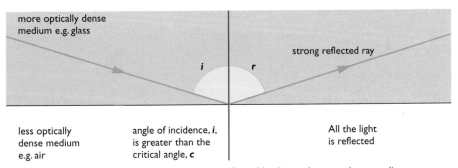

Figure 13.16 *Above the critical angle, the light is reflected back into the more dense medium.*

The value of the critical angle depends upon the media on either side of the boundary. Assuming that the less dense medium is air, then the critical angle for glass is typically 42° and the critical angle for water is 49°.

The critical angle for a particular medium is related to its refractive index by this equation:

$$\sin c = \frac{1}{n}$$

Worked example

Example 2

The refractive index for a type of glass is 1.45. Calculate the critical angle.

$$\sin c = \frac{1}{n}$$

$$\sin c = \frac{1}{1.45}$$

$$\sin c = 0.69$$

$$c = 43.6°$$

Using total internal reflection

If we look carefully at the image of an object created by a plane mirror we may see several faint images around the main central image. These multiple images are due to several partial internal reflections at the non-silvered glass surface of the mirror.

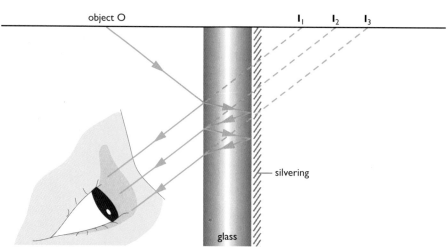

Figure 13.17 *The faint multiple images we can sometimes see in a mirror are caused when some of the light is reflected at the non-silvered surface of the mirror.*

To avoid this problem, particularly when high quality images are required, glass prisms are often used to alter the direction of the light rather than mirrors.

The prismatic periscope

Light passes normally through the surface AB of the first prism (that is, it enters the prism at 90°) and so is undeviated. It then strikes the surface AC of the prism at an angle of 45°. The critical angle for glass is 42° so the ray is totally internally reflected and is turned through 90°. On emerging from the first prism the light travels to a second prism which is positioned such that the ray is again totally internally reflected. The ray emerges parallel to the direction in which it was originally travelling.

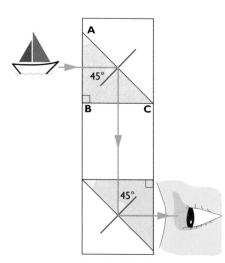

Figure 13.18 *Prisms can be used in periscopes instead of plane mirrors.*

The final image created by this type of periscope is likely to be sharper and brighter than that produced by a periscope that uses two mirrors, as no multiple images are created.

Reflectors

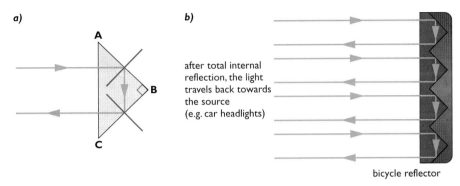

a)

b)

after total internal reflection, the light travels back towards the source (e.g. car headlights)

bicycle reflector

Figure 13.19 *Prisms can also be used as reflectors.*

Light entering the prism in Figure 13.19 undergoes total internal reflection twice. It emerges from the prism travelling back in the direction from which it originally came. This arrangement is used in bicycle reflectors and binoculars.

Optical fibres

One of the most important applications for total internal reflection is the **optical fibre**. This is a very thin strand composed of two different types of glass. There is a central core of optically dense glass (high refractive index) around which is a "cladding" or "coat" of optically less dense glass.

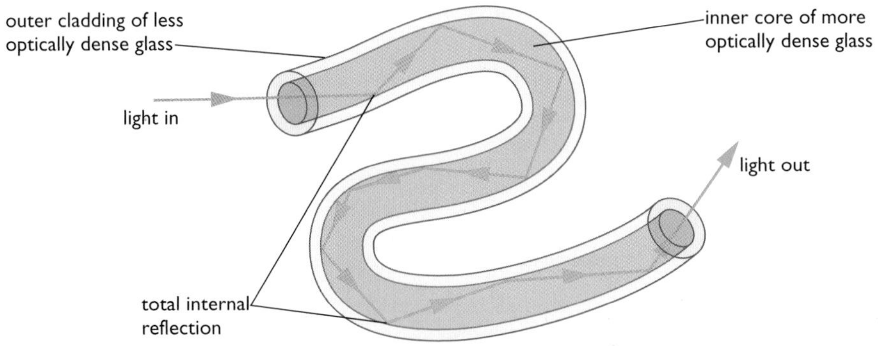

Each side of a pair of binoculars contains two prisms to reflect the incoming light. Without the prisms, binoculars would have to be very long to obtain large magnifications and would look like a pair of telescopes.

outer cladding of less optically dense glass

inner core of more optically dense glass

light in

light out

total internal reflection

Figure 13.20 *In an optical fibre, light undergoes total internal reflection.*

As the fibres are very narrow, light entering the inner core always strikes the boundary of the two glasses at an angle that is greater than the critical angle. No light escapes across this boundary. The fibre therefore acts as a "light pipe" providing a path that the light follows even when the fibre is curved.

Large numbers of these fibres fixed together form a **bundle**. Bundles can carry sufficient light for images of objects to be seen through them. If the fibres are tapered it is also possible to produce a magnified image.

Figure 13.21 *Optical fibres*

Using optical fibres to see what they are doing, surgeons can carry out operations through small holes made in the body, rather than making large incisions. This is called "keyhole surgery". It causes less distress to patients and usually leads to a more rapid recovery.

Figure 13.22 shows optical fibres in an endoscope. The endoscope is used by doctors to see the inside the body – for example, to examine the inside of the stomach. Endoscopes can also be used by engineers to see inaccessible parts of machinery.

Light travels down one bundle of fibres and illuminates the object to be viewed. Light reflected by the object travels up a second bundle of fibres. An image of the object is created by the eyepiece.

Optical fibres in telecommunications

Modern telecommunications systems use optical fibres rather than copper wires to transmit messages. Electrical signals from a telephone are converted into light energy by tiny lasers, which send pulses of light into the ends of optical fibres. A light-sensitive detector at the other end changes the pulses back into electrical signals, which then flow into a telephone receiver (ear piece).

The endoscope

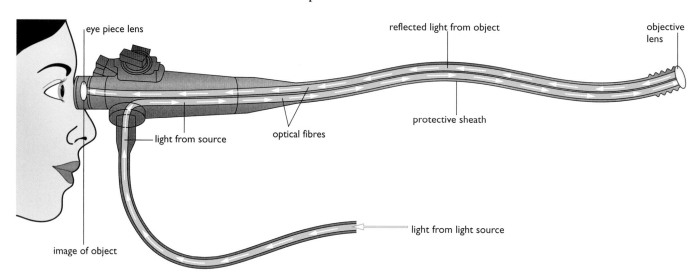

Figure 13.22 *Optical fibres are used in endoscopes to see inside the body.*

Dispersion

You can investigate refraction using glass blocks of different shapes. When white light passes through a prism (Figure 13.23), it emerges as a band of colours called a **spectrum**. The spectrum is formed because white light is a mixture of colours and each colour travels through the prism at a slightly different speed, so each colour is refracted by a different angle. The prism has a different refractive index for each colour. Because of this, each of the colours emerges from the prism travelling in a slightly different direction. The process is called **dispersion**. The speed of red light is changed least and so red has the smallest deviation. The speed of violet light is changed the most and so violet has the largest deviation.

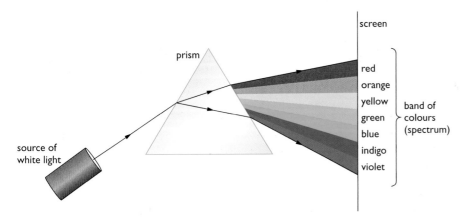

Figure 13.23 *A prism separates white light into its colours because the prism has a slightly different refractive index for each of the colours.*

End of Chapter Checklist

You will need to be able to do the following:

✓ recall that light waves are transverse waves that can be reflected, refracted and diffracted

✓ describe how light is reflected from a plane surface so that the angle of incidence is equal to the angle of reflection

✓ draw ray diagrams to show how an image is created in a plane mirror

✓ recall that light bends towards the normal as it enters an optically denser medium, and bends away from the normal when it enters an optically less dense medium

✓ recall and use the equation
$$n = \frac{\sin i}{\sin r}$$

✓ recall the conditions under which total internal reflection takes place

✓ recall and use the equation
$$\sin c = \frac{1}{n}$$

✓ describe experiments to investigate the refraction of light, including finding the refractive index and the critical angle

✓ describe several applications of total internal reflection, including optical fibres and prisms.

Questions

More questions on refraction can be found at the end of Section C on page 126.

1 Draw a ray diagram to show how a ray of light can be turned through 180° using three plane mirrors. Mark on your diagram a value for the angle of incidence at each of the mirrors.

2 a) Draw an accurate diagram to show how a plane mirror creates an image of an object.

   b) State five properties of an image created in a plane mirror.

   c) A man stands 5 m in front of a plane mirror. How far is he from his image?

   d) The man walks towards the mirror at a speed of 1 m/s. At what speed are the man and his image approaching each other?

3 a) Draw a diagram to show the path of a ray of light travelling from air into a rectangular glass block at an angle of about 45°.

   b) Show the path of the ray as it emerges from the block.

   c) Explain why the ray changes direction each time it crosses the air/glass boundary.

   d) Draw a second diagram showing a ray that travels through the block without being deviated.

4 In an experiment to measure the refractive index of a type of glass, the angle of refraction was found to be 31° when the angle of incidence was 55°.

   a) Calculate the refractive index of the glass.

   b) What would the angle of refraction be for a ray with an angle of incidence of 45°?

   c) Calculate the critical angle for the glass.

5 a) Draw a diagram to show how a prism can cause dispersion.

   b) Explain why the white light is dispersed.

6 Draw three ray diagrams to show what happens to a ray of light travelling in a more dense medium if it strikes the boundary with a less dense medium at an angle:

   a) less than the critical angle

   b) equal to the critical angle

   c) greater than the critical angle.

7 *a)* What is meant by "total internal reflection of light" and under what conditions does it occur?

b) Draw a diagram to show how total internal reflection takes place in a prismatic periscope.

c) Give one advantage of using prisms in a periscope rather than plane mirrors.

d) Draw a second diagram to show how a prism could be used to turn a ray of light through 180°. Give one application of a prism used in this way.

8 *a)* Explain why a ray of light entering an optical fibre is unable to escape through the sides of the strand. Include a ray diagram in your explanation.

b) What would happen to a ray of light inside an optical fibre if the outer glass had a higher optical density than the inner glass?

c) Explain how doctors use optical fibres to see inside the body.

Chapter 14: Sound

Sound waves are longitudinal waves, rather than transverse waves like light, but they can be reflected and diffracted in just the same way. In this chapter you will learn about the nature and behaviour of sound waves, and find out about some properties of vibrations.

The photograph in Figure 14.1 shows just part of the sound system used by a pop group playing at a concert. This equipment must produce sounds that are loud enough to be heard by all the audience and the sound quality must be good enough for the music to be appreciated. In this chapter, we are going to look at how sounds are made, how they travel as waves and some of the uses of sound waves.

Sound waves

Sounds are produced by objects that are vibrating. We hear sounds when these vibrations, travelling as sound waves, reach our ears.

Figure 14.1 *The sound produced by the speakers must be loud but also of good quality.*

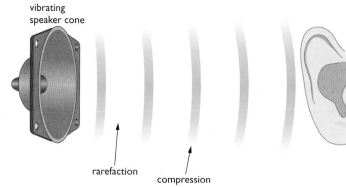

Figure 14.2 *The loudspeaker vibrates and produces sound waves.*

As the speaker cone moves to the right, it pushes air molecules closer together, creating a **compression**. These particles then push against neighbouring particles so that the compression appears to be moving to the right. Behind the compression is a region where the particles are spread out. This region is called a **rarefaction**. After the cone has vibrated several times, it has created a series of compressions and rarefactions travelling away from it. This is a **longitudinal sound wave** (see page 92). Like all other waves, sound waves can be reflected, refracted and diffracted.

When the waves enter the ear, they strike the eardrum and make it vibrate. These vibrations are changed into electrical signals, which are then detected by the brain.

Sound waves in different materials

Sound waves can travel through:

1 solids – this is why you can hear someone talking in the next room, even when the door is closed

2 liquids – this is why whales can communicate with each other when they are under water

3 gases – the sound waves we create when we speak travel through gases (in the air).

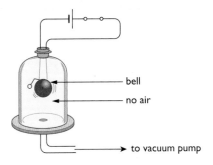

Figure 14.3 *We can only hear the bell when there is air in the jar.*

Sound waves cannot travel through a vacuum because there are no particles to carry the vibrations. We can demonstrate this with the experiment shown in Figure 14.3.

When there is air in the bell jar, the bell can be seen and heard to ring. However, if the air is removed using a vacuum pump, we can see that the bell is still ringing but it cannot be heard. This simple experiment demonstrates that light waves can travel through a vacuum (because we can still see the bell) but sound waves cannot (because we cannot hear the bell any more).

The speed of sound in air is approximately 340 m/s, although this value does vary a little with temperature and pressure. In liquids and solids the particles are much closer together. This means that they are able to transfer sound energy more quickly. The speed of sound in seawater is approximately 1500 m/s. The speed of sound in a solid such as concrete or steel is approximately 5000 m/s.

Measuring the speed of sound

You can measure the speed of sound in the laboratory in several different ways.

Measuring the speed of sound using echoes

You can measure the speed of sound by asking a friend to make a noise by banging two pieces of wood together. If you stand some distance away, you can use a stopwatch to find the time from when you can see the pieces of wood banging together and when you can hear the sound. However your reaction time is likely to make this quite inaccurate.

You can obtain a more accurate measurement using echoes. Stand 50 m away from a large, blank wall and clap or bang two pieces of wood together. Listen for the echo. Set up a rhythm of claps so that the echo comes exactly between two claps. Ask a friend to time 20 claps. During this time the sound has travelled 2000 m (to the wall and back 20 times), and you can divide this distance by the time to work out the speed of the sound (see page 1).

Measuring the speed of sound using a resonance tube and tuning forks

If you waggle one end of a length of rope that is fastened at the far end, you can set up a standing wave (Figure 14.4). This happens because the wave you send down the rope by moving your hand is reflected where the rope is fastened to the wall. If you move your hand at the correct frequency, the wave and its reflection add together to make a standing wave.

A similar thing happens when air vibrates inside a tube. The sound wave is reflected, and if the tube is the correct length, the reflected wave reinforces the original one. This gives a wave with a larger amplitude. This effect is known as resonance. You can use resonance to measure the speed of sound.

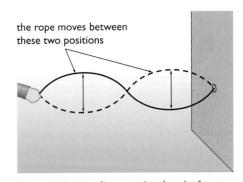

the rope moves between these two positions

Figure 14.4 *A standing wave in a length of rope.*

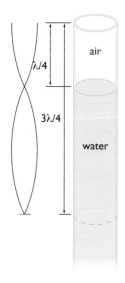

Figure 14.5 *A resonance tube.*

A resonance tube is a Perspex tube with a water reservoir. The height of the water in the tube can be adjusted to change the length of the tube, as the sound waves will be reflected at the water surface. A sound of a known frequency is made by striking a tuning fork and holding it above the open end of the tube. The water column is adjusted until the loudest sound can be heard. As Figure 14.5 shows, the first resonance will be heard when the length of the air in the tube is equal to a quarter of the wavelength. You can check your result by lowering the water level to find the next resonance, at ¾ of the wavelength. The speed of sound is then calculated using the formula $v = f \times \lambda$ (see page 93).

Measuring the speed of sound using an oscilloscope

Figure 14.6 shows how you can use two microphones to measure the speed of sound. Set the signal generator to give a sound with a frequency of about 1 kHz. Start with the microphones close together, and observe how the two traces on the oscilloscope compare. Then move one microphone further away from the loudspeaker until it is one complete wavelength away from the first – you know you have arrived at this point when the traces on the oscilloscope screen are exactly above one another. Measure the distance between the microphones to get the wavelength of the sound, and use the oscilloscope screen to find an accurate value for the frequency. The speed of sound can then be worked out using the formula $v = f \times \lambda$.

Figure 14.6 *Using microphones and an oscilloscope to measure the speed of sound.*

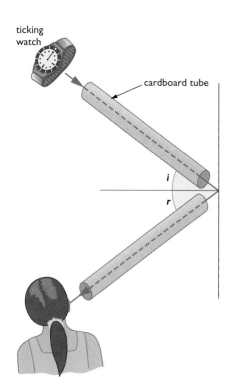

Figure 14.7 *Sound waves are reflected in the same way that light rays are reflected.*

Reflection

Sound waves behave in the same way as any other wave.

When a sound wave strikes a surface it may be **reflected**. Like light waves, sound waves are reflected from a surface so that the angle of incidence is equal to the angle of reflection. A reflected sound wave is called an **echo**.

Ships often use echoes to discover the depth of the water beneath them. This is called **echo sounding**. Sound waves are emitted from the ship and travel to the seabed. Equipment on the ship detects some of the sound waves that are reflected by the seabed. The depth of the sea can be calculated from the time between sending the sound wave and detecting the echo. The system of using echoes in this way is called sonar (SOund, Navigation And Ranging).

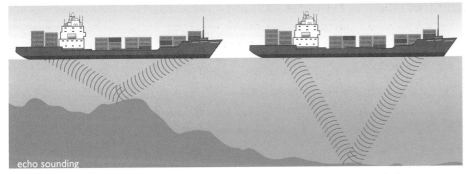

Figure 14.8 *Reflected sound can be used to tell ships about the depth of the sea beneath them.*

Diffraction

We can often hear sounds even when the sound waves cannot travel in a straight line from the source to our ears. Sound can be **diffracted**.

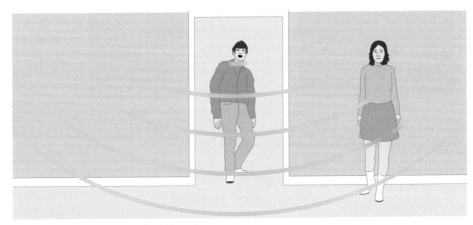

Figure 14.9 *Sound waves can be diffracted.*

The wavelength of some sound waves is approximately the same as the width of a doorway. These waves will therefore spread out as they pass through the door. If the waves did not diffract there would be "sound shadows" where no sound waves would reach.

Pitch and frequency

Small objects, such as the strings of the violin in Figure 14.10, vibrate quickly and produce sound waves with a high **frequency**. These sounds are heard as notes with a high **pitch**.

Larger objects, such as the strings of the cello, vibrate more slowly and produce waves with a lower frequency. These sounds have a lower pitch.

The frequency of a source is the number of complete vibrations it makes each second. We measure frequency in **hertz** (Hz). If a source has a frequency of 50 Hz this means that it vibrates 50 times each second and therefore produces 50 waves each second.

Figure 14.10 *The violin produces notes that are higher pitched than those from the cello.*

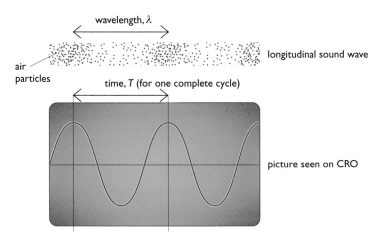

Figure 14.11 *Although we cannot see an actual sound wave we can see a representation of it by connecting a microphone to a piece of apparatus called a **cathode ray oscilloscope** (CRO).*

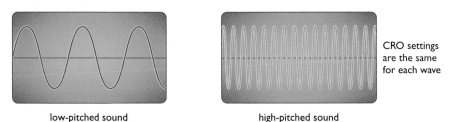

Figure 14.12 *High-pitched sounds and low-pitched sounds seen on a CRO. A low pitched sound has fewer complete waves per second – so fewer complete waves are seen on the CRO.*

You can find the frequency of a sound using a CRO if you find the time period (T) for one complete wave. The relationship between the frequency and the time period is:

$$f = \frac{1}{T}$$

Worked example

Example 1

An oscilloscope trace shows that the time period for a sound is 0.005 s. What is the frequency of the wave?

$$f = \frac{1}{T}$$

$$f = \frac{1}{0.005\,s}$$

$$f = 200\,Hz$$

The relationship between the frequency (f), wavelength (λ) and speed of a sound wave (v) is described by the equation:

$$v = f \times \lambda$$

Worked example

Example 2

Calculate the wavelength of a sound wave that is produced by a source vibrating with a frequency of 85 Hz. The speed of sound in air is 340 m/s.

Using $v = f \times \lambda$

$340 \text{ m/s} = 85 \text{ Hz} \times \lambda$

$\lambda = \dfrac{340 \text{ m/s}}{85 \text{ Hz}}$

$\lambda = 4 \text{ m}$

The wavelength is 4 m.

Audible range

The average person can only hear sounds that have a frequency higher than 20 Hz but lower than 20 000 Hz. This spread of frequencies is called the **audible range** or **hearing range**. The size of the audible range varies slightly from person to person and usually becomes narrower as we get older. You can demonstrate this by using a signal generator and a loudspeaker to produce sounds at different frequencies. You will be able to hear higher frequency notes than your teacher!

Some objects vibrate at frequencies greater than 20 000 Hz. The sounds they produce cannot be heard by human beings and are called **ultrasounds**. Some objects vibrate so slowly that the sounds they produce cannot be heard by human beings. These are called **infrasounds**.

Figure 14.13 *Some animals can make and hear sounds that lie outside the human audible range. Dolphins can communicate using ultrasounds. Elephants can communicate using sounds that have frequencies too low for us to hear.*

Loudness

Figure 14.14 *If you strike a drum hard, you get a louder sound than if you beat it gently.*

If the drum in Figure 14.14 is struck hard, lots of energy is transferred to it from the hammer. The drum skin vibrates up and down with a large **amplitude** and creates regions of very compressed air molecules. As these compressions move away from the source they carry lots of energy, which we hear as a loud sound. If the drum is struck more gently the compressions created are less dense and less energy is transferred by the sound waves. We hear these as quieter sounds.

It is important to remember that sound waves are longitudinal. CROs display all waves as if they are transverse, because they show the amplitude of the wave against **time** on the horizontal scale.

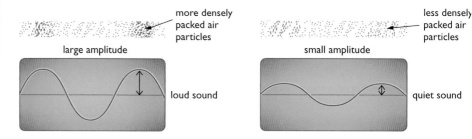

more densely packed air particles

large amplitude

loud sound

less densely packed air particles

small amplitude

quiet sound

Figure 14.15 *Loud sounds and quiet sounds on a CRO.*

The amplitude of a wave gives us some idea of the energy it is transferring. For a sound wave, its amplitude is a measure of its loudness.

Figure 14.16 *The photo above shows a scientist measuring the sound level as a speedboat passes him.*

You will need to be able to do the following:

✓ recall that sound waves are longitudinal waves that can travel through solids, liquids and gases; like other waves, they can be reflected, refracted and diffracted

✓ describe how to measure the speed of sound in air

✓ understand that sounds are produced when objects vibrate

✓ understand that the greater the amplitude of the vibration the louder the sound

✓ understand that the higher the frequency of the vibration the higher the pitch

✓ describe the amplitudes and frequencies of sounds as shown on a cathode ray oscilloscope

✓ understand that humans have an audible range, or hearing range; sounds with frequencies higher than this range are called ultrasounds.

Questions

More questions on sound and vibrations can be found at the end of Section C on page 126.

1 *a)* Name a musical instrument that is used to produce high-pitched notes.

  b) Explain why the musical instrument you have named in part *a)* produces high-pitched notes.

  c) Explain how you would produce loud sounds from this musical instrument.

  d) Draw the trace you might expect to see on a CRO when this instrument is producing a loud, high-pitched note.

2 *a)* What is an echo?

  b) Explain how echoes are used by ships to find the depth of the ocean beneath them.

  c) A ship hears the echo from a sound wave 4 s after it has been emitted. If the speed of sound in water is 1500 m/s, calculate the depth of the water beneath the ship.

3 *a)* What is meant by the phrase "a person's audible range is 20 Hz to 20 000 Hz"?

  b) What are ultrasonic sounds?

  c) Calculate the wavelength of ultrasonic waves whose frequency is 68 000 Hz. Assume that the waves are travelling through air at a speed of 340 m/s.

4 *a)* Two astronauts stand 2 m apart on the surface of the Moon. Their radio link is broken. Both men shout as loud as they can. But neither of them can hear what the other is saying. Explain why the astronauts are unable to hear each other. (Hint: What is the atmosphere like on the Moon?)

  b) The two astronauts move closer together so that their helmets touch. Explain why they can now hear each other.

5 *a)* Sound waves are emitted from a source that is vibrating with a large amplitude, and from a source that is vibrating with a small amplitude. Explain, using diagrams, the difference between the two sets of sound waves.

  b) Draw two diagrams to show how these waves would appear on a CRO.

End of Section C Questions

1 The diagram below shows water waves passing through the entrance of a model harbour.

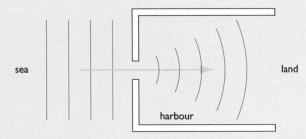

a) Describe what happens to the waves as they leave the gap between the harbour walls. *(1 mark)*

b) What is this process called? *(1 mark)*

c) Describe one change that could be made to the above arrangement in order to reduce this effect. *(1 mark)*

The diagram below shows a cross-section of the water waves.

d) Copy this diagram and mark on it:

　　i) the wavelength of the wave (λ)

　　ii) the amplitude of the wave (A). *(2 marks)*

e) A water wave travelling at 20 m/s has a wavelength of 2.5 m. Calculate the frequency of the wave. *(3 marks)*

Total 8 marks

2 The diagram below shows a ray of light travelling down an optical fibre.

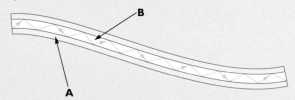

a) What is A? *(1 mark)*

b) What is B? *(1 mark)*

c) Why is light reflected from the boundary between A and B? *(2 marks)*

d) Describe one medical use for optical fibres. *(1 mark)*

Total 5 marks

3 a) i) Explain the difference between a longitudinal wave and a transverse wave.

　　ii) Give one example of each type of wave. *(4 marks)*

A girl stands 500 m from a tall building and bangs two pieces of wood together. At the same instant her friend starts a stopwatch. The sound waves created by the two pieces of wood strike the building and are reflected. When the two girls hear the echo they stop the stopwatch and note the time. The girls repeat the experiment four more times. The results are shown in the table below.

Experiment	Time in seconds
1	2.95
2	3.00
3	2.90
4	3.20
5	2.95

b) Why did the girls repeat the experiment five times? *(1 mark)*

c) Calculate the speed of sound using the above results. *(6 marks)*

d) One of the girls thought that their answer might be affected by wind. Was she correct? Explain your answer. *(2 marks)*

Total 13 marks

4 The electromagnetic spectrum contains the following groups of waves: infra-red, ultraviolet, X-rays, radio waves, microwaves, visible spectrum and gamma rays.

a) Put these groups of waves in the order they appear in the electromagnetic spectrum starting with the group that has the longest wavelength. *(2 marks)*

b) Write down four properties that all of these waves have in common. *(4 marks)*

c) Write down one use for each group of waves. *(7 marks)*

d) Which three groups of waves could cause cancer? *(3 marks)*

e) Which three groups of waves can be used to communicate? *(3 marks)*

Total 19 marks

Chapter 15: Energy Transfers

Whenever anything happens, energy is transferred from one form to another – indeed, without energy things simply can't happen! In this chapter, you will learn that energy can be transferred into many different forms, including sound, light, movement, heat and potential energy. You will also find out that, although energy is never destroyed, in every energy conversion some energy is "lost" to the surroundings, often as heat.

Figure 15.1 *Energy comes in different forms – as sound, movement, light and heat, for example.*

For things to happen we need energy! Energy is used to transport people and goods from place to place, whether it is by train, boat or plane or on the backs of animals or people. Energy is needed to lift objects, make machinery work and run all the electrical and electronic equipment we take for granted in our modern world. Energy is needed to make heat and light. The demand for energy increases every day because the world's population is increasing. People consume energy in the form of food and need energy for the basics of life, like warmth and light. As people become wealthier they demand much more than the basics, so the need for energy grows!

Types of energy

Energy comes in many different forms. We get our energy from the food we eat. Food provides stored **chemical energy** that we can burn to turn it into other types of energy. We use the energy from food to generate **thermal energy** (heat energy) to help to keep us warm. Our muscles convert the chemical energy into **movement energy** (kinetic energy). Some of this movement energy is used as we speak producing energy in the form of **sound**.

We need heat for our homes, schools and workplaces. We also need to convert energy to **light** for our buildings, vehicles and roads. Most of the energy needed for these purposes is converted from **electrical energy**. We shall see later (see Chapter 18) that electrical energy can be made from other forms of energy, like chemical or nuclear energy. Some electrical energy is produced from the **gravitational potential energy** stored in water kept in reservoirs in mountainous areas. We can also use the energy stored in the hot core of the Earth. We see the evidence of this huge supply of heat in volcanoes and thermal springs. Energy from the heat underground is called **geothermal energy**.

Energy can also be stored in springs as **elastic potential energy**. This type of stored energy is used in things like clocks, toys and catapults.

The main source of energy for the Earth is our Sun. This provides us with heat, light and other forms of energy.

Energy transfer and conversion

For energy to be useful, we need to be able to transfer it from place to place and to be able to convert it into whatever form we require. Unfortunately when we try to do either of these things there is usually some energy converted to unwanted forms. We often refer to these unwanted forms as "wasted" energy because it is not being used for a useful purpose.

Here are some examples of wasted energy.

- An electric heater may be used to heat water in a house. The hot water will be stored in a tank for use when required. Although the tank may be well insulated, some energy will escape from the water and some will be used to heat up the copper that the tank is made from. Both processes mean that some of the energy that is converted from electricity to heat is lost because it is not doing what we want it to do – it is not making the water hot.

- When we fill a car with petrol, the main purpose is to convert the chemical energy stored in the fuel into movement energy, with a small amount doing other things like providing electrical energy for the lights or radio. But the process of converting the energy is not perfectly **efficient**, as not *all* of the energy is used to do what we want. (A formal definition of efficiency is given on page 131.) A considerable amount of the energy supplied by the fuel is converted to heat, most of which is lost or wasted by heating up the surroundings. Some of the energy is converted to sound, which can be unpleasant for people both inside and outside the car. A lot of energy is used to overcome the various friction forces that oppose movement of parts within the car and the car's movement along the road. Friction causes energy conversion to occur too, usually producing unwanted heat energy.

Sound energy can be used to break up small stones that can form inside a person's body, without the need for an operation. Sound energy is also used in medicine to examine the inside of the body, as an alternative to X-rays.

Unwanted energy conversions during energy transfer reduce efficiency. This problem is the same whether the system is a small one like a car, or a large system like the nationwide electricity generation and distribution industry. We need to be aware of where our energy is going if we are to find ways of using it to best effect.

Energy conversions

We have many ways of converting energy from one form to another.

   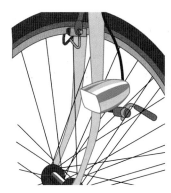

Figure 15.2 *Energy is converted from one form to another, and to another, and so on.*

In Figure 15.2, stored chemical energy in the food is needed to help our bodies make a range of other chemicals. Some of these – like carbohydrates – are used to produce heat to maintain our body temperature and energy for movement through muscle activity. Having eaten a meal, the cyclist in Figure 15.2 is converting the chemical energy stored in his body into movement energy. The movement is initially in the cyclist's legs and is then transferred to the machine (the bicycle). The cyclist is also producing additional heat energy, which is lost to the surroundings. Friction in various parts of the bicycle will also result in energy being converted from movement into heat and sound.

The dynamo or generator fitted to the bicycle's wheel converts some of the movement energy of the wheel into electrical energy. The lamp then converts the electrical energy into light and heat. As the electric current flows in the dynamo–lamp circuit, heat will be produced in the conducting wires too.

Examples of other energy conversions are given in the questions at the end of the chapter.

Conservation of energy

The Law of Conservation of Energy is a very important rule. It states that:

> **Energy is not created or destroyed in any process.**
> **(It is just converted from one type to another.)**

We often hear about the energy crisis: as our demand for more energy increases our reserves of energy in the form of fuels like oil and gas are rapidly being used up. The Law of Conservation of Energy makes it seem as if there is no real problem – that energy can never run out. We need to understand what the law really means.

Physicists believe that the amount of energy in the Universe is constant – energy can be changed from one form to another but there is never any more or any less

Even though the amount of energy in the Universe is constant it is becoming more spread out and so less usable. Some scientists think that all the energy in the Universe is ultimately going to be converted into heat and that everywhere in the Universe will end up at the same, very low temperature. This "end of the world" scenario is sometimes referred to by the dramatic name of "heat death". If the Universe does end up this way, it is not expected to do so for some time yet, so carry on working for those exams!

of it. This means we cannot use energy up. However, if we consider our little piece of the Universe, the problem becomes more obvious. As we make energy do useful things – for example, move a car – some of it will be converted to heat. Some of this heat energy will be radiated away from the Earth and lost (not destroyed or used up). Lost in this sense means not available for us to use any more. This is just like a badly insulated house; if heat energy escapes, it is lost from the system we call our home, and is no longer available to keep us warm.

Energy diagrams

We use different ways to show how energy is transferred and converted. Energy transfer diagrams show the energy input, the energy conversion process and the energy output. The system may be a very simple one with just one main energy conversion process taking place. An example of a simple system with its energy transfer diagram is shown in Figure 15.3.

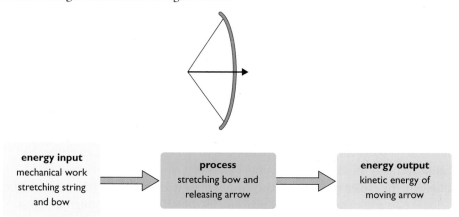

Figure 15.3 *Energy transfer diagram for an arrow being fired from a bow.*

Sankey diagrams are a simpler and clearer way of showing what becomes of an energy input to a system. The energy flow is shown by arrows *whose width is proportional to the amount of energy involved*. Broad arrows show large energy flows, narrow arrows show small energy flows.

Figure 15.4 shows a Sankey diagram for a complex system – the energy flow for a car. Chemical energy in the form of petrol is the input to the car. The energy outputs from the car are:

- electrical energy (from the alternator) to drive lights, radio and so on, to charge the battery (conversion to chemical energy) and provide ignition

- movement (kinetic) energy from the car engine

- wasted energy as electrical heating in wiring and lamp filaments, as frictional heating in various parts of the engine and alternator, and as noise.

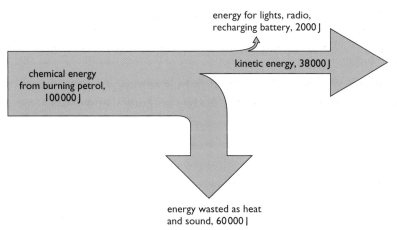

Figure 15.4 *Sankey diagram showing the energy flow in a typical car.*

Efficiency

Whenever we are considering energy transfers, we have to remember that a proportion of the energy input is wasted. Remember that wasted means converted into forms other than the useful form required. We would like our energy conversion systems to be perfect with *all* the input energy being converted to the form that we want – for example, all the input energy for an electric lamp being converted into light rather than some being converted to heat. Real systems do not achieve this level of complete, or 100%, **efficiency**. The efficiency of an energy conversion system is defined as:

$$\text{efficiency} = \frac{\text{useful energy output from the system}}{\text{total energy input to the system}}$$

Efficiency does not have a unit because it is a ratio. It is always a number between 0 and 1. This number represents the fraction of the energy input that is converted to the form of energy that we want. Sometimes efficiency is given as a percentage:

$$\text{efficiency} = \frac{\text{useful energy output from the system}}{\text{total energy input to the system}} \times 100\%$$

If you calculate the efficiency of a system and get an answer greater than 1 (or 100%) then you have put the numbers into the formula the wrong way round!

Worked example

Example 1

A 60 W tungsten filament lamp uses 60 J of energy every second. It is 5% efficient. How much useful light energy does it emit per second?

$$\text{efficiency} = \frac{\text{useful energy output from the system}}{\text{total energy input to the system}} \times 100\%$$

So, $5\% = \dfrac{\text{useful light energy output from the lamp}}{60\,\text{J}} \times 100\%$

∴ useful light energy output from the lamp $= \dfrac{5 \times 60}{100}$

$$= 3\,\text{J per second}$$

End of Chapter Checklist

You will need to be able to do the following:

✓ recognise that energy exists in the following forms: heat (thermal), light, electrical, sound, movement (kinetic), chemical, nuclear, and potential (stored) as both gravitational and elastic potential energy

✓ understand how energy may be converted from one form to another

✓ recall that energy is conserved

✓ appreciate that energy conversions usually involve some energy being converted to unwanted forms or being transferred to places other than where it is needed

✓ draw Sankey diagrams for a variety of everyday and scientific situations

✓ carry out efficiency calculations using

$$\text{efficiency} = \frac{\text{useful energy output from the system}}{\text{total energy input to the system}}$$

Questions

More questions on the need for energy can be found at the end of Section D on page 160.

1 Describe the main energy conversions taking place in the following situations:

   a) turning on a torch

   b) lighting a candle

   c) rubbing your hands to keep them warm

   d) bouncing on a trampoline.

2 Copy and complete the following Sankey diagrams. Remember that the width of the arrows must be proportional to the amount of energy involved. This has been done for you in example a).

   a) For an electric lamp:

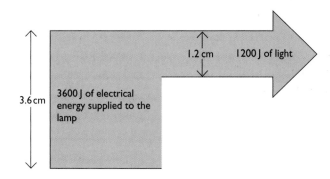

b) For a washing machine:

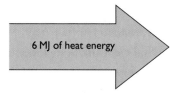

1.2 MJ of kinetic energy to rotate the drum

6 MJ of heat energy

0.8 MJ of energy wasted as heat and sound

3 *a)* Draw a Sankey diagram for the following situation. An electric kettle is used to heat some water. 350 kJ of energy are used to heat the water, 10 kJ raise the temperature of the kettle and 40 kJ escape to heat the surroundings.

   b) Calculate the efficiency of the kettle.

4 A ball is dropped. It hits the ground with 10 J of kinetic energy and rebounds with 4 J of kinetic energy.

   a) What happens to 6 J of the energy during the bounce?

   b) Draw a Sankey diagram for the energy flow that takes place during the bounce.

Chapter 16: Thermal Energy

This chapter is about the ways in which thermal (heat) energy is transferred from a hotter place to a cooler place.

Figure 16.1 *Sometimes we want to prevent the transfer of thermal energy – to keep our bodies warm, for example. In other circumstances, the movement of thermal energy from place to place can be useful – for example, rising warm air creates "thermals" that can carry a glider up to great heights.*

Thermal or heat energy is a form of energy that is possessed by "hot" matter. We shall see that "hot" is a relative term. There is a temperature called **absolute zero** that is the lowest possible temperature. Any matter that is above this temperature has some thermal energy. The kinetic energy of the minute particles that make up all matter produces the effect we call heat.

Thermal energy travels from a place that is hotter (that is, at a higher temperature) to one that is colder (at a lower temperature). In this chapter, we shall look at the different ways in which thermal energy is transferred between places that have different temperatures.

Conduction

Thermal conduction is the transfer of thermal (heat) energy through a substance without the substance itself moving.

Figure 16.2 *Metal skewers allow heat to be transferred to parts that are away from the heat.*

"Free electrons" are electrons that are not bound to any particular atom in the structure of a substance. Metals usually have huge numbers of free electrons per unit volume. Copper, for example, has about 10^{29} free electrons in each cubic metre. As these free electrons carry electric charge as well as energy, it is no coincidence that good thermal conductors are usually good conductors of electricity too.

Substances tend to expand when heated because the particles of which they are made have more kinetic energy. As they move around more, the average distance between the particles increases.

If you have ever cooked kebabs on a barbecue with metal skewers, as shown in Figure 16.2, you will have discovered conduction! The metal over the burning charcoal becomes hot and the heat energy is transferred along the skewer by conduction. In metals, this takes place quite rapidly and soon the handle end is almost as hot as the end over the fire. Metals are good **thermal conductors**. If you use skewers with wooden handles you can hold the wooden ends much more comfortably because wood does not conduct thermal energy very well. Wood is an example of a good thermal **insulator**.

The process of energy transfer by conduction is explained in terms of the behaviour of tiny particles that make up all matter. In a hot part of a substance, like the part of the skewer over the glowing charcoal, these particles have more kinetic energy. The more energetic particles transfer some of their energy to particles near to them. These therefore gain energy and then pass energy on to particles near to them. The energy transfer goes on throughout the substance. This process takes place in all materials.

In metals, the process takes place much more rapidly, because metals have **free electrons** that can move easily through the structure of the metal, speeding up the transfer of energy.

Convection

> Convection is the transfer of heat through fluids (liquids and gases) by the upward movement of warmer, less dense regions of fluid.

You may have seen a demonstration of convection currents in water, like the one shown in Figure 16.3. The water is heated just under the purple crystal – the crystal colours the water as it dissolves, which lets you see the movement in the water. The heated water expands and becomes less dense than the colder surrounding water, so it floats up to the top of the beaker. Colder water sinks to take its place, and is then heated too. At the top, the warm water starts to cool, becomes more dense again and will begin to sink, so a circulating current is set up in the water. This is called a **convection** current.

Lava lamps work by convection (Figure 16.4). Two liquids that do not mix are used in a lava lamp – one clear and one coloured. As the coloured liquid at the bottom is heated, it expands. As a result of it expanding, the coloured liquid becomes less

Figure 16.3 *Demonstration of convection currents, using a potassium manganate (VII) crystal in water.*

Figure 16.4 *The "blobs" in a lava lamp move up and then down again in convection currents.*

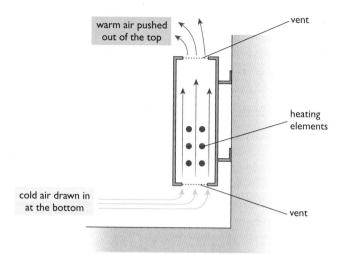

warm air pushed out of the top

vent

heating elements

cold air drawn in at the bottom

vent

Figure 16.5 *A convector heater relies on the effects of convection.*

dense so it floats up to the top. When it eventually cools it sinks back to the bottom, demonstrating convection beautifully!

Convection occurs in any **fluid** substance – that is, in liquids and gases. Convector heaters (Figure 16.5) heat air, which then floats out of the top of the heater to the top of the room. Cold air is drawn in at the bottom and this in turn is heated. In this way, heat energy is eventually transferred to all parts of the room.

In many cooking ovens, the heating element is placed at the bottom of the oven. It heats the air near to it, and this air rises by convection. The top of the oven is generally warmer than the bottom, so you can cook foods at different temperatures. However many modern ovens are fan ovens, when hot air is blown into the oven and provides an even temperature throughout the oven.

Air and water both allow heat transfer to take place readily by convection as they are both fluids, but neither are good thermal conductors (they are insulators). This insulating property of both water and air is put to good use in situations where they are not able to circulate easily. For example, woollen clothing keeps you warm because air gets trapped in the fibres. The trapped air is heated by your body and forms a warm insulating layer that helps to stop you losing heat. In the same way, a wetsuit keeps a diver warm because a thin layer of water is trapped next to the diver's skin.

Radiation

Remember that we are talking about heat transfer – this is *thermal* radiation not *nuclear* radiation!

Figure 16.6 *Heat is transferred from a heater by radiation.*

When you turn on a bathroom heater, as shown in Figure 16.6, you will feel the effect almost instantly. Neither conduction nor convection can explain how heat is getting from the hot element to your hands. Conduction does not occur that rapidly, even in good thermal conductors, and air is a poor thermal conductor. Convection results in heated air floating *upwards* on colder, denser air.

There are two things you should notice about this example.

1 The heat that you feel so quickly is travelling from the heater *in a straight line*.

2 The design of the electric fire includes a specially shaped, very shiny *reflector* similar to the reflector behind a fluorescent light or in a torch.

In this example, heat is travelling in the form of *waves*, like visible light. Heat waves are called **infra-red (IR) waves** or IR radiation. The army and the emergency services use special cameras, called *thermal imaging cameras*, that can detect objects giving out IR waves. These cameras show images of people because of the heat radiation from their bodies, even when there is not enough visible light to actually see them. Thermal imaging is also an important tool in the diagnosis of certain illnesses.

> **Thermal radiation is the transfer of energy by infra-red (IR) waves.**

IR waves are part of the same family of waves as light, radio waves, ultraviolet and so on, called the **electromagnetic (EM) spectrum** (see page 99). IR waves, therefore, have the same properties as all the other waves in the EM spectrum. In particular, IR can travel through a vacuum and does so at the speed of light (3×10^8 m/s). It is important that heat can travel in this way, without the need for matter, otherwise we would not receive heat, as well as light, from the Sun.

IR waves can also be reflected and absorbed by different materials, just like visible light. Highly polished, shiny surfaces are good reflectors of thermal radiation. White surfaces also reflect a lot of IR. Matt black and dark surfaces are *poor* reflectors or, to put it more positively, *good* absorbers of heat radiation. Figure 16.8 shows this fact being put to good effect.

The reflector in an electric fire is a special shape, called a **parabola**. You can see parabolic reflectors in torches and radio telescopes, for example.

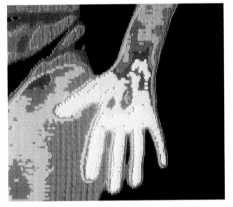

Figure 16.7 *This is a thermal image of a patient showing areas of different temperatures. The hand is white because rheumatoid arthritis gives rise to a temperature increase.*

Figure 16.8 *Shiny and white surfaces reflect thermal radiation, while matt black surfaces absorb it.*

Figure 16.9 a) *A shiny kettle stays warmer longer.*

b) The *heat sink needs to be matt black to lose heat to the surroundings quickly, and so stop the transistor overheating.*

If a surface is a good reflector of IR then it is a poor radiator of IR. This means that a hot object with a shiny surface will emit less heat energy in the form of IR than another object at the same temperature with a dull black surface. The kettle in Figure 16.9a has a shiny surface to reduce the rate of heat loss. The heat sink in Figure 16.9b, designed to stop the transistor overheating, has a matt black surface so that it will radiate heat well.

Energy-efficient houses

We pay for the energy we use in our homes, schools and places of work. Heating is the main use of energy in our homes and – since most domestic heating systems work by burning fuels like coal, oil and gas – it is the main producer of carbon dioxide. (Even if electric heaters are used, most electrical energy is produced by burning fuels in power stations.) Carbon dioxide is a greenhouse gas and contributes to global warming. It is, therefore, in everyone's interest that houses are **energy efficient**.

Energy efficiency means using as much as possible of the energy we produce for the desired purpose. So when we turn on the central heating, we want to keep the inside of our homes warm and not allow the heat to escape. If no heat could escape from a house then we would need only heat it until it reached the desired temperature, then never heat it again.

The key to energy efficient housing is **insulation**. Houses must be designed to reduce the rate at which energy is transferred between the inside and the outside.

How heat is lost

To insulate a house effectively we must look at *all* the ways in which heat energy can escape. Conduction is the main way heat is transferred between the inside of a building and the outside. Next we need to consider the *places* where conduction occurs: the walls, the windows (and doors) and the roof.

Heat loss by conduction through the walls can be reduced by using building materials that are good insulators. However, the materials used for building must also have other suitable properties like strength, durability and availability at a

The greenhouse effect
Infra-red waves from the Sun can pass through ordinary greenhouse glass. The IR waves heat up the ground, which re-radiates the heat. However, the re-radiated heat is in the form of IR waves with much longer wavelengths. The longer wavelength IR waves cannot pass through glass, so they are trapped inside the greenhouse. Carbon dioxide in our atmosphere acts in the same way as the glass in a greenhouse. It traps the Sun's heat.

It is worth remembering that, in some countries, the problem is not keeping warm but keeping cool. Keeping cool also requires energy – to run air-conditioning units, fans and other cooling devices. An energy-efficient house in a hot climate would stay cool by reducing the rate at which heat *entered* the house.

In cooler climates such as that in the UK it is more appropriate to concentrate on keeping heat in, rather than thinking about how to keep it out.

sensible price. For walls, bricks are the common building material. Figure 16.10 shows the typical construction of a modern house in the UK built to conform to current energy efficiency regulations.

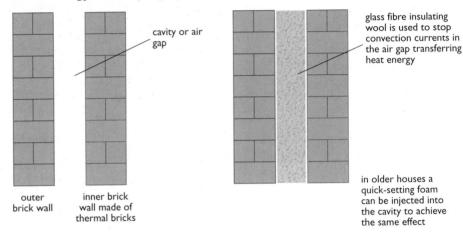

Figure 16.10 *The two-layered wall construction, with the cavity filled with insulation panels, helps to reduce heat loss by conduction, convection and even radiation.*

As you can see, the wall is made with layers of different materials. The outer layer is made with bricks; these have quite good insulating properties, are strong and have good weathering properties. The inner layer is built with thermal bricks with very good insulation properties; they are also light, relatively cheap and quick to work with. The two layers of brick are separated by an excellent thermal insulator in the form of an air cavity or gap.

The walls also stop heat being lost by convection. The cavity or gap between the two walls is wide enough for convection currents to circulate. This means heat is circulated from the warmer surface of one wall to the colder surface of the other. To stop convection currents, the gap in modern houses is filled with insulating panels made of glass fibre matting. This is a lightweight, poor conductor that traps lots of air. The panels are usually surfaced with thin aluminium foil. This highly reflective surface reflects heat in the form of infra-red radiation.

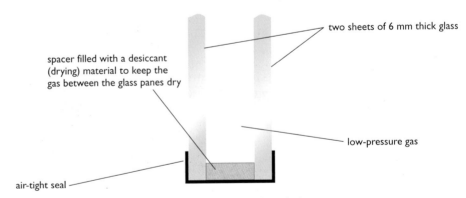

Figure 16.11 *Double glazing helps to stop heat escaping from the home.*

Figure 16.11 shows a cross-section of a typical double glazed window, as used in modern houses. Glass is a poor thermal conductor but is used in thin layers. To improve the insulating properties, two layers of glass are used to trap a layer of air. The thickness of this layer is important. If it is too thin then the insulation effect is reduced, but if it is too thick then convection currents will be able to circulate and carry heat from the hotter surface to the colder one. In very cold countries triple glazing is used. Modern double glazing uses special glass to increase the greenhouse effect (heat radiation from the Sun can get in but radiation from inside the house is mainly reflected back again).

Roof insulation in modern houses uses similar panels to those used in the wall cavities, trapping a thick layer of air. This takes advantage of the poor conducting property of air, whilst also preventing convection currents circulating. Again, reflective foil is used to reduce radiation heat loss. Figure 16.12 shows houses built before loft insulation was a compulsory building regulation. In some, the owners have installed loft insulation – you should be able to identify which!

Figure 16.12 *Loft insulation makes a big difference to heat loss through the roof.*

There are other measures that can be taken to improve the energy efficiency of houses, which do not relate directly to the mechanisms of heat transfer discussed in this chapter. For example, thermostats and computer control systems for central heating can further reduce the heating needs of a house. They stop rooms being heated too much by switching off the heat when a certain temperature is reached. Another important energy saving measure is the reduction or elimination of draughts from poorly fitting doors and windows.

With your understanding of how heat travels you can save your family money, keep warm *and* reduce global warming.

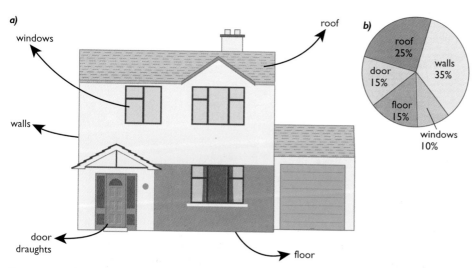

Figure 16.13 a) *How heat energy can be lost from the home.* **b)** *Percentage of energy lost in different ways.*

Insulating people and animals

Earlier in this chapter we saw a picture of a fire fighter in protective clothing designed to reduce the amount of heat getting to their bodies (Figure 16.8). Sometimes we have the opposite problem and want to keep warm. The obvious method of cutting down heat loss from the body is to wear clothes. Clothes that trap air around the body provide insulation because trapped air cannot circulate and is a very poor conductor. A large proportion of body heat is lost from the head, so hats are the human equivalent of loft insulation.

Wind can cause rapid heat loss from the body. It does this by *forced* convection – that is, making air circulate close to the body surface. It may also cause perspiration to evaporate from the skin more quickly, causing rapid cooling. (The purpose of perspiration is to help the body to lose heat by evaporation, but, if it happens because of strong wind on a cold day, the effect can be life threatening.) These cooling effects of wind contribute to what is called the wind-chill factor. To reduce the wind-chill effect, a wind-proof outer garment should be worn.

When people do lose body heat at too great a rate they may become **hypothermic**, which means their body temperature starts to fall. If the heat loss is not drastically reduced the condition is potentially fatal. When people are rescued from mountains suffering from the effects of cold they are usually wrapped in thin, highly reflective blankets. The interior reflective surface reflects heat back to their bodies while the outer reflective surface is a poor radiator of heat. Marathon runners are often cloaked in these blankets at the end of the race to keep them warm when their energy reserves are low (Figure 16.1).

Animals keep warm in different ways. You may have noticed birds fluffing up their feathers on cold days in winter. This increases the thickness of the trapped air layer around their bodies, so reducing heat loss by conduction. Some birds, like penguins, will huddle together for warmth (Figure 16.14). Other animals will curl into small balls. This cuts down heat loss by minimising the surface area of their bodies exposed to the cold.

Figure 16.14 *Penguins huddle together for warmth.*

You will need to be able to do the following:

✓ understand that heat energy is transferred from places at high temperature to places at lower temperature

✓ describe how heat can be transferred by conduction, convection and radiation

✓ understand how heat transfer by these processes can be reduced by using insulation.

Questions

More questions on thermal energy can be found at the end of Section D on page 160.

1 Explain the following observations, referring to the appropriate process of heat transfer in each case.

  a) Two cups of tea are poured at the same time. They are left to stand for ten minutes. One of the cups has a metal teaspoon left in it. The tea in this cup is cooler than the tea in the other at the end of the ten-minute period.

  b) Two fresh cups of tea are poured out. (The others had gone cold!) A thin plastic lid is placed on top of one of the cups. The tea in this cup keeps hot for longer.

2 *a)* Kettles heated on stoves used to be made of copper. Was this a good choice?

  b) Copper kettles were usually kept highly polished. If it is not polished, copper turns dull and eventually blackens as it reacts with oxygen in the air. Apart from making the kettle look nice, what is a sound physics reason for keeping a kettle polished?

3 The diagrams below show a physics demonstration about thermal conduction.

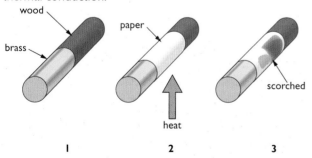

A cylinder is made from a piece of brass fitted to a piece of wood. A strip of paper is glued around the middle. The paper is then heated over a Bunsen burner flame. After a while one end of the paper is noticeably more scorched than the other. Explain why this happens.

4 There are two bench seats in a park, one made of metal, the other made of wood. The metal seat feels much colder to sit on than the wooden one. A student says that it is because the metal seat is at a lower temperature than the wooden one. Explain why this explanation is incorrect, and give a correct explanation of why the metal seat seems colder than the wooden one.

5 *a)* Why is the heating element in an electric kettle positioned very close to the bottom of the kettle?

  b) Where would you expect the cooling element to be placed in a freezer?

6 One of the latest computers does not use a fan to keep the electronic circuits inside it cool, unlike other PCs. A student notices that the ventilation slots on a PC are positioned on the side, but the slots are on the top and bottom surfaces of this new computer. The designer has applied some physics to the problem of keeping the computer cool. Explain why the new computer does not need a fan.

7 The diagram below shows how Roman mines used to be ventilated.

The mine system had a shaft with a fire lit at the bottom. Explain how this kept the air in the mine system fresh.

Work is calculated by multiplying the force applied by the distance through which the force moves – the bigger the force, or the longer the distance through which it moves, the more work is done. Work always involves an energy transfer. Power is the rate at which energy is transferred, and efficiency is a measure of how much of the input energy to a system is converted to useful output energy. In this chapter you will learn how to calculate the work done in a system and its power as energy is transferred.

The unit of energy is named after James Joule. It was Joule who realised that heat was a form of energy. He showed that kinetic energy could be converted into heat. At that time heat was measured in calories. In 1843, Joule worked out "the mechanical equivalent of heat", or, more simply, he found the "exchange rate" between calories and the unit then used for work and energy (the foot-pound weight).

Calories are still used when we talk about the energy content of food. If you look at dietary information on the side of a food product packet, like the one shown in Figure 17.2, you will notice that the energy content is given in kilojoules as well as the kilocalorie equivalent.

Figure 17.1 *James Joule (1818–1889) was the son of a wealthy Manchester brewer. He was tutored by James Dalton and carried out scientific research in his own laboratory, built in the basement of his father's home.*

GUIDELINE DAILY AMOUNTS

EACH DAY	WOMEN	MEN
Calories	2000	2500
Fat	70g	95g

NUTRITIONAL INFORMATION

	Typical value per 100 g	30 g serving with 125 ml of semi-skimmed milk
ENERGY	1550 kJ 370 kcal	700 kJ* 170 kcal
PROTEIN	8g	7g

* Energy contribution of 125 ml of semi-skimmed milk 250 kJ (60 kcal)

Figure 17.2 *Dietary information panel from a packet of cornflakes.*

Energy and work

> Energy is the ability to do work.

This statement tells us what energy *does* rather than what energy *is*. We know that energy comes in a wide variety of different forms but we are really interested in what energy can *do* – the answer is that energy does **work**.

We need to define work in a way that is measurable. Some types of work are not easy to quantify. Mechanical work, like lifting heavy objects, is easy to measure: if you lift a heavier object, you do more work; if you lift an object through a greater distance, again, you do more work. The definition of work in physics is:

work done, W = force applied, F × distance through which it is applied, d
   (in joules)   (in newtons)   (in metres)
$$W = F \times d$$

The unit of work and, therefore, energy is the **joule**. Work done is equal to the amount of energy transferred.

1 J of work is done when a force of 1 N is applied through a distance of 1 m in the direction of the force.

Worked example

Example 1

height lifted 2 m

weight 500 N

Figure 17.3

Figure 17.3 shows a weightlifter raising an object that weighs 500 N through a distance of 2 m. To calculate the work done we use:

$W = F \times d$

$= 500\,N \times 2\,m$

$= 1000\,J$

This work done on the weight has increased its energy. This is explained in the section on gravitational potential energy (page 144).

Worked example

Example 2

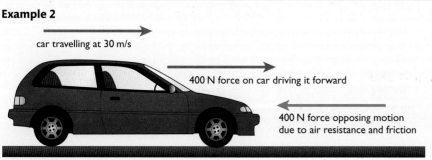

car travelling at 30 m/s

400 N force on car driving it forward

400 N force opposing motion due to air resistance and friction

Figure 17.4

In the example shown in Figure 17.4 the force acting on the car is not accelerating it – instead, it is being used to balance the forces opposing its motion. The resultant force on the car is zero, so it keeps moving in a straight line at constant speed. To work out the work done on the car in one second we substitute the force required, 400 N, and the distance through which it acts in one second, 30 m, in the equation:

$W = F \times d$

$= 400\,N \times 30\,m$

$= 12\,000\,J$ or $12\,kJ$

Gravitational potential energy (GPE)

In the weight-lifting example given on page 143, the weightlifter has used some chemical energy to do the work. We know that energy is conserved so what has happened to the chemical energy that the weightlifter used? Some has been converted to heat in the weightlifter's body. The remainder has been transferred to the weight because he has increased its height in the gravitational field of the Earth. The energy that the weight has gained is called **gravitational potential energy** or GPE.

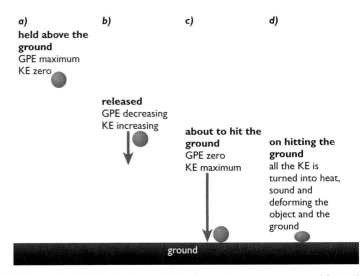

Figure 17.6 *When a raised object falls, its gravitational potential energy is converted first to kinetic energy and then to heat and sound.*

In Figure 17.6, we can see the GPE possessed by the weight being converted into other forms as the weight falls. The weight accelerates because of the force of gravity acting on it, so it gains kinetic energy. When it reaches the ground all the initial GPE is converted to kinetic energy. When it hits the ground all the movement energy is then converted into other forms, mainly heat and sound.

The *change* in GPE of an object is defined as:

change in GPE (in joules)	=	mass of object, m (in kilograms)	×	gravitational field strength, g (in newtons/ kilogram)	×	distance raised against gravitational force, h (in metres)

$$GPE = m \times g \times h$$

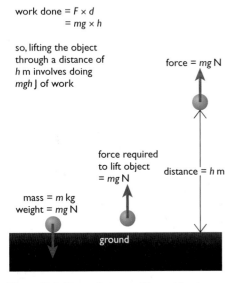

work done $= F \times d$

$= mg \times h$

so, lifting the object through a distance of h m involves doing mgh J of work

force $= mg$ N

force required to lift object $= mg$ N

distance $= h$ m

mass $= m$ kg

weight $= mg$ N

ground

Figure 17.5 *The work done to lift an object is equal to the GPE the object has at its new height.*

Kinetic energy (KE) is the energy possessed by moving objects.

Reminder: Gravitational field strength is the force acting per kilogram on a mass affected by gravity. The gravitational field strength, g, on the surface of the Earth is approximately 10 N/kg. Since the weight of an object is mg, increase in GPE is a special version of the equation $W = F \times d$, with $F = mg$ and $d = h$.

This change in the GPE of an object will be an *increase* if we apply a force on it in the *opposite direction* to the pull of gravity – that is, if we lift it off the ground. For the sake of simplicity, we usually assume that an object has no GPE before we do work on it.

Meteorites and kinetic energy

The amount of energy possessed by a moving object depends on its speed and its mass. As the Earth travels through space, orbiting the Sun, it runs the risk of colliding with chunks of matter that are drawn into the gravitational field of the Solar System. In fact, this is a common occurrence. If you have ever seen a shooting star – or, to give it its proper name, a **meteor** – you have seen the streak of light produced as a small piece of space debris burns up on entering our atmosphere. This is an example of kinetic energy being converted to heat and light by the friction produced between the air and the object passing through it.

The meteorite that caused the Arizona crater is thought to have hit the Earth travelling at 11 000 m/s and to have had a mass of 10^9 kilograms. It hit the ground with an energy equivalent to a 15 megaton hydrogen bomb, 1000 times greater than the atomic bomb dropped on Hiroshima at the end of the Second World War.

Figure 17.8 *This crater was created when a meteorite collided with Earth in Arizona.*

Figure 17.7 *Meteors burn up on entering our atmosphere – we see them as 'shooting stars'.*

Small pieces of space debris do not present a threat to life on this planet. Friction against the atmosphere converts their kinetic energy into so much heat that they are vaporised into minute, harmless particles. Bigger pieces of matter are not completely burned up before reaching the Earth's surface, so they hit the ground still carrying kinetic energy.

Small meteorites cause little damage and most impacts are in uninhabited regions or in the oceans. Large meteorites, however, can carry enormous amounts of kinetic energy and the energy conversions on impact with the Earth are devastating.

The kinetic energy of a moving object is calculated using the formula:

$$KE = \frac{1}{2}mv^2$$

where KE = kinetic energy (in joules)
m = mass of object (in kilograms)
v = speed of object (in metres/second)

Meteors are called **meteorites** when they hit the ground.

Example 3

Calculate the kinetic energy carried by a meteorite of mass 500 kg (less than that of an average-sized car) hitting the Earth at a speed of 1000 m/s.

$$KE = \frac{1}{2}mv^2$$

$$= \frac{1}{2} \times 500 \text{ kg} \times (1000 \text{ m/s})^2$$

$$= 250\,000\,000 \text{ J (or 250 MJ)}$$

Calculations using work, GPE and KE

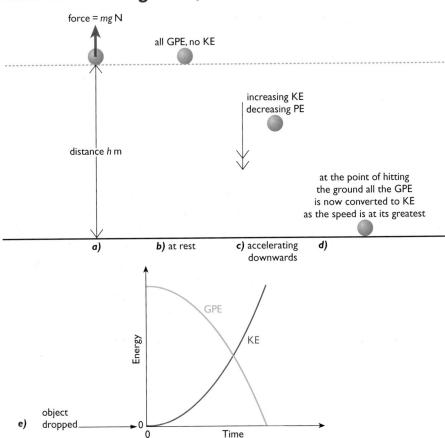

Figure 17.9 *GPE and KE of a falling object:*
a) *doing work to lift an object,* **b)** *all GPE,* **c)** *GPE converting to KE during fall,* **d)** *all KE at end of fall,* **e)** *graph showing relationship between GPE and KE as the object falls.*

Work transfers energy to an object: $W = Fd$. An object of mass, m, weighs $m \times g$ newtons so the force, F, needed to lift it is mg (Figure 17.9). If we raise the object through a distance h, the work done on the object is $mg \times h$. This is also the gain in GPE.

When the object is released, it falls – it loses GPE, but gains speed and so gains KE. At the end of the fall, all the initial GPE of the stationary object has been converted into the KE of the moving object. The graphs in Figure 17.9 show how the GPE of the object is changing into KE as it falls. The sum of the two graphs is always the same. Energy is conserved, so the loss of GPE is equal to the gain in KE.

work done lifting object = gain in GPE = gain in KE of the object just before hitting the ground

Example 4

If you throw an object vertically upwards with an initial speed of 20 m/s you can work out how high it will reach before falling back to Earth. At the highest point of its flight all the initial KE you have given it will be converted to GPE, according to the formula:

$$\frac{1}{2}mv^2 = mgh$$

(You can see that you don't need to know the mass of the object for this calculation. But the mass will affect how much energy you must use to throw it at a particular speed.)

Substituting v = 20 m/s and g = 10 N/kg:

$$\frac{1}{2} \times m\,\text{kg} \times (20\ \text{m/s})^2 = m\,\text{kg} \times 10\,\text{N/kg} \times h\,\text{m}$$

$$\frac{1}{2} \times m\,\text{kg} \times 400\ \text{m}^2/\text{s}^2 = m\,\text{kg} \times 10\,\text{N/kg} \times h\,\text{m}$$

$$m\,\text{kg} \times 200\ \text{m}^2/\text{s}^2 = m\,\text{kg} \times 10\,\text{N/kg} \times h\,\text{m}$$

$$h = \frac{m\,\text{kg} \times 200\ \text{m}^2/\text{s}^2}{m\,\text{kg} \times 10\,\text{N/kg}}$$

$$h = 20\ \text{m}$$

Worked example

This calculation has assumed that the effect of air resistance is very small. In practice, air resistance will reduce the height that an object will reach when thrown in the air. Neglecting air resistance, we can use $h = (v^2)/2g$ to work out the height reached.

Power

James Watt (Figure 17.10) is remembered as the inventor of the steam engine and is said to have been inspired by watching the lid on a kettle being forced up by the pressure of the steam forming inside. Neither story is accurate, but what is true is that Watt, working in partnership with Matthew Boulton, patented improvements to the steam engine that made it a commercial product and revolutionised industry and transport. Potential customers wanted to know just how fast these engines could do work, so Watt calculated the rate of working of his engines in comparison with the rate at which a typical horse could work – the unit was the "horsepower".

The horsepower is only used in the car industry these days. The modern unit of power is named in honour of James Watt. The watt (W) is the rate of transfer or conversion of energy of one joule per second (1 J/s).

> power, P (in watts) = $\dfrac{\text{work done } W \text{ (in joules)}}{\text{time taken, } t \text{ (in seconds)}}$
>
> $$P = \frac{W}{t}$$

Some power calculations

You may have done a simple experiment involving running up a flight of stairs to measure your output power. You do work as you raise your GPE, and to find your power output in watts you divide the work done by the time taken. The experiment is described in Figure 17.11. Notice that calculating the work you do against gravity using force × distance works just as well as using the formula for GPE (mass × gravitational field strength × height).

Power is the measure of how fast energy is transferred or transformed.

Figure 17.10 *James Watt (1736–1819) was a Scottish engineer who improved the performance of the steam engine and can be said to have started the Industrial Revolution – the beginning of the machine age.*

1 horsepower is equivalent to 746 watts.

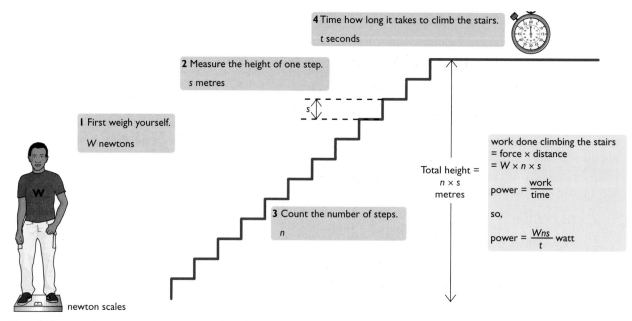

4 Time how long it takes to climb the stairs.

t seconds

2 Measure the height of one step.

s metres

I First weigh yourself.

W newtons

s

Total height =
n × *s*
metres

work done climbing the stairs
= force × distance
= *W* × *n* × *s*

$$power = \frac{work}{time}$$

so,

$$power = \frac{Wns}{t} \text{ watt}$$

3 Count the number of steps.

n

newton scales

If you don't have scales measuring in newtons, simply multiply your mass in kg by 10 to convert to newtons.

Figure 17.11 *An experiment to measure your output power.*

A more convenient way of raising your GPE and getting to a higher floor in a building is to take a lift. The lift will convert its energy input, usually electrical, into kinetic energy and then, if you are going up, into GPE. As usual, unwanted energy conversions are inevitable – sound and heat will be produced. If we know the weight of the lift and its contents and the height through which it moves, we can calculate the work done in the usual way. If we measure the time that the lift journey takes we can then calculate the power output of the lift motor. (Strictly this will be the *useful* power output – it will not take account of the wasted power due to unwanted energy conversions.)

Worked example

Example 5

Suppose a lift and passengers have a combined weight of 4000 N and the lift moves upwards with an average speed of 3 m/s. What is the useful power output of the lift motor?

To keep the lift moving upwards at a steady speed, the lift motor must provide an upward force to balance the weight of the lift. This is 4000 N. In each second, this force is applied through a vertical distance of 3 m, so:

work done/second = 4000 N × 3 m/s

= 12 000 J/s

= 12 000 W

motor

4000 N

3 m/s

lift and passengers weight 4000 N

Figure 17.12

You will need to be able to do the following:

✓ recall and apply the relationship work done = force × distance

✓ understand that doing work involves the transfer of energy

✓ understand that the gravitational potential energy (GPE) of an object is increased when it is moved against the pull of gravity

✓ calculate the increase in GPE using the formula GPE = mgh

✓ recall that moving objects possess kinetic energy (KE) and calculate KE using KE = $\frac{1}{2}mv^2$

✓ appreciate that, as an object falls, gravity does work on the object converting its GPE into KE

✓ explain that power is the rate of doing work or converting energy, and carry out power calculations using: power = work done/time.

Questions

More questions on work, power and efficiency can be found at the end of Section D on page 160. In the questions below, where necessary, take the strength of the Earth's gravity to be 10 N/kg.

1 James Joule showed that heat is a form of energy. He did this by showing that heat can be produced by using mechanical energy.

   a) Describe how you would convert mechanical energy into heat energy.

   b) How could you convert heat energy into mechanical energy?

2 **a)** What is the unit of work?

   b) Define the unit of work.

   c) How much work is done in each of the following situations?

   i) A bag of six apples each weighing 1 N is lifted through 80 cm.

   ii) A rocket with a thrust of 100 kN travels to a height of 200 m.

   iii) A weightlifter raises a mass of 60 kg through a height of 2.8 m.

   iv) A lift of mass 200 kg lifts three people of mass 50 kg each through a distance of 45 m.

3 Water from a hydroelectric power station reservoir is piped from a reservoir at a height of 800 m above sea level to turbines in the power station itself. The power station is 250 m above sea level. The reservoir holds 200 million (2×10^8) litres of water. If a litre of water has a mass of 1 kg, how much gravitational potential energy is stored in the water in the reservoir?

4 **a)** Explain how to calculate the kinetic energy possessed by a moving object.

   b) Work out the kinetic energy of the following:

   i) a man of mass 80 kg running at 9 m/s

   ii) an air rifle pellet of mass 0.2 g travelling at 50 m/s

   iii) a ball of mass 60 g travelling at 24 m/s.

5 A catapult fires a stone of mass 0.04 kg vertically upwards. If the stone has an initial kinetic energy of 48 J, how high will it travel before it starts to fall back to the ground?

6 If a coin is dropped from a height of 80 m, how fast will it be travelling when it hits the ground? State any assumptions you may need to make.

7 Define *power* and state its unit.

8 A person with a mass of 40 kg runs up a flight of stairs in 12 s. The flight of stairs has 20 steps and the height of each step is 20 cm.

   a) How much does the person weigh, in newtons?

   b) What is the total height that the person has climbed?

   c) How much work is done in climbing the stairs?

   d) What is the power output of the person running up the stairs?

9 A drag car, of mass 500 kg, accelerates from rest to a speed of 144 km/h in 5 s.

   a) What is its final speed in:

   i) m/h (metres per hour)

   ii) m/s?

   b) What is the increase in KE of the drag car?

   c) What is the average power developed by the drag car's engine?

Chapter 18: Energy Resources and Electricity Generation

In this chapter, you will learn about different sources of energy that are available to us on Earth. You will learn that some resources are renewable, while others cannot be replaced once used. As the demand for energy increases with the human population, there is a danger that non-renewable resources will run out. We therefore need to use fuel efficiently and to exploit more renewable resources.

Figure 18.1 *Humans consume vast amounts of fuel for transport, heating and cooking.*

The demand for energy increases all the time. The growth of the world population means more people need food and warmth. More people want to be able to travel. The fuels that we use to produce energy are being used up too quickly. We must use our remaining fuel supplies efficiently and look for new sources of energy. In Chapter 16, we saw how we can use energy more efficiently in heating our homes. Clearly we can make the energy supplies we have available last longer by being energy efficient.

We also need to understand what energy resources we have available on the Earth. In this chapter we shall look at different types of energy resource and the advantages and disadvantages of each resource for generating electricity. In particular we shall distinguish between renewable and non-renewable energy resources. New sources of energy are being researched all the time to meet our growing needs. We must also consider the effect that the use of different energy resources has on our environment. Some types of energy resource can cause long-term damage to our environment.

Non-renewable energy resources

Fossil fuels

Figure 18.2 *Fossil fuels include coal, oil and natural gas.*

One of the main energy resources available on our planet is its supply of **fossil fuels**. Coal, oil and natural gas are all fossil fuels. They have been formed in the ground from dead vegetation or tiny creatures by a process that has taken millions of years. Once we have used them, it will take millions of years for new reserves of these fuels to be formed. Fossil fuels are, therefore, examples of **non-renewable** energy resources.

> A non-renewable energy resource is one that effectively cannot be replaced once it has been used.

Burning fossil fuels affects the environment, mainly by releasing carbon dioxide into the atmosphere. Carbon dioxide is a greenhouse gas. Greenhouse gases trap the Sun's heat in the Earth's atmosphere and cause the average temperature of the atmosphere to rise. This effect is called **global warming** and causes changes in the world's climate and melting of the polar ice caps. Burning coal releases more carbon dioxide into the atmosphere than burning oil or gas. Of the fossil fuels, natural gas produces the least carbon dioxide for the same energy output. There is no practical way of avoiding the release of carbon dioxide into the atmosphere when fossil fuels are burned, although some energy companies are researching ways of capturing it and storing it underground.

Most types of coal and oil contain some sulphur. When they are burned, this is converted to sulphur dioxide. Sulphur dioxide is then released into the atmosphere where it combines with water to form acid rain. Acid rain causes damage to people, plants and buildings. It is possible to remove the sulphur from these fuels but this increases the cost of the energy produced. It is also possible to remove sulphur dioxide from the waste gases when the fuel is burned, but this also increases the cost. International agreements are forcing companies who emit large quantities of

Figure 18.4 *William Perkin discovered the first synthetic dye in 1856 using substances produced from coal tar.*

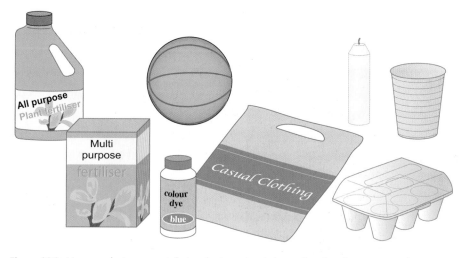

Figure 18.3 *Many products are manufactured using extracts from oil and coal.*

sulphur dioxide to clean up their waste gases, and acid rain is now less of a problem in Europe than it used to be. Acid rain is still a problem in many countries in the developing world.

Fossil fuels also provide valuable chemicals that can be used in the manufacture of a wide range of useful products (Figure 18.3). Once burned for energy production, these chemical resources are lost permanently. Burning such resources may be a very wasteful way of using them.

Nuclear fuel

Nuclear reactors use uranium to produce energy. For the nuclear process, a particular form or **isotope** (see page 202) of uranium is needed. Although a reactor only needs a small amount of uranium fuel, uranium is in limited supply. The uranium in the Earth was formed before the Solar System was formed, so once it has been used there will be no further supplies. It is, therefore, another example of a non-renewable resource.

Power generated from nuclear processes has the advantage of being "clean". It is clean because the process does not involve the production of greenhouse or other polluting gases. The cost per unit of electricity is very low, but nuclear power stations are expensive to build. The disadvantages of nuclear power are the risk of accidents and the problem of disposal of radioactive material once a power station is finished with. Accidents that release radioactive materials like uranium and plutonium into the atmosphere cause long-lasting risks to living things.

Electricity

Electricity is not an energy resource, because it has to be generated using other sources of energy. At present, most of the electricity used in the world is generated in power stations like the one shown in Figure 18.5.

Heat from nuclear fuel or from burning fossil fuels is used to heat water. This produces high-pressure steam that makes the blades of a turbine spin. A turbine is like a windmill or a fan, but with many more blades. The turbine is used to turn the

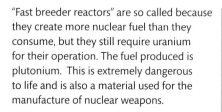

"Fast breeder reactors" are so called because they create more nuclear fuel than they consume, but they still require uranium for their operation. The fuel produced is plutonium. This is extremely dangerous to life and is also a material used for the manufacture of nuclear weapons.

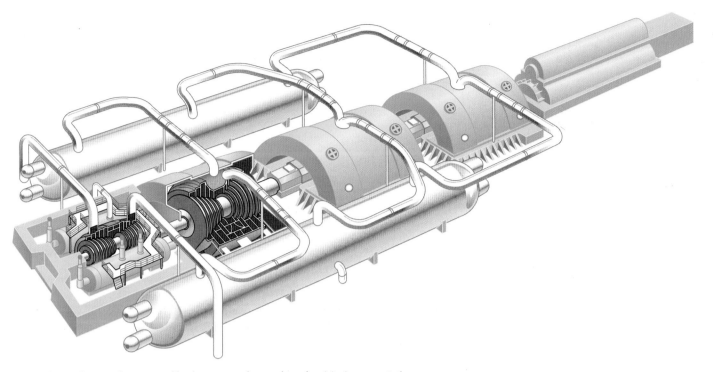

Figure 18.5 *Turbines and generators like these are used to produce electricity in power stations.*

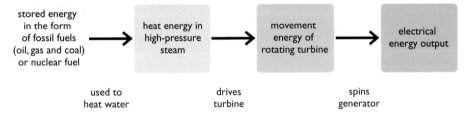

Figure 18.6 *Several energy changes are involved in producing electricity.*

generator, which generates the electricity (you will learn more about this in Chapter 22). The energy changes involved are shown in Figure 18.6.

Electricity can also be generated using renewable energy resources.

Renewable energy resources

A renewable energy resource is one that will not run out.

Wood is an example of a **renewable** energy resource. As wood is cut for fuel, new fast-growing trees are planted to replace those cut down. With careful management the supply of wood fuel can be maintained indefinitely. However, burning wood produces pollution and greenhouse gases. Wood is also more valuable if it is not burned, because it can be used in building or making furniture.

The demand for fuel and our worries about global warming and pollution have made us search for alternative energy resources. We need renewable energy resources that do not pollute the world or contribute to global warming.

Figure 18.7 *Moving water is a renewable energy resource.*

Hydroelectric power

The kinetic energy available in large quantities of moving water has been harnessed for many hundreds of years. Water wheels have been used to convert the energy possessed by water in rivers to grind corn and power industrial machinery. A different kind of water wheel, called a turbine, is used to turn the generators in a **hydroelectric** power station. These power stations use the stored gravitational potential energy (GPE) of water in high reservoirs built in mountains. The GPE is converted to kinetic energy (KE) as the water flows down the mountain to the power station below.

The energy produced in this way is renewable. The Sun causes water to evaporate continuously and to be drawn up into the atmosphere. This water then falls as rain to be collected in reservoirs and used again. Moving water is a renewable resource.

Although hydroelectricity is a very clean, renewable resource, building reservoirs and power stations can spoil the landscape. The reservoir may also destroy or alter the natural habitat for wildlife.

Tidal power

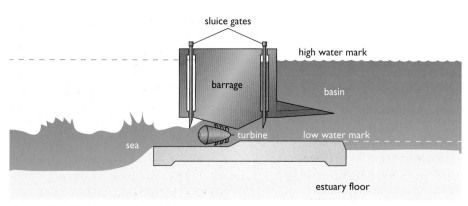

Figure 18.8 a) *Tidal power also involves harnessing the energy in moving water.*

b) *Tidal power station at La Rance in Brittany.*

The tides also involve the movement of huge amounts of water. Tidal power generation schemes, like that at La Rance in Brittany (Figure 18.8b), generate power by turning turbines as the tide flows into a dammed river estuary. As the tide falls and the water flows out of the estuary the turbines are spun again.

The energy for the movement of the tides is provided by the gravitational pull of the Moon and Sun. This is renewable energy using a small fraction of the continuous supply of gravitational energy.

There are not many places around the world suitable for building dams for tidal energy. If a dam is built, it affects the rise and fall of water in the estuary, and this is likely to damage habitats for wildlife. Some energy companies are now developing 'tidal stream turbines', which are like underwater wind turbines. These will be driven by tidal currents.

Wave energy

Energy can also be extracted from waves. The continuous movement of the surface of the seas and oceans is the result of a combination of tides and wind. A variety of methods have been developed to make use of the rise and fall of water due to waves. Figure 18.10 shows a system that has been developed to use the energy of waves. Again, this energy is renewable, as the movement energy of the waves is continuously available.

Water power is clean, producing no greenhouse gases or unwanted waste products.

Figure 18.9 *The turbine has angled blades. As water is forced between the blades, they start to spin. The rotating turbine is connected to a generator to make it spin too.*

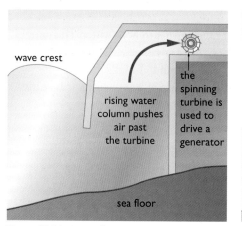
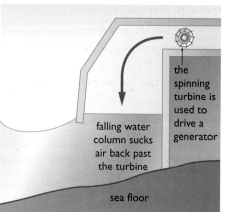

Figure 18.10 *An oscillating water column system for using wave energy.*

Wind power

Winds are powered by the Sun's heat energy. Wind is a renewable source of energy that has been used for many centuries. Windmills have been used to grind corn and power machinery like pumps to drain lowland areas. Today, wind turbines drive generators to provide electrical energy.

The energy produced is clean, but wind power can only be harvested in regions where the wind blows with enough energy for a significant proportion of the year. Wind farms can cause environmental damage, as they change the appearance of the landscape. They also cause some noise pollution, and may kill birds and bats.

Solar power

There are two methods of gathering and using energy directly from the Sun.

Photovoltaic cells (solar cells) convert light energy directly into electrical energy. They are not very efficient and are expensive. They also require quite bright sunlight to produce useful amounts of electrical energy. These factors limit the

Figure 18.11 *Old and new uses for the wind.*

usefulness of photovoltaic cells to countries with a high number of sunshine hours. In the UK, they are only suitable for applications that need small amounts of energy, like calculators and low-power garden lighting. Figure 18.12 shows photovoltaic cells being used to power the Hubble Space Telescope, and a motorway emergency telephone in southern Europe. Both are remote locations with plenty of sunlight.

Figure 18.12 *Photovoltaic cells produce electricity when sunlight falls on them.*

Figure 18.13 *Solar heating panels can be used to heat water, even in the UK climate.*

The design of efficient solar heating panels involves all the methods of heat transfer discussed in Chapter 16. Solar panels are often used in questions about heat transfer.

Solar heating panels absorb thermal radiation and use it to heat water. The panels are placed to receive the maximum amount of the Sun's energy. In the northern hemisphere, they must face south and be angled so that light falls on them as directly as possible for as long as possible. The structure of a typical solar heating panel is shown in Figure 18.14.

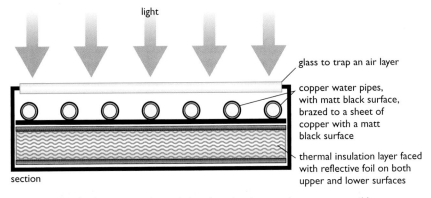

Figure 18.14 *Solar heating panels are designed to absorb as much energy as possible.*

Water is pumped through copper pipes fixed onto a copper sheet. Copper is used because it is an excellent thermal conductor. The surfaces of the sheet and the pipes have a matt black finish as this is the best absorber of heat radiation. The glass traps a layer of air above the copper to help insulate the unit and retain the heat. The backing is also designed to stop heat escaping to the surroundings. This kind of panel is reasonably efficient and the energy produced is more cost efficient than that from photovoltaic cells. Solar heating panels are used widely to provide water heating.

Electricity can also be generated using solar heating. Curved mirrors are used to focus thermal radiation onto a boiler or pipes containing water to produce steam. The steam can be used to drive turbines which can be used to drive electricity generators.

Geothermal energy

Geothermal energy is heat energy stored deep inside the Earth. The heat in regions of volcanic activity was produced by the decay of radioactive elements like uranium. Volcanoes are evidence of the enormous heat and energy beneath the Earth's surface but do not provide a safe or reliable energy resource. However, heat from the ground *can* be used safely. In some areas of the world, like Iceland (Figure 18.15), geothermally heated water is readily available in springs and geysers. This is used to drive the turbines in electricity generation stations. The hot water is also used to provide domestic heating by piping it directly to houses. This resource is renewable, does not produce pollution and does not have a great impact on the environment. There are many areas of the world where geothermally heated springs can, and are, being used to provide energy.

Geothermal energy can also be used in areas with no hot springs. There are some areas where the rocks beneath the ground are hot enough to produce steam. Geothermal energy can also be used to heat houses, by burying long pipes full of water a few metres below the ground. The water is warmed by the ground. The temperature change is not very big, but hotter water can be produced using a heat pump, which is a bit like a refrigerator in reverse. The hot water leaving the heat pump is warm enough to heat homes and to use for bathing.

Figure 18.15 *A geothermal electricity generating station in Iceland, with a huge swimming lagoon heated geothermally.*

Supply and demand

Many different energy resources can be used to generate electricity, and they all have advantages and disadvantages. Some of the environmental disadvantages have already been discussed, but supply and demand also need to be taken into account. Different types of power station differ in the speed with which they can meet changes in the demand for electricity.

The demand for electricity varies from hour to hour, day to day and season to season. The way that the demand varies can be predicted to some extent. For example, there is a surge in demand in the early morning as people wake up, turn on lights and heaters and start to make breakfast, and of course in winter the demand for heat is much greater than in summer. Some sudden surges in demand are less predictable. A popular TV soap with an exciting episode can keep millions of viewers glued to their television sets – if they all decide to make a cup of tea as soon as the adverts come on, electricity consumption will suddenly increase (electric kettles use a lot of power). The companies that supply electricity must be able to cope with these changes in demand, otherwise they are forced to cut off electricity to some consumers. This is not good for customer relations and, of course, means a reduction in the amount of electricity sold.

Nuclear power stations cannot be turned on instantly. The process of starting the fission reaction and heating up the core of the nuclear reactor is a lengthy one. Clearly nuclear power stations cannot meet sudden variations in demand.

Power stations that burn fossil fuels can be started more quickly but can still take many hours to start producing electricity. Coal-fired stations take longer than oil-fired stations to develop the heat required to drive steam through the turbines. Gas-fired stations can respond most quickly to demand surges.

Hydroelectric power stations provide a very reliable energy source with the advantage of being able to respond very quickly to changes in the national demand for electricity. Unlike other types of power station, they are able to operate in reverse. This means that they can use surplus electricity produced by other power stations that cannot be shut down quickly to pump water back up into the high-level reservoirs. This converts the electrical energy back into gravitational potential energy, which can then be reconverted when needed at a later time. This is the only realistic way of "storing" large amounts of surplus electrical energy.

Wind power is dependent on the strength, direction and frequency of wind. Although wind farms are sited in windy areas, they cannot be relied upon to produce electricity at the times when it is needed most. Tidal power is not available continuously, but the times at which it will be available are predictable.

Cost

The US Department of Energy has proposed the building of a nuclear waste storage facility beneath the Yucca Mountains. High-level nuclear waste will be placed in concrete casks that are supposed to contain the nuclear radiation safely for 300 to 1000 years.

Planners must also look at the financial costs of electricity generation. Nuclear power uses a relatively cheap fuel. Uranium produces huge amounts of energy, so the cost of energy per unit of fuel used is low. However, building a nuclear power station is very expensive. Nuclear power requires complex technology and very high standards of safety. On top of these "start-up" costs, planners must also consider the expense of decommissioning a nuclear power station at the end of its useful working life. For conventional power stations, this is a routine demolition job, but for nuclear power stations the task is not as straightforward. Radioactive materials must be handled with great care and stored in a way to ensure that none escapes.

We see that, although the running costs of nuclear power are relatively low, the pay-back time is very long. (The pay-back time is how long it takes for the income from selling electricity to cover the cost of building the power station.)

The cost of setting up a wind farm is much lower than the cost of building a nuclear power station and there are no fuel costs. However, the amount of energy produced by wind farms is comparatively low. The pay-back time for wind generators is therefore quite long.

You will need to be able to do the following:

✓ understand the difference between renewable and non-renewable energy resources

✓ appreciate that fossil fuels (natural gas, oil and coal) cannot be replaced once used and all produce greenhouse gases and other pollution when burned

✓ understand what is meant by "clean" energy resources

✓ recall the following sources of renewable energy – wood, wind, the Sun, waves, water and geothermal energy

✓ understand that different types of power station can respond to changes in the demand for electricity at different rates

✓ appreciate the many different cost considerations in the choice of a power station; these include the cost of fuel, the cost of building, maintaining and decommissioning the power station, and the effect of the power station on the environment

✓ discuss the advantages and disadvantages of different energy resources.

Questions

More questions on energy resources can be found at the end of Section D on page 160.

1 a) Explain what is meant by a non-renewable energy resource.

   b) Give three examples of types of non-renewable energy resources.

2 a) What is the greenhouse effect?

   b) How can we reduce the greenhouse effect on the Earth?

3 a) What are fossil fuels?

   b) Explain why fossil fuels are not a clean method of producing energy.

4 Nuclear power generation does not produce greenhouse gases. This is a significant advantage of nuclear power over power stations that burn fossil fuels.

   a) What other advantages are there in using nuclear power?

   b) What are the disadvantages of nuclear power?

5 Give three examples of renewable energy resources that can be used to generate electricity. Compare their advantages and disadvantages.

6 a) The demand for electricity varies on a hourly and daily basis. Sometimes the changes in demand are predictable, but sometimes they are not. Give two examples of predictable changes in demand and two examples of unpredictable demand variations.

   b) Electricity is generated by a number of different types of power station. Give three examples of different types of power station and compare how well they are able to respond to sudden changes in demand.

7 "Tidal power stations provide energy at zero cost and produce no pollution." Give one argument in support of this view, and one argument against it.

1 Windmills, tidal power and solar panels are all examples of renewable energy sources.

   a) Explain what is meant by a renewable energy source.

   (2 marks)

   b) What advantage do solar panels have over windmills as a source of energy? *(2 marks)*

   Windmills and tidal power can both be used to generate electricity.

   c) Explain which of these two energy resources has the least environmental impact. *(2 marks)*

   d) Give one advantage and one disadvantage of tidal power in terms of the supply and demand of electricity. *(2 marks)*

   Total 8 marks

2 A hydroelectric power station has turbines that are fed by a reservoir in the mountains, as shown in the diagram.

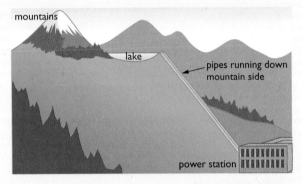

   The reservoir is 400 metres above the power station. As water falls from the reservoir to the turbines in the power station it gains kinetic energy. The kinetic energy is converted to electrical energy by generators driven by the turbines.

   a) How much kinetic energy does each kilogram of water gain as it falls to the turbines? (Take *g* as 10 N/kg.)

   (2 marks)

   b) The turbines are 60% efficient. What is the power output of the station if 300 kg of water passes through the turbines each second? *(4 marks)*

   c) Give two advantages of hydroelectric power stations in terms of the supply and demand of electricity. *(2 marks)*

   Total 8 marks

3 The diagram shows a lift powered by an electric motor. The lift and its load of passengers have a total weight of 8000 N.

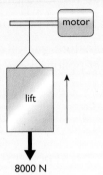

   a) What is the work done when the lift is moved up by 30 m? *(3 marks)*

   b) If the lift takes 7.5 seconds to move up 30 m, what is the useful power output of the electric motor? *(3 marks)*

   c) The system is not 100% efficient. Describe the ways in which energy is wasted in this system. *(4 marks)*

   Counterweights are used to reduce the energy needed to operate a lift. These are shown in the diagram below.

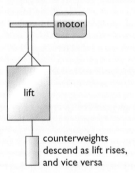

   d) What weight should these counterweights have? *(2 marks)*

   e) How do the counterweights save energy? *(3 marks)*

   Total 15 marks

4 The chart below shows the proportion of heat energy lost from different parts of a house.

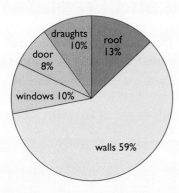

The householder is considering different ways of reducing the annual heating cost.

a) Explain how double glazing cuts down energy loss from a house. Your answer must consider all the mechanisms of heat transfer. *(6 marks)*

b) Explain how the walls of the house can be insulated, and why this works. *(2 marks)*

Total 8 marks

5 A fan heater is used to heat up an office. The energy transfers taking place are shown in the diagram. The "useful" energy output is heat.

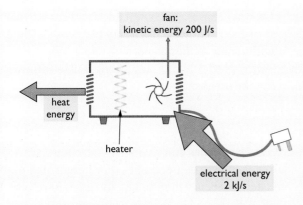

a) Draw a labelled Sankey diagram for this system. *(4 marks)*

b) Calculate the efficiency of the fan heater. *(3 marks)*

c) This heater does not have a fan. Explain how it can heat a whole room, even without a fan. *(4 marks)*

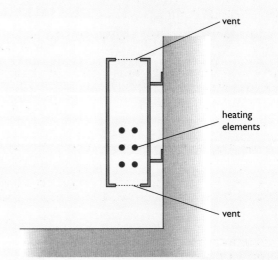

Total 11 marks

6 The diagram below shows the structure of a vacuum flask. Explain how its design makes it more difficult for heat energy to be transferred between the inside of the flask and the outside environment. *(6 marks)*

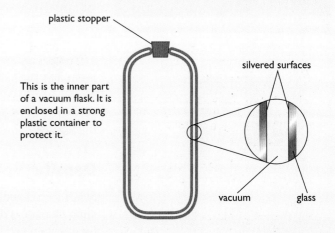

This is the inner part of a vacuum flask. It is enclosed in a strong plastic container to protect it.

Total 6 marks

Section E: Solids, Liquids and Gases

Figure 19.1 *Some effects of density and pressure.*

Chapter 19: Density and Pressure

One way of characterising materials is by their density. This chapter looks at density and at how materials can affect things around them by exerting pressure.

The properties of a material affect how it behaves, and how it affects other materials around it. The balloon can fly because the gas inside it has a very low density. The skis spread the weight of the skiers over the snow so they do not sink into it. The submersible is designed to explore the sea bed – it has a very strong hull to withstand the high pressure from water deep in the oceans.

Density

Solids, liquid and gases have different properties and characteristics. One such characteristic is **density**. Solids are often very dense, that is, they have a high mass for a certain volume. Liquids are often less dense than solids, and gases have very low densities.

The density (ρ) of a material can be calculated if you know the mass (m) of a certain volume (V) of the material, using this equation.

ρ is the Greek letter rho and is the usual symbol for density.

$$\text{density}, \rho = \frac{\text{mass}, m}{\text{volume}, V}$$

$$\rho = \frac{m}{V}$$

The units for density depend on the units used for mass and volume. If mass is measured in kilograms and volume in cubic metres, the units for density are kilograms per cubic metre (kg/m^3). Density can also be measured in grams per cubic centimetre (g/cm^3).

Example 1

A piece of iron has a mass of 390 kg and a volume of 0.05 m³. What is its density?

density, $\rho = \dfrac{\text{mass, } m}{\text{volume, } V}$

$\rho = \dfrac{m}{V}$

$= \dfrac{390\,\text{kg}}{0.05\,\text{m}^3}$

$= 7800\,\text{kg/m}^3$

The density of a substance can be determined by measuring the mass and volume of a sample of the material, and then calculating the density.

Worked example

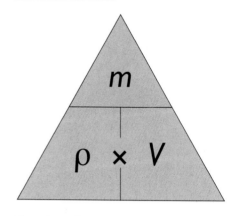

Figure 19.2 *The equation for density can be rearranged using the triangle method.*

If an examination question asks you to write out the formula for calculating density, mass or volume, always give the actual equation (such as $\rho = m/V$). You may not be awarded the mark if you just draw the triangle.

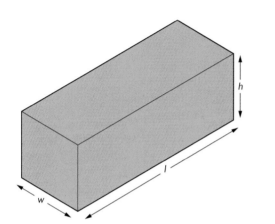
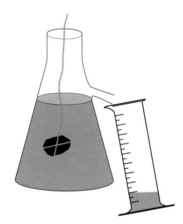

Figure 19.3 **a)** *The volume of a regular solid can be calculated by multiplying its length (l), width (w) and height (h).* **b)** *The volume of an irregular object can be determined using a displacement can and a measuring cylinder.*

Example 2

Worked example

The mass of 50 cm³ of a liquid and a measuring cylinder is 146 g. The mass of the empty measuring cylinder is 100 g. What is the density of the liquid in kg/m³?

Mass of 50 cm³ liquid = 146 g − 100 g

$= 46\,\text{g}$

$= 0.046\,\text{kg}$

50 cm³ = 0.000 05 m³

$\rho = \dfrac{m}{V}$

$= \dfrac{0.046\,\text{kg}}{0.000\,05\,\text{m}^3}$ or $= \dfrac{46\,\text{g}}{50\,\text{cm}^3}$

$= 0.92\,\text{g/cm}^3$

$= 920\,\text{kg/m}^3$ $= 920\,\text{kg/m}^3$

Check the units when you are working out density – don't mix up g and m³, for example. Also check which units the question asks for in your final answer.

1 kg = 1000 g

To convert kg to g, divide by 1000.

1 m³ = 1 000 000 cm³

To convert cm³ to m³, divide by 1 000 000 (or 10⁶).

Alternatively, work out the density in g/cm³, then multiply your answer by 1000.

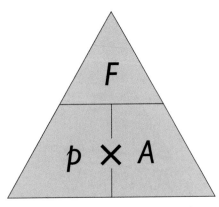

Figure 19.4 *The equation for pressure can be rearranged using the triangle method.*

If an examination question asks you to write out the formula for calculating pressure, force or area, always give the actual equation (such as p = F/A). You may not be awarded the mark if you just draw the triangle.

Pressure under a solid

You can push a drawing pin into a piece of wood quite easily, but you cannot make a hole in the wood with your thumb, no matter how hard you push! The small point of the drawing pin concentrates all your pushing force into a tiny area, so the pin goes into the wood easily. Similarly, it is easier to cut things with a sharp knife than a blunt one, because with a sharp knife all the force is concentrated into a much smaller area.

Pressure is defined as the force per unit area. Force is measured in newtons (N) and area is measured in square metres (m²). The units for pressure are pascals (Pa), where 1 Pa is equivalent to 1 N/m².

Pressure (p), force (F) and area (A) are linked by the following equation:

$$\text{pressure, } p \text{ (in pascals)} = \frac{\text{force, } F \text{ (in newtons)}}{\text{area, } A \text{ (in square metres)}}$$

$$p = \frac{F}{A}$$

Worked example

Example 3

An elephant has a weight of 40 000 N, and her feet cover a total area of 0.1 m².
A woman weighs 600 N and the total area of her shoes in contact with the ground is 0.0015 m². Who exerts the greatest pressure on the ground?

Elephant:

$$p = \frac{F}{A}$$

$$= 40\,000\,\text{N}/0.1\,\text{m}^2$$

$$= 400\,000\,\text{Pa (or 400 kPa)}$$

Woman:

$$p = \frac{F}{A}$$

$$= 600\,\text{N}/0.0015\,\text{m}^2$$

$$= 400\,000\,\text{Pa (or 400 kPa)}$$

They both exert an equal pressure.

a)

b)

Figure 19.5 a) *The caterpillar tracks on this vehicle spread its weight over a large area.* **b)** *Camels have large feet so they are less likely to sink into loose sand.*

Some machines, including cutting tools like scissors, bolt cutters and knives, need to exert a high pressure to work well. In other applications, a low pressure is important. Tractors and other vehicles designed to move over mud have large tyres that spread the vehicle's weight. The pressure under the tyres is relatively low, so the vehicle is less likely to sink into the mud. Caterpillar tracks used on bulldozers and other earth-moving equipment serve a similar purpose.

Pressure in liquids and gases

The submersible shown in Figure 19.1 has a very strong hull to withstand the high pressure exerted on it by sea water. Pressure in liquids acts equally in all directions, as long as the liquid is not moving. You can easily demonstrate this using a can with holes punched around the bottom, as shown in Figure 19.6. When the can is filled with water, the water is forced out equally in all directions.

Figure 19.6 *Pressure in liquids acts equally in all directions. A can of water with holes can be used to demonstrate this.*

Gases also exert pressure on things around them. The pressure exerted by the atmosphere on your body is about 100 000 Pa (although the pressure varies slightly from day to day). However the pressure inside our bodies is similar, so we do not notice the pressure of the air.

One of the first demonstrations of the effects of air pressure was carried out by Otto van Guericke in 1654, in Magdeburg, Germany. Van Guericke had two large metal bowls made, put them together and then pumped the air out. The bowls could not be pulled apart, even when he attached two teams of horses to the bowls.

Figure 19.7 *Van Guericke's experiment at Magdeburg.*

You can do the same experiment in the laboratory, using much smaller bowls called Magdeburg hemispheres. When air is inside the spheres, the pressure is the same inside and outside. If the air is sucked out, pressure is only acting from the outside. The hemispheres cannot be pulled apart until air is let back into them.

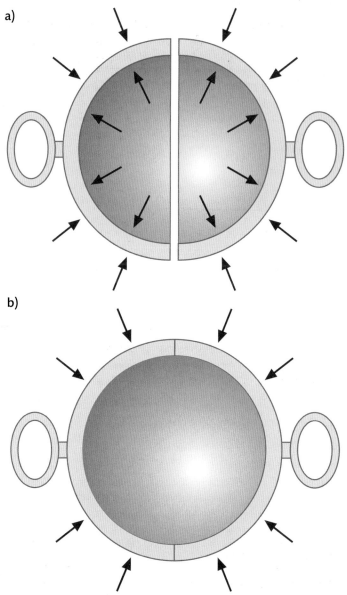

a)

b)

Figure 19.8 a) *When the hemispheres are full of air, the forces are the same inside and outside.*
b) *When the air is taken out, there is only a force on the outside of the hemispheres.*

Worked example

Example 4

A laboratory set of Magdeburg hemispheres has a surface area of 0.045 m². What is the total force on the outside of the hemispheres?

$F = p \times A$
$\quad = 100\,000\,\text{Pa} \times 0.045\,\text{m}^2$
$\quad = 4500\,\text{N}$

Pressure and depth

The experiment shown in Figure 19.9 demonstrates that the pressure in a liquid increases with depth. We can work out the pressure difference by thinking about a column of water, as shown in Figure 19.10.

The force at the bottom of the column is equal to all the weight of water above it. The volume of this water (V) is found by multiplying the area of its base (A) by the height (h) of the column. We can work out the mass (m) of the water by multiplying the volume by the density (ρ).

$$\text{mass of water} = A \times h \times \rho$$

The force (F) on the bottom of the water column is equal to the weight of this volume of water, which is the mass multiplied by the gravitational field strength (g) (see page 29).

$$F = A \times h \times \rho \times g$$

As we are concerned with the pressure on the base of the column, we divide the force by the area.

$$F = \frac{A \times h \times \rho \times g}{A}$$

The area of the column therefore does not matter, and we can calculate the pressure difference between two points in a liquid using the equation:

> **pressure difference, p (in Pa) = height, h (in m) × density, ρ (in kg/m³)**
> **× g (in N/kg)**
>
> **$p = h \times \rho \times g$**

The same equation can be used for calculating pressure differences in other liquids or gases, as long as you know the density.

Figure 19.9 *Pressure in a liquid increases with depth.*

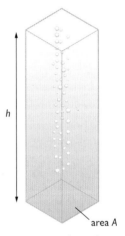

Figure 19.10 *We can work out the pressure difference between two points in a liquid by considering a column of the liquid.*

Example 5

The first experiments on air pressure were carried out using a simple barometer. This was made by filling a long glass tube with mercury, and then inverting it into a bowl of mercury. The mercury falls until the weight of the column is supported by the pressure of the air on the mercury in the bowl.

If the column of mercury is 0.74 m high, what is the air pressure? The density of mercury is 14 000 kg/m³. Take the gravitational field strength as 10 N/kg.

$$\begin{aligned} p &= h \times \rho \times g \\ &= 0.74\,\text{m} \times 14\,000\,\text{kg/m}^3 \times 10\,\text{N/kg} \\ &= 103\,600\,\text{Pa} \end{aligned}$$

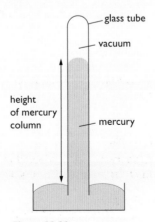

Figure 19.11

Worked example

The unit for pressure is named after Blaise Pascal (1623–1662). He was the first person to demonstrate that air pressure decreases with height. He persuaded his brother-in-law to take a mercury barometer up a mountain and measure the air pressure at different stages in the climb. He also arranged for someone at the base of the mountain to measure the air pressure at different times during the day. The measurements showed that the pressure of the air does decrease as you climb.

End of Chapter Checklist

You will need to be able to do the following:

✓ recall and use the relationship between density, mass and volume, $\rho = m/V$

✓ describe how to work out the density of a material

✓ recall and use the relationship between pressure, force and area, $p = F/A$

✓ recall that the pressure at a point in a liquid or gas acts equally in all directions

✓ recall and use the equation for calculating pressure difference in a liquid or gas, $p = h \times \rho \times g$.

Questions

More questions on density and pressure can be found at the end of Section E on page 178.

1 A Greek scientist called Archimedes was asked to check the purity of the gold in a crown. He did this by comparing the density of the crown with the density of pure gold.

   a) Describe how he could have measured the density of an irregular-shaped object such as a crown.

   b) Pure gold has a density of 19 000 kg/m³. Suppose the crown had a volume of 0.0001 m³. What mass should the crown be if it is made of pure gold?

2 People working on the roofs of buildings often lay a ladder or plank of wood on the roof. They walk on the ladder rather than the roof itself.

   a) Explain why using a ladder or plank will help to prevent damage to the roof.

   b) A workman's weight is 850 N, and each of his boots has an area of 210 cm². Calculate the maximum pressure under his feet when he is walking. Give your answer in pascals. (Hint: remember that all your weight is on one foot at some point while you are walking. To convert cm² to m²: divide by 10 000 or 10⁴.)

   c) The workman lays a plank on the roof. The plank has an area of 0.3 m² and a weight of 70 N. What is the maximum pressure under the plank when he is walking on it?

3 A manometer can be used to find the pressure of a gas. The difference in the level of the liquid in each side of the tube indicates the pressure of the gas.

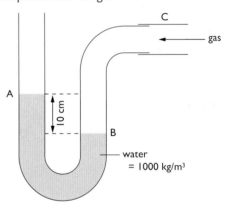

   a) What is the difference in pressure between A and B? Use g = 10 N/kg.

   b) What is the pressure of the gas in tube C?

   c) Explain why this pressure is the pressure of the gas above atmospheric pressure.

Chapter 20: Solids, Liquids and Gases

All matter is made up of particles that are continuously moving. The arrangement and movement of the particles determine the properties of the material. In gases, scientists have discovered laws that describe the relationship between pressure, temperature and volume. In this chapter, you will learn what these laws are and how this relationship can be explained in terms of the behaviour of the particles.

We think that all matter is made up of tiny particles that are moving. The way that the particles are arranged and the way that they move determine the properties of a material, such as its state at room temperature or its density.

The states of matter

Some of the properties of a substance depend on the chemicals it is made from. However, substances can exist in different states. The main states of matter are solid, liquid and gas. We are used to finding some substances in each state in everyday life – for example, water is familiar as ice, as water and as steam. There are other substances that we usually see in only one state – for example, we rarely see iron in any other state than solid, or experience oxygen in any other state than as a gas.

Substances can change state by the processes of melting, evaporation, boiling, freezing and condensing.

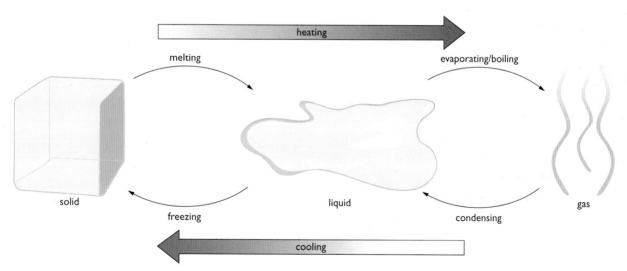

Figure 20.1 *Changes of state.*

Properties of the different states of matter

Most of this chapter will be about the properties of gases, but we shall mention solids and liquids for completeness.

Solids

Solids have a definite rigid shape and they are often very dense. The density of a substance is a measure of how tightly packed the particles are.

Some solids have high densities because the particles that they are made from are very closely packed in a regular arrangement. There are strong forces between the particles, which give solid objects their definite shape and, in some materials, a great deal of strength.

Although the particles are held together by strong forces, they can still move. They vibrate about their fixed positions in the solid. When we supply energy to a solid, by heating it, the particles vibrate more – they move more quickly. We notice the increase in the kinetic energy of the particles in a substance as an increase in the *temperature* of the substance.

Liquids

Liquids share a property with gases – they have no definite shape. However, the particles that make up liquids tend to stick together, unlike gas particles. Liquids will occupy the lowest part of any container but gases will expand to fill any container that they are in. Liquids have much greater densities than gases. This is because the particles in liquids are still very close together, like they are in solids. Because the particles in liquids are close together, they still attract one another and hold together. In liquids, there is no fixed pattern and the particles can move around more freely than in solids. As we heat liquids, the movement of the particles becomes more energetic.

Gases

In gases the particles are very spread out, with large spaces between them. This means that the forces holding them together are small. Gases have very low densities and no definite shape. Gases can also be squashed into a smaller space (compressed). Particles of a gas are moving randomly all the time. The particles will bump into anything in the gas, or into the walls of the container, and the forces caused by these collisions are responsible for the pressure that gases exert.

Solids and liquids are very difficult to compress because the particles in them are almost as close together as they can be.

Summary of the properties of solids, liquids and gases

Property	Solids	Liquids	Gases
definite shape	yes	no	no
can be easily compressed	no	no	yes
relative density	high	high	low
can flow (fluid)	no	yes	yes
expands to fill all available space	no	no	yes

The particles (molecules) in a solid (Figure 20.2a):

- are tightly packed
- are held in a fixed pattern or crystal structure by strong forces between them
- vibrate around their fixed positions in the structure.

The particles (molecules) in a liquid (Figure 20.2b):

- are tightly packed
- are not held in fixed positions but are still bound together by strong forces between them
- move at random.

The particles (molecules) in a gas (Figure 20.2c):

- are very spread out
- have no fixed positions and the forces between them are very weak
- move with a rapid, random motion.

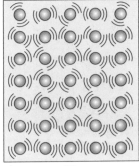

a)   solid

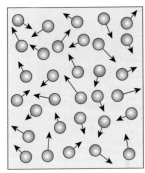

b)   liquid

Brownian motion

One piece of evidence for the continual motion of particles in a liquid or a gas is Brownian motion. This is named after the Scottish botanist Robert Brown (1773–1858). In 1827 he was observing pollen grains in water through a microscope, and he noticed that the grains appeared to jerk around in random movements. At first he thought that the motion was due to a kind of "life force" in the pollen, but he also observed other tiny non-living particles in water and found that they were moving in a similar way. A similar effect can be seen with particles in a gas.

Brownian motion was not explained until the theory that all substances are made from particles was developed. Particles of a liquid or gas are moving around continually and bump into each other and into tiny particles such as pollen grains. Sometimes there will be more collisions on one side of a pollen grain than on another, and this will make the pollen grain change its direction or speed of movement.

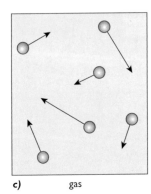

c)   gas

Figure 20.2 *The different arrangements of the particles in solids, liquids and gases.*

The gas laws

We are now going to focus our attention on the properties of gases. We shall explain the different properties in terms of the movement of particles.

We have already said that gases are made up of particles that are moving. We believe that the particles in gases are spread out and constantly moving in a random, haphazard way.

Boyle's Law

The scientist Robert Boyle (Figure 20.3) discovered something that you have probably noticed if you have ever used a bicycle pump: air is squashy! He noticed that you can squeeze air in a cylinder and that it springs back to its original volume when you release it. You can try this for yourself with a plastic syringe (Figure 20.4).

Figure 20.3 *Robert Boyle (1627–1691) was an Anglo-Irish chemist and philosopher. As well as discovering the law that bears his name, he worked with Robert Hooke at Oxford developing the air pump.*

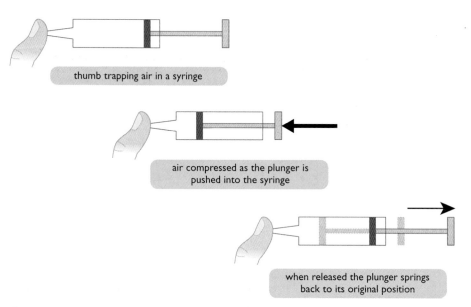

thumb trapping air in a syringe

air compressed as the plunger is pushed into the syringe

when released the plunger springs back to its original position

Figure 20.4 *Air is squashy!*

Figure 20.5 *A modern version of Boyle's experiment to see how the volume of a gas depends on the pressure exerted on it.*

Boyle devised an experiment to see how the volume occupied by a gas depends on the pressure exerted on it. **Pressure** is the force acting per unit area. This is measured in N/m². One N/m² is called a pascal (Pa). A version of Boyle's experiment is shown in Figure 20.5.

Boyle took care to make sure that the trapped gas he was studying stayed at the same temperature. He increased the pressure on the gas and made a note of the new volume. His results looked like the graph shown in Figure 20.6a.

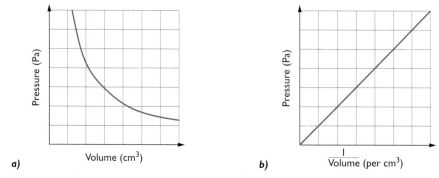

a)

b)

Figure 20.6 a) *Graph to show how the pressure of a gas at constant temperature varies with the volume,* **b)** *graph of pressure against 1/volume.*

Boyle noticed that when he doubled the pressure, the volume of the gas halved. If we plot pressure (p), against 1/volume ($\frac{1}{V}$), as in Figure 20.6b, we can see from the straight line passing through the origin that p is proportional to $\frac{1}{V}$.

This discovery, called Boyle's Law, is expressed in the equation:

$$p_1V_1 = p_2V_2$$

This means that if you take a fixed mass of gas that has a pressure p_1 and a volume V_1 and change either the pressure or the volume, the new pressure (p_2) multiplied by the new volume (V_2) will be the same as $p_1 \times V_1$.

Example 1

Atmospheric pressure is 100 kPa (100 000 Pa). Some air in a sealed container has a volume of 2 m³ at atmospheric pressure. What would be the pressure of the air if you reduced its volume to 0.2 m³?

First write down what we know:

$$p_1 = 100\,\text{kPa}$$
$$V_1 = 2\,\text{m}^3$$
$$V_2 = 0.2\,\text{m}^3$$
$$p_1 V_1 = p_2 V_2$$
$$\text{so } p_2 \times 0.2\,\text{m}^3 = 100\,\text{kPa} \times 2\,\text{m}^3$$
$$p_2 = 100\,\text{kPa} \times 2\,\text{m}^3/0.2\,\text{m}^3$$
$$= 1000\,\text{kPa}$$

You can do all your working in kPa if you wish, rather than converting the pressure to pascals. You can also use cubic centimetres for volume if these units are given in the question. It does not matter which units you use, as long as you use the same ones throughout the question.

Gases can be compressed because the particles are very spread out. When a gas is squashed into a smaller container it presses on the walls of the container with a greater pressure. This is explained in terms of particle theory as follows.

If the gas is kept at the same temperature, the average speed of the particles stays the same. (Remember that temperature is an indication of the kinetic energy of the particles.) If the same number of particles is squeezed into a smaller volume, they will hit the container walls more often. Each particle exerts a tiny force on the wall with which it collides. More collisions per second means a greater average force on the wall and, therefore, a greater pressure.

Absolute zero

Boyle took care to conduct his experiment at constant temperature. He was aware that temperature also had an effect on the pressure of a gas. Figure 20.7 shows an experiment to investigate how the pressure of a gas depends on its temperature.

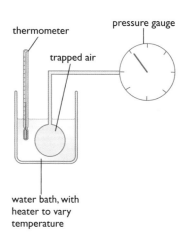

Figure 20.7 *Simple apparatus to measure the pressure of a fixed volume of gas at a range of temperatures.*

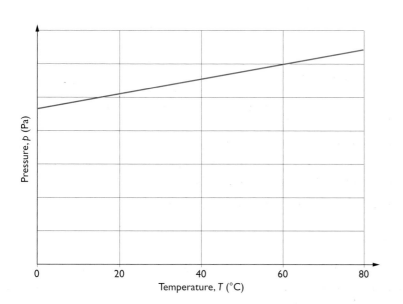

Figure 20.8 *Graph to show how the pressure of a fixed volume of gas varies with temperature.*

The gas is kept at constant volume, and its pressure is measured at a range of temperatures. The graph in Figure 20.8 shows typical results for this experiment.

The graph shows that the pressure of the gas increases as the temperature increases. We could also say that the gas pressure gets smaller as the gas is cooled.

What happens if we keep cooling the gas? The graph in Figure 20.9 shows this.

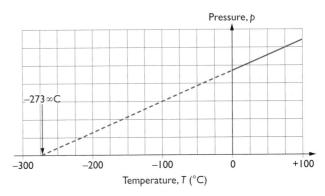

Figure 20.9 *At a temperature of –273 °C, the pressure of the gas would be zero. This temperature is known as "absolute zero".*

As we cool the gas, the pressure keeps decreasing. The pressure of the gas cannot become less than zero. This suggests that there is a temperature below which it is not possible to cool the gas further. This temperature is called **absolute zero**. Experiments show that absolute zero is approximately –273 °C.

The **kelvin** temperature scale starts from absolute zero. The kelvin temperature of a gas is proportional to the average kinetic energy of its molecules.

To convert a temperature on the Celsius scale (in °C) to a kelvin scale temperature (in K), add 273 to the Celsius scale temperature:

> temperature in K = temperature in °C + 273
>
> temperature in °C = temperature in K – 273

Worked example

Example 2

a) At what temperature does water freeze, in kelvin?

Water freezes at 0 °C. To convert 0 °C to kelvin:

$T = (0\,°C + 273)\,K$

$= 273\,K$

b) What is room temperature, in kelvin?

Typical room temperature is 20 °C, so:

$T = (20\,°C + 273)\,K$

$= 293\,K$

c) What temperature is 400 K on the Celsius scale?

$T = (400\,K - 273)\,°C$

$= 127\,°C$

If we redraw the graph of pressure against temperature using the absolute or kelvin temperature scale, we get a graph that is a straight line passing through the origin, as shown in Figure 20.10. This shows that the pressure of the gas is proportional to its kelvin temperature. For example, if you heat a gas from 200 K (−73 °C) to 400 K (127 °C), its pressure will double.

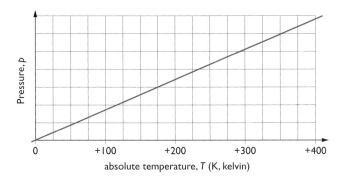

Figure 20.10 *Graph of pressure against absolute temperature for a fixed amount of gas at constant volume.*

For a fixed mass of gas at a constant volume,

$$\frac{p_1}{T_1} = \frac{p_2}{T_2}$$

NB *T* must be measured in kelvin.

Worked example

Example 3

You take an empty tin and put the lid on tightly. You heat it using a Bunsen burner until the temperature of the air inside is 50 °C. What is the pressure of the air inside the tin? The temperature of the room is 20 °C

First write down what we know:

p_1 = 100 kPa (this is atmospheric pressure)

T_1 = 20 °C, but we must change this to kelvin, so T_1 = 20 + 273 K = 293 K

T_2 = 50 °C, so T_2 = 50 + 273 K = 323 K

$$\frac{p_1}{T_1} = \frac{p_2}{T_2} \qquad\qquad \text{so } p_2 = p_1 \times \frac{T_2}{T_1}$$

$$p_2 = 100\,\text{kPa} \times 323\,\text{K}/293\,\text{K}$$

$$= 110\,\text{kPa}$$

The relationship can be explained as follows.

The number of gas particles and the space, or volume, they occupy remain constant. When we heat the gas the particles continue to move randomly, but with a higher average speed. This means that their collisions with the walls of the container are harder and happen more often. This results in the average pressure exerted by the particles increasing.

When we cool a gas the kinetic energy of its particles decreases. The lower the temperature of a gas the less kinetic energy its particles have – they move more slowly. At absolute zero the particles have no thermal or movement energy, so they cannot exert a pressure.

Cooling things further becomes more and more difficult as they get closer to 0 K. Scientists have managed to cool gases down to within a few thousandths of a degree above absolute zero. At this temperature even gases like helium and hydrogen can be liquefied.

End of Chapter Checklist

You will need to be able to do the following:

✓ understand that matter is made up of particles (molecules or atoms) that are in continuous motion

✓ recall the arrangement of particles in the three states of matter

✓ appreciate that the average kinetic energy of particles in a substance increases with temperature

✓ recall that gases exert a pressure because of the collisions that gas particles make with other matter

✓ understand that when you change the volume of a gas without changing the temperature its pressure changes because the particles hit the walls of the container at a different rate

✓ explain the changes in pressure and volume of a gas as the gas temperature changes in terms of the motion of the particles of the gas

✓ understand the reasons we believe that there is an absolute zero of temperature and know how to convert Celsius temperature to absolute or kelvin temperature

✓ recall and apply the gas law equations

$$\frac{p_1}{T_1} = \frac{p_2}{T_2} \quad \text{and} \quad p_1V_1 = p_2V_2$$

Questions

More questions on solids, liquids and gases can be found at the end of Section E on page 178.

1 a) Draw up a table to summarise the way that particles are arranged in solids, liquids and gases.

b) How do these different arrangements of particles explain the physical properties of solids, liquids and gases?

2 Copy and complete the following paragraph about the particle theory of matter.

Matter is made up of _____ that are in continuous _____ . When we supply heat energy to matter the _____ move _____ . Gases exert a pressure on their containers because the _____ are continually _____ with the walls. The pressure will _____ when the gas is heated in a container of fixed volume because the _____ are moving _____ .

3 Explain how ideas about particles can account for the absolute zero of temperature.

4 a) Convert the following Celsius temperatures to kelvin temperatures.

　　i) 0 °C

　　ii) 100 °C

　　iii) 20 °C

b) Convert the following kelvin temperatures to Celsius temperatures.

　　i) 250 K

　　ii) 269 K

　　iii) 305 K

5 State what happens in the situations shown in the diagram. Explain your answers using ideas about particles.

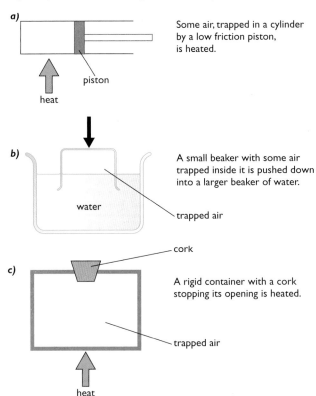

a)

Some air, trapped in a cylinder by a low friction piston, is heated.

piston

heat

b)

A small beaker with some air trapped inside it is pushed down into a larger beaker of water.

water

trapped air

c)

cork

A rigid container with a cork stopping its opening is heated.

trapped air

heat

6 *a)* A fixed amount of gas occupies a volume of 500 m³ when under a pressure of 100 kPa. Calculate the volume that this amount of gas will occupy when its pressure is increased to 125 kPa. You should show each stage of your calculation.

b) What do you need to assume about the temperature of the gas? Explain your answer.

7 *a)* You put the lid on a jar in a kitchen where the air temperature is 20 °C. The jar gets left out in the winter, and the air temperature drops to –5 °C. What is the air pressure in the cold jar?

b) Explain why it might be difficult to remove the lid of the jar when it is cold.

1 Copy and complete the following passage about the properties of gases, filling in the spaces.

The average speed of the particles in a gas _____ with increasing temperature. _____ zero is the temperature at which it is not possible to _____ a gas further. This temperature is approximately _____ °C, which is zero on the _____ temperature scale.

If you compress a gas at a constant temperature, the particles bump into the walls of their container more often, so the _____ increases. If the temperature is increased at a constant volume the pressure will _____ because the particles will hit the walls _____ and more often.

Total 8 marks

2 Show all the stages in your calculations when answering this question.

A shipping company packs metal bars into crates. Each bar has a volume of 0.0004 m³, and each crate can only take 70 kg of metal.

a) If the bars are made of gold (density = 19 000 kg/m³), how many bars can be packed into a crate? You may assume that the shape of the bars will not limit the number that can go into the crate. *(5 marks)*

b) A different crate has 64 kg of iron bars packed into it. The density of iron is 8000 kg/m³. How many bars are in the crate? *(4 marks)*

Total 9 marks

3 A scuba diver descends to 30 m in the sea. The density of the water is 1030 kg/m³. Take the gravitational field strength to be 10 N/kg.

a) What is the increase in pressure on her body at this depth compared to when she is swimming just below the surface? *(3 marks)*

b) How deep would she be if the additional pressure was only 20 kPa? *(3 marks)*

c) She does a similar dive in fresh water. The increase in pressure on her when she is 20 m down is 197 000 Pa. What is the density of the fresh water? *(3 marks)*

Total 9 marks

4 A bicycle pump has a stroke volume of 50 cm³ (that is, it pumps 50 cm³ of air on each stroke). Thirty strokes of the pump are used to put air into a bicycle tyre, whose final volume is 1000 cm³.

a) What is the total volume of air at atmospheric pressure that is put into the tyre? *(2 marks)*

b) What is the pressure of the tyre when it is pumped up? You may assume that the temperature of the air stays the same and that atmospheric pressure is 100 kPa. Show all the stages in your working. *(4 marks)*

Total 6 marks

5 Boiling jam is poured into a jar, and the lid is put on a couple of minutes later. During that time the heat from the jam has heated the air above it to 60 °C.

a) What is the air pressure in the jar when the jam has cooled to 20 °C? You can assume that the atmospheric pressure when the jar was sealed was 100 kPa. Show all the stages in your calculation. *(4 marks)*

b) The lid of the jar has an area of 0.001 m². How big is the force keeping the jar closed? (Hint: First work out the difference between the pressure of the air in the jar and atmospheric pressure.) *(5 marks)*

Total 9 marks

Chapter 21: Magnetism and Electromagnetism

A magnet has a magnetic field around it. A current-carrying wire also has a magnetic field around it while current is flowing. This means we can make electromagnets that can be switched on and off. In this chapter you will learn about the factors affecting the magnetic field around an electromagnet and how electromagnets are used in several important devices.

Figure 21.1 *Electromagnets can be used to lift iron or steel objects.*

The huge electromagnet in Figure 21.1 is being used in a scrapyard to pick up large objects that contain iron or steel. When the objects have been moved to their new position the electromagnet is turned off and the objects fall. This chapter explains how magnets and electromagnets are used in everyday devices.

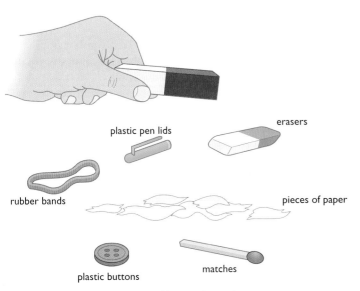
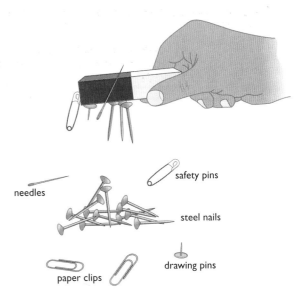

plastic pen lids
erasers
rubber bands
pieces of paper
plastic buttons
matches
needles
safety pins
steel nails
paper clips
drawing pins

Figure 21.2 *Magnets attract some objects and not others.*

Magnetism and magnetic materials

Magnets are able to attract objects made from **magnetic materials** such as iron, steel, nickel and cobalt. Magnets cannot attract objects made from other materials such as plastic, wood, paper or rubber. These are **non-magnetic materials**.

The strongest parts of a magnet are called its **poles**. Most magnets have two poles. These are called the **north pole** and the **south pole**.

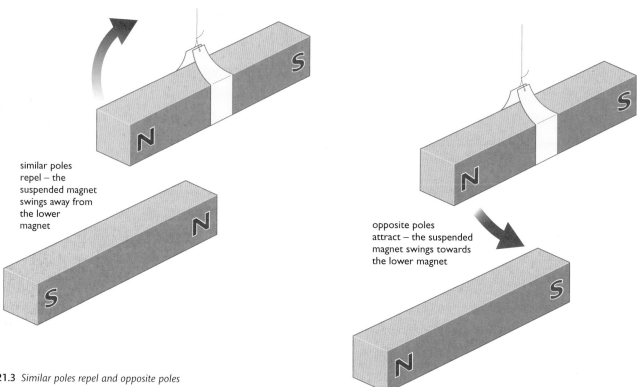

similar poles repel – the suspended magnet swings away from the lower magnet

opposite poles attract – the suspended magnet swings towards the lower magnet

Figure 21.3 *Similar poles repel and opposite poles attract.*

Ancient travellers would construct a crude compass by placing a splinter of magnetised rock called **lodestone** onto a piece of wood floating in water. The splinter would turn to align itself in a north–south direction.

If two similar poles are placed near to each other they **repel**. If two dissimilar (opposite) poles are placed near to each other they **attract**.

Permanent magnets like those shown in Figure 21.3 are made from a **magnetically hard** material such as steel. A magnetically hard material retains its magnetism once it has been **magnetised**. Iron is a **magnetically soft** material and would not be suitable for a permanent magnet. Magnetically soft materials lose their magnetism easily and are therefore useful as temporary magnets.

Magnetism can be induced in a magnetic material by leaving it in a magnetic field. This may be done deliberately to make a magnet. However it can also happen to steel food cans – if they are left in one position in a cupboard the Earth's magnetic field will gradually induce magnetism in them.

Magnetic fields

Around every magnet there is a volume of space where magnetism can be detected. This volume of space is called a **magnetic field**. Normally a magnetic field cannot be seen but we can use iron filings or plotting compasses to show its shape and discover something about its strength and direction.

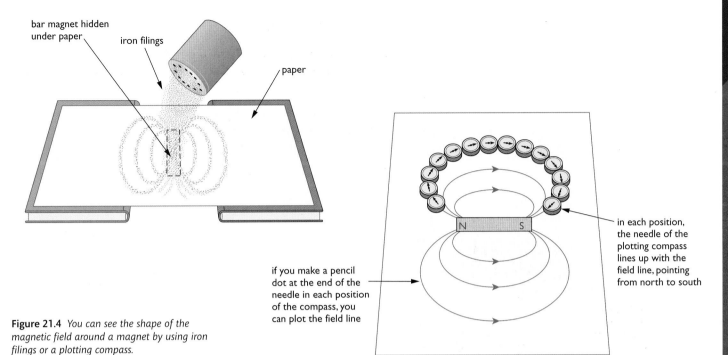

Figure 21.4 *You can see the shape of the magnetic field around a magnet by using iron filings or a plotting compass.*

if you make a pencil dot at the end of the needle in each position of the compass, you can plot the field line

in each position, the needle of the plotting compass lines up with the field line, pointing from north to south

If two magnets are placed near each other, their magnetic fields affect each other. Figure 21.6 shows the various field patterns possible. Note that when North and South poles are placed near each other there is an almost uniform field between the two poles.

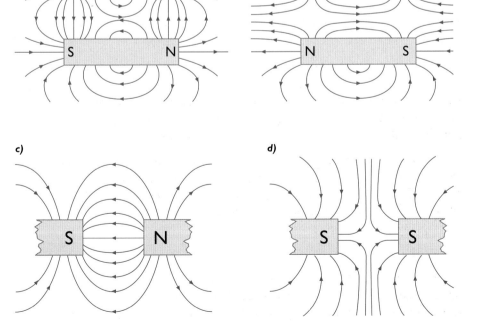

a)

b)

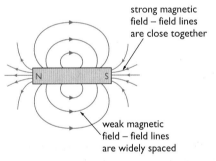

strong magnetic field – field lines are close together

weak magnetic field – field lines are widely spaced

Figure 21.5 *The magnetic field around a bar magnet follows a pattern like this.*

c)

d)

We draw magnetic fields using **lines of force** or **flux lines**. Like contour lines on a map, flux lines don't really exist but they are an aid in helping us visualise the main features of a magnetic field.

The magnetic lines of force:

- show the *shape* of the magnetic field
- show the *direction* of the magnetic field – the field lines "travel" from north to south
- show the *strength* of the magnetic field – the field lines are closest together where the magnetic field is strongest.

Figure 21.6 *Magnetic fields around pairs of magnets.*

Electromagnetism

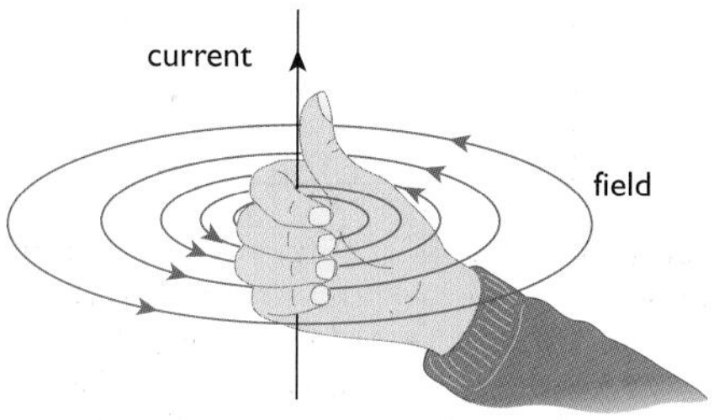

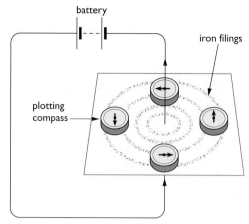

Figure 21.7 *A current-carrying wire has a magnetic field around it.*

The shape and direction of the magnetic field around a current-carrying wire can be seen using iron filings and plotting compasses.
Changing the direction of the current changes the direction of the magnetic field.

Figure 21.8 *You can work out the direction of the field using the right-hand grip rule (for fields).*

With the thumb of your right hand pointing in the direction of the current, your fingers will curl in the direction of the field.

When a current flows through a wire a magnetic field is created around the wire. This phenomenon is called **electromagnetism**. The field around the wire is quite weak and circular in shape. The direction of the magnetic field depends upon the direction of the current and can be found using the **right-hand grip rule** (**for fields**).

If the wire is made into a flat, circular coil, the magnetic field around the wire is as shown in Figure 21.9.

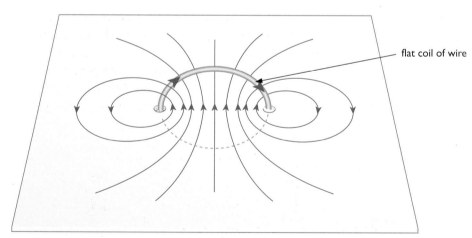

Figure 21.9 *The magnetic field around a flat coil.*

The strength of the magnetic field around a current-carrying wire can be increased by:

1 increasing the current in the wire

2 wrapping the wire into a coil or **solenoid** (a solenoid is a long coil).

The shape of the magnetic field around a solenoid is the same as that around a bar magnet. The positions of the poles can be determined using the **right-hand grip rule** (**for poles**).

If the direction of the current flowing through the solenoid is reversed, so too are the positions of the poles.

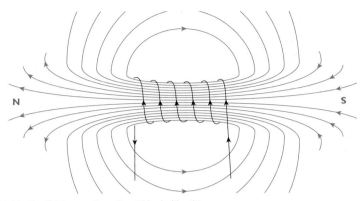

Figure 21.11 *The field around a solenoid looks like this.*

The strength of the field around a solenoid can be increased by:

1 increasing the current flowing through the solenoid

2 increasing the number of turns on the solenoid

3 wrapping the solenoid around a magnetically soft core such as iron – this combination of soft iron core and solenoid is often referred to as an **electromagnet**.

Using electromagnets

The electric bell

In Figure 21.12, when the bell push is pressed the circuit is complete and current flows. The soft iron core of the electromagnet becomes magnetised and attracts the iron armature. When the armature moves, the hammer strikes the bell and at the same time a gap is created at the contact screw. The circuit is incomplete and current stops flowing. The electromagnet is now turned off so the spring's armature returns to its original position. The circuit is again complete and the whole process begins again.

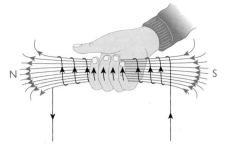

Figure 21.10 *You can work out the polarity of the solenoid by imagining that your right hand is wrapped around it. Your fingers curl in the direction of the current and your thumb points to the north pole of the solenoid. This is the right-hand grip rule (for poles).*

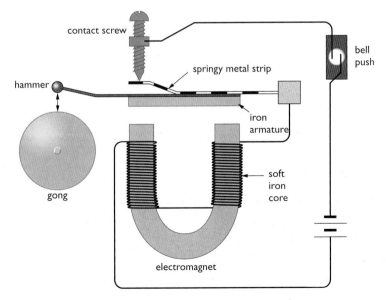

Figure 21.12 *An electric bell relies upon an electromagnet.*

Circuit breaker

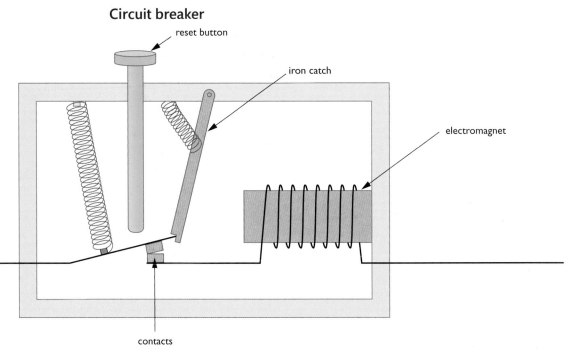

Figure 21.13 *Circuit breakers also use electromagnets.*

The circuit breaker in Figure 21.13 uses an electromagnet to cut off the current if it becomes larger than a certain value. If the current is too high the electromagnet becomes strong enough to pull the iron catch out of position so that the contacts open and the circuit breaks. Once the problem in the circuit has been corrected the catch is repositioned by pressing the reset button.

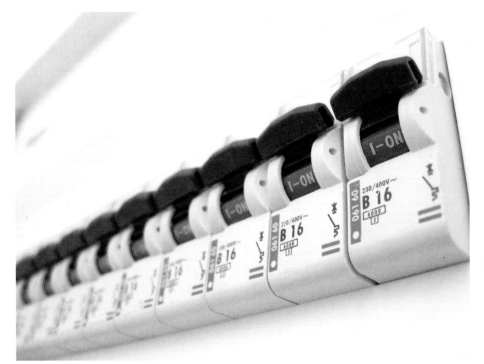

Figure 21.14 *These circuit breakers control the supply of electricity to different circuits in a building. The circuit breaker will 'trip' if there is something wrong with the circuit and the current is too high.*

The relay switch

When large currents flow in a circuit there is always the danger of the user receiving a severe electric shock. Even turning the circuit on and off can be hazardous. To get around this problem we often use **relay switches**. A relay switch uses a small current in one circuit to turn on a second circuit that may be carrying a much larger current.

In Figure 21.15, when switch S is closed a small current flows around the circuit on the left. As current passes through coil C the soft iron core becomes magnetised and attracts the iron armature. Because the armature is pivoted at X, its lower end Y pushes the contacts of the second circuit together. The circuit is complete and current flows without the user coming into contact with the potentially more dangerous circuit. If the switch S is opened the electromagnet is turned off, the iron armature moves back to its original position and the contacts spring apart, turning the right-hand circuit off. An arrangement similar to this is used in car ignition circuits.

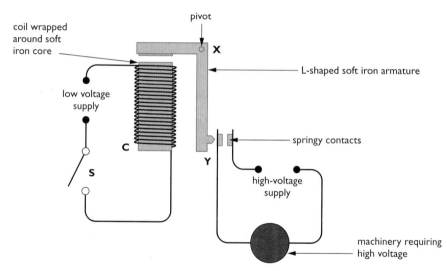

Figure 21.15 *A relay switch uses a small current in one circuit to switch on a larger current in another circuit.*

End of Chapter Checklist

You will need to be able to do the following:

✓ recall that magnets repel and attract other magnets and attract magnetic materials

✓ understand that magnetically hard and magnetically soft materials have different properties

✓ sketch and explain the magnetic field patterns for bar magnets

✓ recall that magnetism can be induced in some materials when they are placed in a magnetic field

✓ recall that a current flowing in a wire or coil produces a magnetic field

✓ sketch the magnetic field around a wire, a flat coil and a solenoid

✓ describe some applications of electromagnetism.

Questions

More questions on electromagnetism can be found at the end of Section F on page 198.

1 *a)* Draw a diagram to show the shape of the magnetic field around a solenoid.

b) How does your diagram show where the magnetic field is strong or weak?

c) Explain what happens to the magnetic field if the direction of the current flowing through the solenoid is reversed.

2 In 1819 a scientist named Hans Christian Oersted was using a cell to pass a current through a wire. Close to the wire there was a compass. When current passed through the wire, Oersted noticed – much to his surprise – that the compass needle moved.

a) Why did the compass needle move?

b) When current is passed through a horizontal wire, the needle of a compass placed beneath the wire comes to rest at right angles to the wire, pointing from left to right. In which direction will the compass needle point if it is held above the wire? Explain your answer.

c) Would your answer to part *b)* still be correct if the direction of the current in the wire was changed? Explain your answer.

3 The diagram below shows a simple electromagnet.

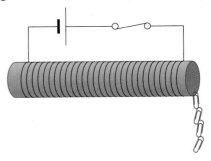

a) Explain why the core of an electromagnet is made of soft iron and not steel.

b) Suggest two ways in which the strength of this electromagnet could be increased.

Chapter 22: Electric Motors and Electromagnetic Induction

Trains in many cities use electric motors to transport millions of people to and from work each day. In the first part of this chapter, we are going to look at how an electric motor works. An electric motor creates motion from an electric current. Generators, on the other hand, transfer movement into electrical energy, by electromagnetic induction. The second part of this chapter looks at this process.

Figure 22.1 *Electric train in Bangkok (the Skytrain).*

Movement from electricity

A charged particle moving through a magnetic field experiences a force, as long as its motion is not parallel to the field. As an electric current is a flow of electrons (which are charged particles), we can see this effect when a wire carrying the current is put into a magnetic field.

Overlapping magnetic fields

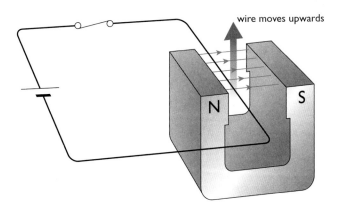

wire moves upwards

N   S

Figure 22.2 *The wire moves as a current flows through it.*

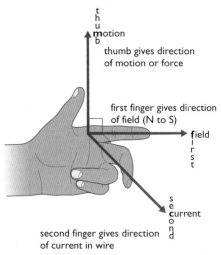

Figure 22.4 *Fleming's left-hand rule helps you to work out the direction of the force.*

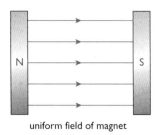

uniform field of magnet

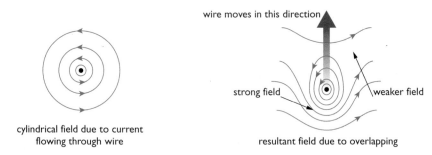

cylindrical field due to current
flowing through wire

resultant field due to overlapping

Figure 22.3 *The field around the wire and the field around the magnet overlap. The current in the wire is flowing towards us, out of the paper.*

If we pass a current through a piece of wire held at right angles to the magnetic field of a magnet, as shown in Figure 22.2, the wire will move. This motion is the result of a force created by overlapping magnetic fields around the wire and the magnet.

As we have seen in Chapter 21, when a current flows along a wire a cylindrical magnetic field is created around the wire. If the wire is placed between the poles of a magnet, the two fields overlap. In certain places, the fields are in the same direction and so reinforce each other, producing a strong magnetic field. In other places, the fields are in opposite directions, producing a weaker field. The wire experiences a force, pushing it from the stronger part of the field to the weaker part. This is called the **motor effect**. A stronger force will be produced if the magnetic field is stronger or if the current is increased.

If the direction of the current or the direction of the magnetic field is reversed, the wire experiences a force in the opposite direction. We can predict the direction of the motion of the wire using **Fleming's left-hand rule**.

The moving-coil loudspeaker

The moving-coil loudspeaker uses the motor effect to change electrical energy into sound energy.

Signals from a source, such as an amplifier, are fed into the coil of the speaker as currents that are continually changing in size and direction. The overlapping fields of the coil and the magnet therefore create rapidly varying forces on the wires of the coil, which cause the speaker cone to vibrate. These vibrations create the sound waves we hear.

The electric motor

As current passes around the loop of wire in Figure 22.6, one side of it will experience a force pushing it upwards. The other side will feel a force pushing it downwards, so the loop will rotate. Because of the split ring, when the loop is vertical, the connections to the supply through the brushes swap over, so that the current flowing through each side of the loop changes direction. The wire at the bottom is now pushed upwards and the wire at the top is pushed downwards – so the loop carries on turning. The arrangement of brushes and split ring changes the direction of the current flowing through the loop every half turn, which means that rotation can be continuous.

Figure 22.5 *A loudspeaker turns electrical energy into sound energy.*

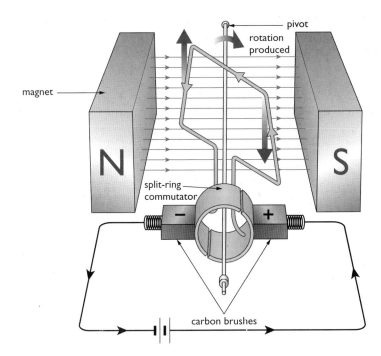

Figure 22.6 *A simple electric motor.*

Figure 22.7 *A motor.*

To increase the rate at which the motor turns we can:

1 increase the number of turns or loops of wire (to make a coil)

2 increase the strength of the magnetic field

3 increase the current flowing through the loop of wire.

Practical motors differ from that described in Figure 22.6 in several ways.

- The permanent magnets are replaced with curved electromagnets capable of producing very strong magnetic fields.

- The single loop is replaced with several coils of wire wrapped on the same axis. This makes the motor more powerful and allows it to run more smoothly.

- The coils are wrapped on a laminated soft iron core. This makes the motor more efficient and more powerful.

Electromagnetic induction

Motors use electricity to produce movement. Generators make electricity from movement.

The workers shown in Figure 22.8 need electricity for their machines and their lights. Rather than connecting into the mains supply, as we do at home, the workers have their own generator, which produces the electrical energy they need. In fact, the mains supply itself is produced by large generators in power stations. In this next section, you will discover how a generator produces electricity.

Figure 22.8 *Generators are used to produce electricity for the lights and machinery used on motorway roadworks.*

The generator

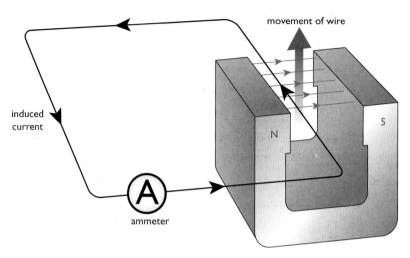

Figure 22.9 *When a wire moves through a magnetic field a voltage is generated in the wire.*

If we move a wire across a magnetic field at right angles, as shown in Figure 22.9, a voltage is **induced** or generated in the wire. If the wire is part of a complete circuit, a current flows. This phenomenon is called **electromagnetic induction**.

The size of the induced voltage (and current) can be increased by:

1 moving the wire more quickly

2 using a stronger magnet

3 wrapping the wire into a coil so that more pieces of wire move through the magnetic field.

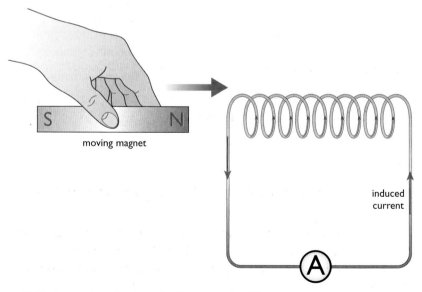

Figure 22.10 *A magnet moving in a coil will generate electricity.*

We can also generate a voltage and current by pushing a magnet into a coil. The size of the induced voltage (and current) can be increased by:

1 moving the magnet more quickly

2 using a stronger magnet

3 using a coil with more turns

4 using a coil with a larger cross-sectional area.

The factors listed above show that:

- a voltage and current are generated when a conductor such as a wire cuts through the magnetic field lines

- the faster the lines are cut the larger the induced voltage and current.

Michael Faraday was the first person to observe how the size of an induced voltage depends upon the rate at which the magnetic lines of flux (field lines) are being cut. He summarised his observations in **Faraday's Law of Electromagnetic Induction**. This states that:

> **The size of the induced voltage across the ends of a wire (coil) is directly proportional to the rate at which the magnetic lines of flux are being cut.**

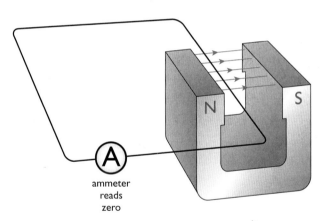

Figure 22.11 *When the field lines are not cut there is no voltage or current produced.*

If we hold the wire or magnet stationary there is no cutting of the field lines so no voltage or current is generated. If we move the wire horizontally between the poles of the magnet, again there are no lines being cut and therefore no voltage or current is generated (Figure 22.11).

The direction of the induced current in Figures 20.9 and 20.10 depends upon the direction of the motion. If the direction of movement is reversed, so too is the direction of the induced current.

Using generators

Figure 22.12 shows a small generator or dynamo used to generate electricity for a bicycle light.

As the cyclist pedals, the wheel rotates and a small magnet within the dynamo spins around. As this magnet turns, its magnetic field cuts through the surrounding coil inducing a current in it. This current can be used to work the cyclist's lights.

Figure 22.13 shows a much larger generator used in power stations to generate the mains electricity we use in our homes. The size of the induced voltage is greater

Figure 22.13 *This generator produces electricity on an industrial scale.*

Most alternators use electromagnets rather than permanent magnets, as these can produce stronger magnetic fields, and it is the electromagnet which is rotated inside a stationary coil.

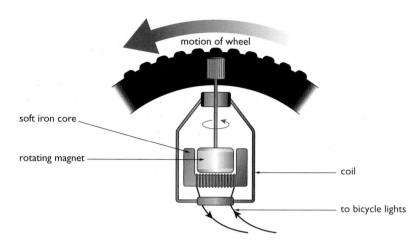

Figure 22.12 *A dynamo is a simple generator.*

than in the bicycle dynamo because these generators use much stronger magnets, have many more turns of wire on the coil, and spin the coil much faster.

As the coil rotates, its wires cut through magnetic field lines and a current is induced in them. If we watch just one side of the coil, we see that the wire moves up through the field and then down for each turn of the coil. As a result, the current induced in the coil flows first in one direction and then in the opposite direction. This kind of current is called **alternating current**. A generator that produces alternating current is called an **alternator**.

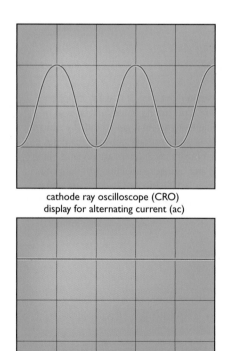

cathode ray oscilloscope (CRO)
display for alternating current (ac)

CRO display for direct current (dc)

Figure 22.15 *Direct currents (dc) flow in one direction. Alternating currents (ac) keep changing direction.*

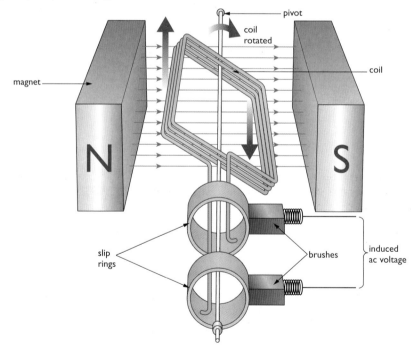

Figure 22.14 *The alternator produces alternating current.*

The frequency of an alternating current is the number of complete cycles it makes each second. If an alternator coil rotates twice in a second, the frequency of the alternating current it produces is 2 Hz (2 cycles per second). The frequency of the UK mains supply is 50 Hz.

The transformer

When alternating current is passed through a coil, the magnetic field around it is continuously changing. As the size of the current in the coil increases the field grows. As the size of the current decreases the field collapses. If a second coil is placed near the first, this changing magnetic field will pass through it. As it cuts through the wires of the second coil, a voltage is induced across that coil. The size and direction of the induced voltage changes as the voltage applied to the first coil changes. (The first coil is more usually called the **primary coil**.) An alternating voltage applied across the primary coil therefore produces an alternating voltage across the **secondary coil**. This combination of two magnetically linked coils is called a **transformer**.

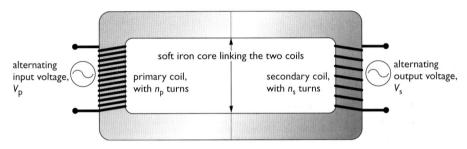

Figure 22.16 *The size of the voltage generated in the secondary coil of a transformer depends on the voltage in the primary coil and the numbers of turns on each coil.*

The relationship between the voltages across each of the coils is described by the equation:

$$\frac{\text{input voltage}}{\text{output voltage}} = \frac{\text{number of turns on primary coil}}{\text{number of turns on secondary coil}}$$

$$\frac{V_p}{V_s} = \frac{n_p}{n_s}$$

> Remember that transformers only work if the magnetic field around the primary coil is *changing*. Transformers will therefore only work with ac currents and voltages. They will not work with dc currents and voltages.

Worked example

Example 1

A transformer has 100 turns on its primary coil and 500 turns on its secondary coil. If an alternating voltage of 2V is applied across the primary, what is the voltage across the secondary coil?

$$\frac{V_p}{V_s} = \frac{n_p}{n_s}$$

$$\frac{2\,V}{V_s} = \frac{100}{500}$$

$$V_s = \frac{500 \times 2\,V}{100}$$

$$V_s = 10\,V$$

A transformer that is used to *increase* voltages, like the one in Example 1, is called a **step-up** transformer. One that is used to *decrease* voltages is called a **step-down** transformer.

If a transformer is 100% efficient then the electrical energy entering the primary coil each second equals the electrical energy leaving the secondary coil each second:

$$P_{in} = P_{out}$$
$$V_p \times I_p = V_s \times I_s$$

Worked example

Example 2

When a voltage of 12 V ac is applied across the primary coil of a step-down transformer, a current of 0.4 A flows through the primary coil. Calculate the current flowing through the secondary coil if the voltage induced across it is 2 V ac. Assume that the transformer is 100% efficient.

Using $V_p \times I_p = V_s \times I_s$

$12\,V \times 0.4\,A = 2\,V \times I_s$

$$I_s = \frac{12\,V \times 0.4\,A}{2\,V}$$

$I_s = 2.4\,A$

Figure 22.17 *A transformer.*

Transformers and the UK National Grid

The UK National Grid is a network of wires and cables that carries electrical energy from power stations to consumers such as factories and homes. As current passes through a wire, energy is lost in the form of heat. If the current flowing through the wire is kept to a minimum, the heat losses are also reduced. Transformers are used in the National Grid so that the electricity is transmitted as low currents and at high voltages.

Immediately after generation, electric currents from the alternators are passed through step-up transformers. Here the voltage of the electricity is increased to approximately 400 kV and the size of the electric current is greatly decreased. High voltages like these can be extremely dangerous so the cables are supported high above the ground on pylons. As the cables enter towns and cities they are buried underground. Close to where the electrical energy is needed, the supply is passed through a step-down transformer that decreases the voltage to approximately 230 V, whilst at the same time increasing the current.

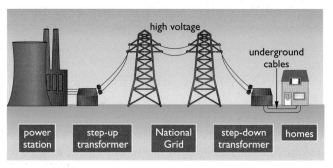

Figure 22.18 *Transformers are used in the UK National Grid.*

End of Chapter Checklist

You will need to be able to do the following:

✓ understand why a current-carrying conductor placed in a magnetic field experiences a force

✓ recall and use Fleming's left-hand rule to predict the direction of the force and consequent movement

✓ recall that the size of the force can be increased by increasing the strength of the magnetic field or the size of the current flowing in the wire

✓ explain how electromagnetic effects are used in the simple dc motor

✓ understand that when a wire cuts through a magnetic field, or vice versa, a voltage is induced across the wire; if the wire is part of a complete circuit this induced voltage will cause a current to flow

✓ recall that the size of the induced voltage increases as the rate at which the magnetic field lines are being cut increases

✓ explain how electricity can be generated by rotating a coil in a magnetic field or rotating a magnet inside a coil of wire

✓ recall and explain the structure of a transformer

✓ recall that when an ac voltage is applied to the primary coil of a transformer an ac voltage is produced across the secondary coil

✓ recall and use the relationships $\dfrac{V_p}{V_s} = \dfrac{n_p}{n_s}$ and $V_p I_p = V_s I_s$

✓ describe the use of transformers in the large-scale transmission of electrical energy.

Questions

More questions on electric motors and electromagnetic induction can be found at the end of Section F on page 197.

1 The diagram below shows a long wire placed between the poles of a magnet.

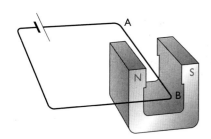

Describe what happens when:

a) current is passed through the wire flowing from A to B

b) the direction of the current is reversed – that is, it flows from B to A

c) with the current flowing from B to A, the poles of the magnet are reversed

d) a larger current is passed through the wire.

2 *a)* Draw a diagram of a simple electric motor.

    b) Explain the functions of the split ring and the brushes.

    c) Suggest three ways in which the speed of rotation of the motor could be increased.

    d) State two ways in which the structure of practical motors is different from that of a simple motor.

3 The diagram below shows a bar magnet being pushed into a long coil. A sensitive meter is connected across the coil.

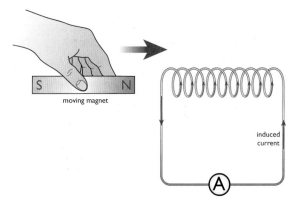

moving magnet

induced current

Ⓐ

Describe what happens to the meter when:

a) the magnet is pushed into the coil quickly

b) the magnet is held stationary inside the coil

c) the magnet is withdrawn from the coil slowly

d) the magnet is held stationary and the coil is moved towards it.

4 *a)* Explain the difference between a step-up transformer and a step-down transformer.

b) Explain where step-up and step-down transformers are used in the UK National Grid.

c) Explain why transformers are used in the UK National Grid.

d) Draw a fully labelled diagram of a transformer.

e) Explain why a transformer will not work if a dc voltage is applied across its primary coil.

f) A transformer has 200 turns on its primary coil and 5000 turns on its secondary coil. Calculate the voltage across the secondary coil when a voltage of 2 V ac is applied across the primary coil.

1 A wire carrying an electric current experiences a _____ when it is in a _____ field. This effect can be used in _____ and electric _____ .

If a wire is moved through a magnetic field, or the magnetic field near a _____ of wire changes, a current can be _____ in the wire. This effect is used in _____ and _____ .

Total 8 marks

2 *a)* Explain how a bicycle dynamo generates current. *(3 marks)*

b) Why does the dynamo produce no current when the cyclist has stopped? *(1 mark)*

c) What is an alternator? *(1 mark)*

d) Explain using diagrams the difference between ac and dc currents. *(3 marks)*

e) Explain what is meant by this statement: "The mains supply in the UK has a frequency of 50 Hz." *(2 marks)*

Total 10 marks

3 The diagram below shows how the electrical energy is transmitted from a power station to our homes.

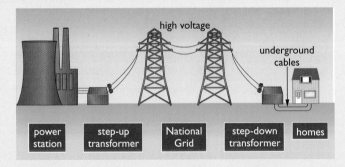

a) Why is the voltage of the supply increased before transmission? *(1 mark)*

b) Why is the voltage of the supply decreased before entering our homes? *(1 mark)*

c) A step-up transformer has 100 turns on its primary coil and 20 000 turns on its secondary coil. Calculate the output voltage of the transformer if the input voltage is 12 V ac. *(3 marks)*

d) Assuming that the transformer is 100% efficient, calculate the current flowing through the secondary coil if the current flowing through the primary coil is 10 A. *(3 marks)*

Total 8 marks

4 The diagram below shows a relay circuit. These circuits can be used to turn other circuits carrying high currents on and off safely.

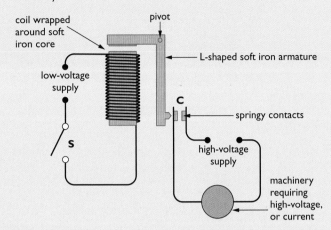

a) What is created around the coil when switch S is closed? *(1 mark)*

b) What happens to the soft iron core around which the coil is wrapped? *(1 mark)*

c) Explain in your own words why, when the contacts at C are closed, the second high-voltage circuit is turned on. *(3 marks)*

d) Explain in detail what happens if switch S is then opened. *(3 marks)*

e) Why would the relay circuit not work if the soft iron core was replaced with one made of steel? *(1 mark)*

Total 9 marks

5 An electric kettle operates at 230 V and draws a current of 13 A. What would the equivalent current be at the following voltages used in the UK National Grid? Show all your working.

a) 33 kV (33 000 V) *(4 marks)*

b) 400 kV *(4 marks)*

Total 8 marks

6 The diagram shows a circuit breaker that uses an electromagnet.

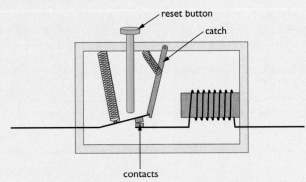

reset button

catch

contacts

a) Explain why the current is cut off by this circuit breaker if it is larger than a certain value. *(3 marks)*

b) Give one advantage of this type of circuit breaker compared with a cartridge fuse. *(1 mark)*

Total 4 marks

7 The diagram below shows the circuit for an electric bell.

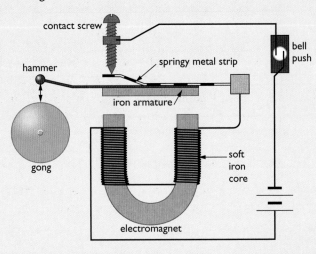

contact screw

hammer

gong

springy metal strip

bell push

iron armature

soft iron core

electromagnet

a) Explain in your own words why the bell will not work if the electromagnet is replaced with a permanent magnet. *(2 marks)*

b) Explain why the core of the electromagnet used in an electric bell must not be made from steel. *(3 marks)*

Total 5 marks

Chapter 23: Atoms and Radioactivity

Atoms are made up of sub-atomic particles called neutrons, protons and electrons. It is the numbers of these particles that give each element its unique properties. In this chapter you will find out how atoms can break up and become transformed into different elements, and about the different types of radiation they give out.

Electrons, protons and neutrons

Atoms are made up of **electrons**, **protons** and **neutrons**. Figure 23.1 shows a simple model of how these particles are arranged.

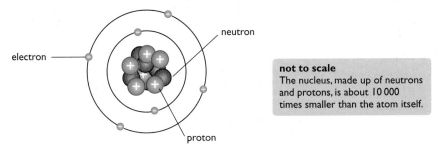

not to scale
The nucleus, made up of neutrons and protons, is about 10 000 times smaller than the atom itself.

Figure 23.1 *A simple model with protons and neutrons in the nucleus of the atom and electrons in orbits around the outside.*

The electron is a very light particle with very little mass. It has a *negative* electric charge. Electrons orbit the nucleus of the atom. The nucleus is very small compared to the size of the atom itself. The diameter of the nucleus is about 10 000 times smaller than the diameter of the atom. If the nucleus of an atom were enlarged to the size of a full stop on this page, the atom would have a diameter of around 2.5 metres.

The nucleus is made up of protons and neutrons. Protons and neutrons have almost exactly the same mass. Protons and neutrons are nearly 2000 times heavier than electrons. Protons carry *positive* electric charge but neutrons, as the name suggests, are electrically neutral or *uncharged*. The amount of charge on a proton is equal to that on an electron but opposite in sign.

The properties of these three atomic particles are summarised in the table below. Protons and neutrons are also called **nucleons** because they are found in the nucleus of the atom.

The *actual* mass of an electron is 9.1×10^{-31} kg and its *actual* charge is -1.6×10^{-19} C. The table shows the approximate relative masses of the particles and the relative amount of charge they carry. The mass in atomic mass units is discussed below.

Atomic particle	Relative mass of particle	Relative charge of particle
electron	1	−1
proton	2000	+1
neutron	2000	0

The atom

The nucleus of an atom is surrounded by electrons. We sometimes think of electrons as orbiting the nucleus in a way similar to the planets orbiting the Sun. It is more accurate to think of the electrons as moving rapidly around the nucleus in a cloud or shell.

An atom is electrically neutral. This is because the number of positive charges carried by the protons in its nucleus is balanced by the number of negative charges on the electrons in the electron "cloud" around the nucleus.

Atomic number

The chemical behaviour and properties of a particular element depend upon how the atoms combine with other atoms. This is determined by the number of electrons in the atom. Although atoms may gain or lose electrons, sometimes quite easily, the number of protons in atoms of a particular element is always the same. The **atomic number** of an element tells us how many protons each of its atoms contains. For example, carbon has six protons in its nucleus – the atomic number of carbon is, therefore, 6. The symbol we use for atomic number is Z. Each element has its own unique atomic number. The atomic number is sometimes called the proton number.

Atomic mass

The total number of protons and neutrons in the nucleus of an atom determines its **atomic mass**. The mass of the electrons that make up an atom is tiny and can usually be ignored. The mass of a proton is approximately 1.7×10^{-27} kg. To save writing this down we usually refer to the mass of an atom by its **mass number** or **nucleon number**. This number is the total number of protons and neutrons in the atom. The mass number of an element is given the symbol A.

Atomic notation – the recipe for an atom

Each particular type of atom will have its own atomic number, which identifies the element, and a mass number that depends on the total number of nucleons, or particles, in the nucleus. Figure 23.2 shows the way we represent an atom of an element whose chemical symbol is X, showing the atomic number and the mass number.

So, using this notation, an atom of oxygen is represented by:

$$^{16}_{8}O$$

The chemical symbol for oxygen is O. The atomic number is 8 – this tells us that the nucleus contains eight protons. The mass number is 16, so there are 16 nucleons (protons and neutrons) in the nucleus. Since eight of these are protons, the remaining eight must be neutrons. The atom is electrically neutral overall, so the +8 charge of the nucleus is balanced by the eight orbiting electrons, each with charge −1.

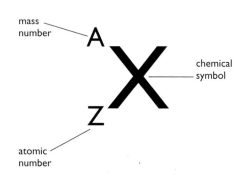

mass number —— A

chemical symbol

Z

atomic number

Figure 23.2 *Atomic notation*

$$\text{mass number, A} = \text{number of neutrons} + \text{number of protons, Z}$$
$$= \text{number of nucleons}$$

So,

$$\text{number of neutrons} = \text{number of nucleons} - \text{number of protons}$$
$$= A - Z$$

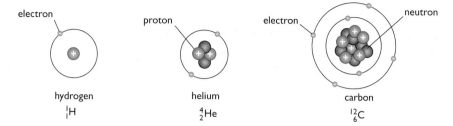

Figure 23.3 *The hydrogen atom has one proton in its nucleus and no neutrons, so the mass number A = 1 + 0 = 1. As it has one proton, its atomic number Z = 1. For helium, A = 4 (2 protons + 2 neutrons) and Z = 2 (2 protons). For carbon, A = 12 (6 protons + 6 neutrons) while Z = 6 (6 protons).*

Figure 23.3 shows some examples of the use of this notation for hydrogen, helium and carbon, together with a simple indication of the structure of an atom of each of these elements. In each case the number of orbiting electrons is equal to the number of protons in the nucleus, so the atoms are electrically neutral.

Isotopes

The number of protons in an atom identifies the element. The chemical behaviour of an element depends on the number of electrons it has and, as we have seen, this always balances the number of protons in the nucleus. However, the number of neutrons in the nucleus can vary slightly. Atoms of an element with different numbers of neutrons are called **isotopes** of the element. The number of neutrons in a nucleus affects the mass of the atom. Different isotopes of an element will all have the *same* atomic number, Z, but *different* mass numbers, A. Figures 23.4 and 23.5 show some examples of isotopes.

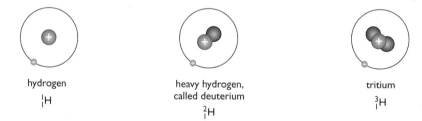

Figure 23.4 *Isotopes of hydrogen – they all have the same atomic number, 1, and the same chemical symbol, H.*

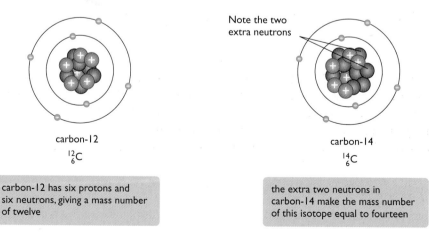

carbon-12 has six protons and six neutrons, giving a mass number of twelve

the extra two neutrons in carbon-14 make the mass number of this isotope equal to fourteen

Figure 23.5 *Two isotopes of carbon – they are referred to as carbon-12 and carbon-14 to distinguish between them.*

The stability of isotopes

Isotopes of an element have different physical properties from other isotopes of the same element. One obvious difference is the mass. Another difference is the **stability** of the nucleus.

The protons are held in the nucleus by the **nuclear force**. This force is very strong and acts over a very small distance. It is strong enough to hold the nucleus together against the **electric force** repelling the protons away from each other. (Remember that protons carry positive charge and like charges repel.) The presence of neutrons in the nucleus affects the balance between these forces. Too many or too few neutrons will make the nucleus **unstable**. An unstable nucleus will eventually **decay**. When the nucleus of an atom decays it gives out energy and may also give out alpha or beta particles.

Ionising radiation

When unstable nuclei decay they give out **ionising radiation**. Ionising radiation causes atoms to gain or lose electric charge, forming **ions**. Unstable nuclei decay at **random**. This means that it is not possible to predict which unstable nucleus in a piece of radioactive material will decay, or when decay will happen. We shall see that we can make measurements that will enable us to predict the probability that a certain proportion of a radioactive material will decay in a given time.

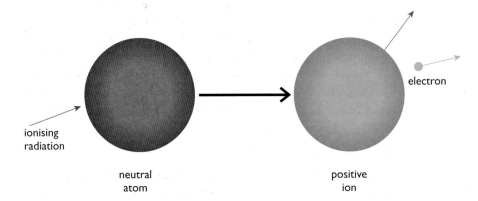

Figure 23.6 *When a neutral atom (or molecule) is hit by ionising radiation it loses an electron and becomes a positively charged ion.*

There are three basic types of ionising radiation: they are **alpha** (α), **beta** (β) and **gamma** (γ) radiation.

Alpha radiation

Alpha radiation consists of fast-moving particles that are thrown out of unstable nuclei when they decay. These are called **alpha particles**. Alpha particles are helium nuclei – helium atoms without their orbiting electrons. Figure 23.7 shows an alpha particle and the notation that is used to denote it in equations.

Alpha particles have a relatively large mass. They are made up of four nucleons and so have a mass number of 4. They are also charged because of the two protons that they carry. The relative charge of an alpha particle is +2.

Alpha particles have a short **range**. The range of ionising radiation is the distance it can travel through matter. Alpha particles can only travel a few centimetres in

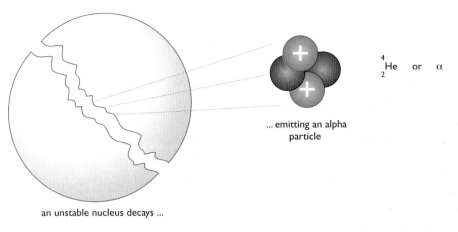

an unstable nucleus decays ...

... emitting an alpha particle

$^4_2$He or α

Figure 23.7 *An unstable nucleus decays, emitting an alpha particle.*

air and cannot penetrate more than a few millimetres of paper. They have a limited range because they interact with atoms along their paths, causing ions to form. This means that they rapidly give up the energy that they had when they were ejected from the unstable nucleus.

Beta radiation

Beta particles are very fast-moving electrons that are ejected by a decaying nucleus. The nucleus of an atom contains protons and neutrons, so where does the electron come from? The stability of a nucleus depends on the proportion of protons and neutrons it contains. The result of radioactive decay is to change the balance of protons and neutrons in the nucleus to make it more stable. Beta decay involves a neutron in the nucleus splitting into a proton and an electron. The proton remains in the nucleus and the electron is ejected at high speed as a beta particle.

Beta particles are very light – they have only 0.000 125 times the mass of an alpha particle. The relative charge of a beta particle is –1.

Beta particles interact with matter in their paths less frequently than alpha particles. This is because they are smaller and carry less charge. This means that beta particles have a greater range than alpha particles. Beta particles can travel long distances through air, pass through paper easily and are only absorbed by denser materials like aluminium. A millimetre or two of aluminium foil will stop all but the most energetic beta particles.

Gamma rays

Gamma rays are electromagnetic waves (see page 103) with very short wavelengths. As they are waves, they have no mass and no charge. They are weakly ionising and interact only occasionally with atoms in their paths. They are extremely penetrating and pass through all but the very densest materials with ease. It takes several centimetres thickness of lead, or a metre or so of concrete, to stop gamma radiation.

Gamma radiation is emitted in 'packets' of energy called **photons**.

Nucleons have roughly 2000 times the mass of an electron, and alpha particles are made up of four nucleons, so an alpha particle has 8000 times the mass of a beta particle.

Summary of the properties of ionising radiation

We have said that ionising radiation causes uncharged atoms to lose electrons. An atom that has lost (or gained) electrons has an overall charge. It is called an **ion**. The three types of radioactive emission all can form ions.

As ionising radiation passes through matter, its energy is absorbed. This means that radiation can only penetrate matter up to a certain thickness. This depends on the type of radiation and the density of the material that it is passing through.

The ionising and penetrating powers of alpha, beta and gamma radiation are compared in the table below. Note that the ranges given in the table are typical but they do depend on the energy of the radiation. More energetic alpha particles will have a greater range than those with lower energy.

Radiation	Ionising power	Penetrating power	Example of range in air	Radiation stopped by
alpha, α	strong	weak	5–8 cm	paper
beta, β	medium	medium	500–1000 cm	thin aluminium
gamma, γ	weak	strong	virtually infinite	thick lead sheet

Nuclear transformations

As we said earlier, an unstable atom, or strictly speaking its nucleus, will decay by emitting radiation. If the decay process involves the nucleus ejecting either an alpha or a beta particle, the atomic number will change. This means that alpha or beta decay causes the original element to transform into a different element.

Alpha (α) decay

Here is an example of alpha decay:

$$^{222}_{88}\text{Ra} \rightarrow \ ^{218}_{86}\text{Rn} + \ ^{4}_{2}\text{He} + \text{energy}$$

radium atom $\rightarrow$ radon atom + alpha particle + energy

The radioactive isotope radium-222 decays to the element radon by the emission of an alpha particle. The alpha particle is sometimes represented by the Greek letter α. Radon is a radioactive gas that also decays by emitting an alpha particle. Note that the atomic number for radon, 86, is two *less* than the atomic number for radium.

The general form of the alpha decay equation is:

$$^{A}_{Z}\text{Y} \rightarrow \ ^{A-4}_{Z-2}\text{W} + \ ^{4}_{2}\text{He} + \text{energy}$$
$$\uparrow$$
alpha
particle, α

In alpha decay, element Y is transformed into element W by the emission of an alpha particle. Element W is two places before element Y in the periodic table. The alpha particle, a helium nucleus, carries away four nucleons, which reduces the mass number (A) by four. Two of these nucleons are protons so the atomic number of the new element is two less than the original element, $Z - 2$. Notice that the mass number and the atomic number are conserved through this equation – that

Reminder: A is the mass number of the element and Z is the atomic number. The letters W and Y are not the symbols of any particular elements as this is the *general equation*.

It is worth pointing out that the mass number refers to the number of nuclear particles, or nucleons, involved in the transformation – not the exact mass. Mass is *not* conserved in nuclear transformations, as some of it is transformed into energy.

is, the *total* numbers of nucleons and protons on each side of the equation are the same.

Beta (β) decay

Here is an example of beta decay:

$$^{14}_{6}\text{C} \quad \rightarrow \quad ^{14}_{7}\text{N} \quad + \quad ^{0}_{-1}\text{e} \quad + \text{ energy}$$

carbon atom $\rightarrow$ nitrogen atom + beta particle + energy

The radioactive isotope of carbon, carbon-14, decays to form the stable isotope of the gas nitrogen, by emitting a beta particle. Remember that the beta particle is formed when a neutron splits to form a proton and an electron. The beta particle is sometimes represented by the symbol β. Figure 23.8 shows the standard atomic notation for a beta particle (see page 200).

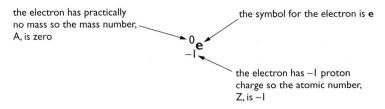

Figure 23.8 *A beta particle.*

The general form of the beta decay equation is:

$$^{A}_{Z}\text{X} \rightarrow ^{A}_{Z+1}\text{Y} + ^{0}_{-1}\text{e} + \textbf{energy}$$
$$\uparrow$$
beta particle, β⁻

In beta decay, element X is transformed into element Y by the emission of a beta particle. Element Y is the next element in the periodic table after element X. The beta particle, an electron, has practically no mass so the mass number, A, is the same in X and Y. As the beta particle has a charge of −1, the atomic number of the new element is increased to Z+1. Again the mass number and the atomic number are conserved through this equation.

Gamma (γ) decay

Gamma radiation is high-energy electromagnetic radiation (see page 100). After an unstable nucleus has emitted an alpha or beta particle it sometimes has surplus energy. It emits this energy as gamma radiation. Gamma rays are pure energy, so they do not have any mass or charge. When a nucleus emits a gamma ray there is no change to either the atomic number or the mass number of the nucleus.

Example 1

An isotope of caesium $^{137}_{55}$Cs decays by emitting a beta particle and forms an atom of barium (Ba). Write a balanced nuclear equation for this transformation.

Write down what you know:

$$^{137}_{55}\text{Cs} \rightarrow\, ^{?}_{?}\text{Ba} +\, ^{0}_{-1}\text{e} + \text{energy}$$

An electron has practically no mass so the mass number does not change. The emission of an electron happens when a neutron becomes a proton and an electron, so the atomic number increases by one. The barium isotope formed is therefore $^{137}_{56}$Ba and the completed equation is:

$$^{137}_{55}\text{Cs} \rightarrow\, ^{137}_{56}\text{Ba} +\, ^{0}_{-1}\text{e} + \text{energy}$$

Example 2

Uranium-234 has an atomic number of 92 and a mass number of 234. Write a balanced nuclear equation for the decay of uranium to thorium (Th) by the emission of an alpha particle.

Write down what you know:

$$^{234}_{92}\text{U} \rightarrow\, ^{?}_{?}\text{Th} +\, ^{4}_{2}\text{He} + \text{energy}$$

The alpha particle has a mass number of 4, so the mass number of the uranium atom must have decreased by 4 to form thorium. Similarly, the atomic number must have gone down by 2. This gives us:

$$^{234}_{92}\text{U} \rightarrow\, ^{230}_{90}\text{Th} +\, ^{4}_{2}\text{He} + \text{energy}$$

End of Chapter Checklist

You will need to be able to do the following:

✓ compare the mass and charge of electrons, protons and neutrons

✓ understand the terms atomic number and mass number and be able to use and interpret notation for a nucleus using these numbers

✓ recall that the same element may exist in the form of several different isotopes

✓ appreciate that some isotopes are unstable because of the proportion of protons to neutrons in their nuclei and that the way they decay depends on this

✓ recall that radioactive nuclei may emit three different types of ionising radiation – alpha, beta and gamma

✓ describe the different properties of alpha, beta and gamma radiation considering ionising and penetrating power

✓ balance nuclear transformation equations with respect to mass number and atomic number

✓ understand that alpha and beta decay result in a nucleus of one element transforming into another.

Questions

More questions on the structure of the atom can be found at the end of Section G on page 232.

1 Copy and complete the table below showing the relative charge and mass of each of the particles that make up atoms.

Atomic particle	Relative mass of particle	Relative charge of particle
	1	–1
		+1
	2000	0

2 Identify the following atomic particles from their descriptions:

a) an uncharged nucleon

b) the particle with the least mass

c) the particle with the same mass as a neutron

d) the particle with the same amount of charge as an electron

e) a particle that is negatively charged.

3 Explain the following statements about the atom.

a) An atom is mainly made up of empty space.

b) Almost all the mass of an atom is in the nucleus.

c) Atoms are electrically neutral.

4 Explain the following terms used to describe the structure of an atom:

a) atomic number

b) mass number.

5 Copy and complete the table below, describing the structures of the different atoms in terms of numbers of protons, neutrons and electrons.

	^3_2He	$^{13}_6C$	$^{23}_{11}Na$
protons			
neutrons			
electrons			

6 Copy and complete the following sentences:

a) An alpha particle consists of four _____ . Two of these are _____ and two are _____ . An alpha particle carries a charge of _____ .

b) A beta particle is a fast-moving _____ that is emitted from the nucleus. It is created when a _____ in the nucleus decays to form a _____ and the beta particle.

c) The third type of ionising radiation has no mass. It is called _____ radiation. This type of radiation is a type of wave with a very _____ wavelength.

d) Gamma radiation is part of the _____ spectrum.

7 *a)* The nuclear equation below shows the decay of thorium. Copy and complete the equation by providing the missing numbers and letters.

$$^{234}_{90}\text{Th} \longrightarrow \boxed{}\ ^{}_{}\text{Pa} + ^{0}_{-1}\text{e}$$

b) What type of decay is taking place in this transformation?

c) The nuclear equation below shows the decay of polonium. Copy and complete the equation by providing the missing numbers and letters.

$$^{216}_{\boxed{}}\text{Po} \longrightarrow ^{}_{82}\text{Pb} + ^{4}_{2}\boxed{}$$

d) What type of decay is taking place in this transformation?

Chapter 24: Radiation and Half-life

In this chapter you will learn about ways of detecting radiation, and where some of the radiation around us comes from. You will also learn why we use a value called half-life to describe the activity of radioactive isotopes.

Detecting ionising radiation

Using photographic film

Henri Becquerel (Figure 24.1) was studying X-rays using uranium ore in 1896. He believed that the uranium emitted X-rays after being exposed to sunlight. To test this idea he placed some wrapped, unused photographic plates in a drawer with some samples of the uranium ore on top of them. He found a strong image of the ore on the plates when he developed them. He had discovered radioactivity.

The unit of radioactivity is named after Becquerel. The **becquerel** (Bq) is a measure of how many unstable nuclei are disintegrating per second – one becquerel means a rate of one disintegration per second. The becquerel is a very small unit. More practical units are the kBq (an average of 1000 disintegrations per second) and the MBq (an average of 1 000 000 disintegrations per second).

Photographic film is still used to detect radioactivity. Scientists who work with radioactive materials wear a strip of photographic film in a badge. If the film becomes fogged it shows that the scientist has been exposed to a certain amount of radiation. These badges are checked regularly to ensure that the safety limit for exposure to ionising radiation is not exceeded.

The Geiger–Müller tube

Figure 24.2 shows the basic construction of a Geiger–Müller (GM) tube. It is a glass tube with an electrically conducting coating on the inside surface. The tube has a thin window made of mica (a naturally occurring mineral that can be split into thin sheets). The tube contains a special mixture of gases at very low pressure. In the middle of the tube, electrically insulated from the conducting coating, there is an electrode. This electrode is connected, via a high value resistor, to a high-voltage supply, typically 300–500 V.

Figure 24.1 *Henri Becquerel (1852–1908) studied X-rays.*

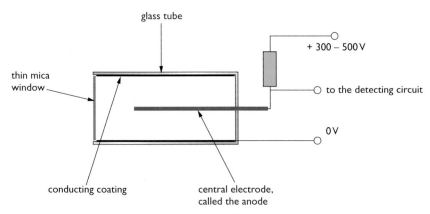

Figure 24.2 *A Geiger–Müller tube is used to measure the level of radiation.*

When ionising radiation enters the tube it causes the low pressure gas inside to form ions. The ions allow a pulse of current to flow from the electrode to the conducting layer. This is detected by an electronic circuit.

The GM tube is usually linked up to a counting circuit. This keeps a count of how many ionising particles (or how much γ radiation) have entered the GM tube. Sometimes GM tubes are connected to rate meters. These measure the number of ionising events per second, and so give a measure of the radioactivity in becquerels. Rate meters usually have a loudspeaker output so the level of radioactivity is indicated by the rate of clicks produced.

Background radiation

Background radiation is low-level ionising radiation that is produced all the time. This background radiation has a number of sources. Some of these are natural and some are artificial.

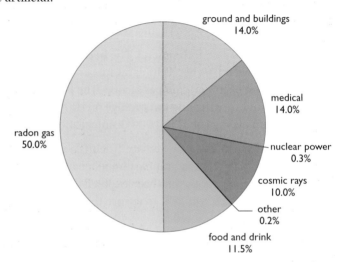

Figure 24.3 *Sources of background radiation in the UK.*

Natural background radiation from the Earth

Some of the radiation we receive comes from rocks in the Earth's crust. When the Earth was formed, around 4.5 billion years ago, it contained many radioactive isotopes. Some decayed very quickly but others are still producing radiation. Some of the **decay products** of these long-lived radioactive materials are also radioactive, so there are radioactive isotopes with much shorter half-lives (see page 212) still present in the Earth's crust.

One form of uranium is a radioactive element that decays very slowly. Two of its decay products are gases. These are the radioactive gases **radon** and **thoron**. Radon-222 is a highly radioactive gas produced by the decay of radium-226. Thoron, or radium-220, is an isotope of radium formed by the decay of a radioactive isotope of thorium (thorium-232).

As these decay products are gases, they seep out of radioactive rocks. They are dense gases so they build up in the basements and foundations of buildings. Some parts of the Earth's crust have higher amounts of radioactive material so the amount of background radiation produced in this way varies from place to place. In Cornwall in the UK, for example, where the granite rock contains traces of

When an atom of a radioactive element decays it gives out radiation and changes to an atom of another element. This may also be radioactive, and decay to form an atom of yet another element. The elements formed as a result of a radioactive element undergoing a series of decays are called decay products.

uranium, the risk of exposure to radiation from radon gas is greater than in some other parts of the UK.

Natural background radiation from space

Violent nuclear reactions in stars and exploding stars called **supernovae** produce very energetic particles and **cosmic rays** that continuously bombard the Earth. Lower energy cosmic rays are given out by the Sun. Our atmosphere gives us fairly good protection from cosmic rays.

Internal radiation

The atoms that make up our bodies were formed in the violent reactions that took place in stars created at the beginning of the Universe. Some of these atoms are radioactive so we carry our own personal source of radiation around with us. Also, as we breathe we take in tiny amounts of the radioactive isotope of carbon, carbon-14. Because carbon-14 behaves chemically just like the stable isotope, carbon-12, we continuously renew the amount of the radioactive carbon in our bodies (see page 219).

Artificial radiation

We use radioactive materials for many purposes. Generating electricity in nuclear power stations has been responsible for the leaking of radioactive material into the environment. The levels are usually small, but there have been a number of major incidents around the world, notably at Three Mile Island in the USA in 1979 and at Chernobyl in the Ukraine in 1986. Testing nuclear weapons in the atmosphere has also increased the amounts of radioactive isotopes on the Earth.

Radioactive tracers are used in industry and medicine. Radioactive materials are also used to treat certain forms of cancer. However the majority of background radiation is natural – the amount produced from medical and civil use in industry is very small indeed.

Radioactive decay

Radioactive decay is a random process, just like tossing a coin. If we toss a coin we cannot say with certainty whether it will come down heads or tails. If we toss a thousand coins we cannot predict which will land heads and which will land tails. The same is true for radioactive nuclei. It is impossible to tell which nuclei will disintegrate at any particular time. However, if we tossed a thousand coins we would be surprised if the number that landed as heads was not around 500. We know that a fair coin has an equal chance of landing as a head or a tail, so if we got 600 heads we would think it was unusual. If the proportion of heads were much greater than this we would be right to think that the coin was not fair.

Experimental demonstration of nuclear decay

We could, if we had the time, take 1000 coins and toss them. We could then remove all the coins that came down heads, note the number of coins remaining and then repeat the process. If we did this for, say, six trials we would begin to see the trend. A set of typical results is shown in the following table and in Figure 24.4.

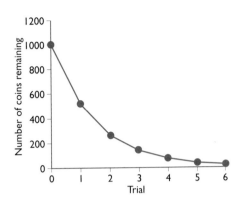

Figure 24.4 *Coin-tossing experiment. Each time the coins are tossed about 50% of them land as "heads" and are removed from the pile. The graph decreases steeply at first but then does so more and more slowly.*

The coin-tossing experiment is a **model** of radioactive decay. A good model will show the features of the real process. We must remember that models have limitations, however, and do not perfectly represent the actual process. One limitation of the experiment is that of scale. In just 1 g of uranium-235 there are millions of nuclei, and our model uses just 1000 coins. The model would be better if we used, say, 1 000 000 coins, but would take too long to perform. If we use a computer model to toss the coins we *could* deal with more realistic numbers.

Trial	Number of coins remaining
0	1000
1	519
2	264
3	140
4	72
5	33
6	19

Notice that the graph in Figure 24.4 falls steeply at first and more slowly after each toss. How quickly the graph falls depends on how many heads occur each toss. But as the number of coins decreases, the number of coins that come up heads also gets smaller. This graph follows a rule: the smaller the quantity, the more slowly the quantity decreases. The quantity here is the number of coins still in the experiment. The name for this kind of decrease proportional to size is called **exponential decay**.

If we have a sample of a radioactive material, it will contain millions of atoms. The process of decay is random, so we don't know when an atom will decay but there will be a probability that a certain fraction of them will disintegrate in a particular time. This is the same as in the coin toss – there was a 50% probability that the coins would land heads each time we conducted a trial. Once an unstable nucleus has disintegrated, it is out of the game – it won't be around to disintegrate during the next period of time. If we plot a graph of number of disintegrations per second against time for a radioactive isotope we would, therefore, expect the rate of decay to fall as time passes because there are fewer nuclei to decay.

Half-life

Our coin-tossing model of radioactive decay shows a graph that approaches the horizontal axis more and more slowly as time passes. The model will produce a number of throws after which all the coins have been taken out of the game. The number is likely to vary from trial to trial because the model becomes less and less reliable as the number of coins becomes smaller. With real radioactive decay we use a measure of activity called the **half-life**. This is defined as follows.

> The half-life of a radioactive sample is the average time taken for half the original mass of the sample to decay. The half-life is different for different radioactive isotopes.

Figure 24.5 shows what this means. After one half-life period, $t_{\frac{1}{2}}$, the amount of the original unstable element has halved. After a second period of time, $t_{\frac{1}{2}}$, the amount has halved again, and so on.

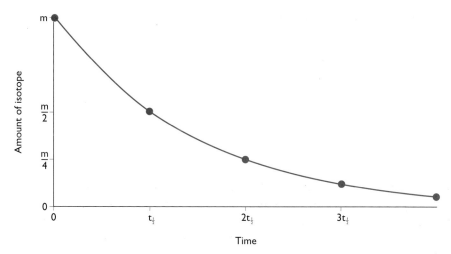

Figure 24.5 *Graph showing the half-life period for a radioactive isotope.*

Measuring the half-life of a radioactive isotope

To measure the half-life of a radioactive material (radioisotope) we must measure the activity of the sample at regular times. This is done using a Geiger–Müller (GM) tube linked to a rate meter. Before taking measurements from the sample, we must measure the local background radiation. We must subtract the background radiation measurement from measurements taken from the sample so we know the radiation produced by the sample itself. We then measure the rate of decay of the sample at regular time intervals. The rate of decay is shown by the count rate on the rate meter. The results should be recorded in a table like the one shown below.

Average background radiation measure over 5 min = x Bq

Time, t (min)	Count rate (Bq)	Corrected count rate, C (Bq)
0	y_0	$y_0 - x$
5	y_5	$y_5 - x$

The rate of decay, C, corrected for background radiation, is proportional to the amount of radioactive isotope present. If we plot a graph of C against time, t, we can measure the half-life from the graph, as shown in Figure 24.6.

As we have already mentioned, different isotopes have widely differing half-lives. Some examples of different half-lives are shown in the table below.

Isotope	Half-life	Decay process
uranium-238	4.5 billion years	α particle emission
radium-226	1590 years	α particle emission, γ ray emission
radon-222	3.825 days	α particle emission
polonium-218	3.05 minutes	α particle emission

Isotopes with short half-lives are suited to medical use (see page 216). This is because the activity of a source will rapidly become very small as the isotope decays quickly.

Isotopes used for dating samples of organic material need to have very long half-lives. This is because the activity will become difficult to measure accurately if it

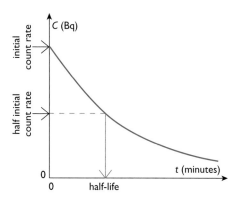

Figure 24.6 *You can find the half-life by reading from the graph the time taken for the count rate to halve.*

drops below a certain level. In Chapter 25, we shall see that there are suitable isotopes for these different applications.

Half-life calculations

Graphs of activity, in becquerels, against time can be used to find the half-life of an isotope, and this half-life information can be used to make predictions of the activity of the radioisotope at a later time.

Worked example

Example 1

The activity of a sample of a certain isotope is found to be 200 Bq.

a) If the isotope has a half-life of 20 minutes, what will the activity of the sample be after one hour?

After 20 minutes the activity will have halved to 100 Bq.

After 40 minutes (two half-lives) it will have halved again to 50 Bq.

After 60 minutes it will have halved again, so the activity will be 25 Bq.

b) What is the level of activity of this sample after three hours?

Three hours = 9 × 20 minutes – that is, nine half-life periods. This means the activity will have halved nine times. The level of activity (and the amount of the radioisotope remaining) will be:

$$\frac{1}{2} \times \frac{1}{2} \times \frac{1}{2} \times \frac{1}{2} \times \frac{1}{2} \times \frac{1}{2} \times \frac{1}{2} \times \frac{1}{2} \times \frac{1}{2}$$

or $\frac{1}{2^9}$ of the original value, and so $\frac{1}{512}$ of the original activity or amount.

You will need to be able to do the following:

✓ recall that the becquerel is a measure of the rate of nuclear decay

✓ describe different methods of detecting ionising radiation

✓ be aware of background radiation and describe its different sources

✓ understand that radioactive decay is a random process

✓ model radioactive decay processes and understand the limitations of such models

✓ understand and be able to measure the half-life of a radioisotope

✓ carry out calculations involving half-life.

Questions

More questions on radioactive decay can be found at the end of Section G on page 232.

1 a) Explain what is meant by background radiation.

  b) Explain the difference between natural background radiation and artificial background radiation.

  c) Give three different sources of background radiation. Say whether your examples are natural or artificial sources.

2 a) Explain, simply, the principle of the Geiger–Müller tube.

  b) The Geiger–Müller tube is often connected to a rate meter. Explain what this instrument measures.

  c) The rate meter is calibrated in kBq. How is this unit defined?

3 A certain radioactive source emits different types of radiation. The sample is tested using a Geiger counter. When a piece of card is placed between the source and the counter, there is a noticeable drop in the radiation. When a thin sheet of aluminium is added to the card between the source and the counter, the count rate is unchanged. A thick block of lead, however, causes the count to fall to the background level.

What type (or types) of ionising radiation is the source emitting? Explain your answer carefully.

4 a) Define what is meant by the half-life of a radioactive material.

  b) Radioactive decay is a random process. Explain what this means.

5 The activity of a radioactive sample is measured. The activity, corrected for background radiation, is found to be 240 Bq. The activity is measured again after 1 hour 30 minutes and is now 30 Bq. What is the half-life of the sample?

6 In another model of radioactive decay, a student fills a burette with water, as shown in the diagram, and starts a timer at the instant the valve at the bottom is opened. She notes the height of the column of water at regular intervals. It takes 35 seconds to empty from 50 ml to 25 ml. Assuming that the arrangement provides a good model of radioactive decay:

  a) How long will it take for three quarters of the water in the burette to drain away?

  b) How much water should remain in the burette after $1\frac{3}{4}$ minutes?

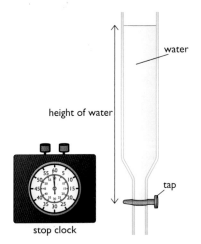

7 A student wants to measure the half-life of a radioactive isotope. He is told the isotope has a half-life of between 10 and 20 minutes. Illustrating your answers as appropriate, describe:

  a) the measurements that he should take

  b) how he should use the measurements to arrive at an estimate of the half-life for the isotope.

Chapter 25: Applications of Radioactivity

Radioactivity can be used in a wide variety of useful applications, including medicine, industry, power generation and archaeology. In this chapter, you will read about these applications and also learn about the hazards associated with the use of radioactivity.

The use of radioactivity in medicine

Using tracers in diagnosis

Radioactive isotopes are used as **tracers** to help doctors identify diseased organs. A radioactive tracer is a chemical compound that emits gamma radiation. The tracer is taken orally by the patient (swallowed) or injected. Its passage around the body can then be traced using a gamma ray camera.

Different compounds are chosen for different diagnostic tasks. For example, the isotope iodine-123 is absorbed by the thyroid gland in the same way as the stable form of iodine. The isotope decays and emits gamma radiation. A gamma ray camera can then be used to form a clear image of the thyroid gland.

The half-life of iodine-123 is about 13 hours. A short half-life is important as this means that the activity of the tracer decreases to a very low level in a few days.

Other isotopes are used to image specific parts of the body. Technetium-99 is the most widely used isotope in medical imaging. It is used to help identify medical problems that affect many parts of the body. Figure 25.1 shows a scan of a patient's kidneys. It shows clearly that one of the kidneys is not working properly.

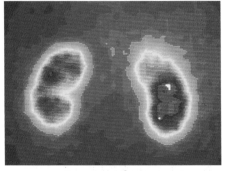

Figure 25.1 *This scan shows the kidneys in a patient's body.*

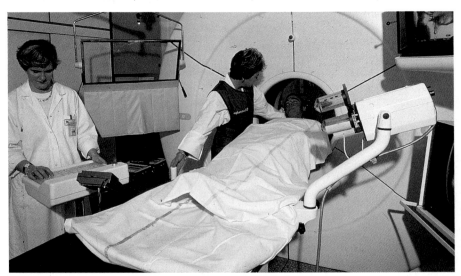

Figure 25.2 *Scanner used to provide 3D images of a patient's body.*

Imaging techniques enable doctors to produce three-dimensional computer images of parts of a patient's body. These are of great value in diagnosis. Figure 25.2 shows the kind of equipment used for three-dimensional (3D) imaging.

Treatment

Radiation from isotopes can have various effects on the cells that make up our bodies. Low doses of radiation may have no lasting effect. Higher doses may cause the normal function of cells to be changed. This can lead to abnormal growth and cancer. Very high doses will kill living cells.

Cancer can be treated by surgery that involves cutting out cancerous cells. Another way of treating cancer is to kill the cancer cells inside the body. This can be done with chemicals containing radioactive isotopes. Unfortunately, the radiation kills healthy cells as well as diseased ones. To reduce the damage to healthy tissue, chemicals are used to target the location of the cancer in the body. They may emit either alpha or beta radiation. Both these types of radiation have a short range in the body, so they will affect only a small volume of tissue close to the target.

The radioisotope iodine-131 is used in the treatment of various diseases of the thyroid gland. It has a half-life of about eight days and decays by beta particle emission.

Sterilisation using radiation

Ionising radiation can kill living cells. It is therefore used to kill micro-organisms on surgical instruments and other medical equipment. The technique is called **irradiation**. The items to be sterilised are placed close to strongly ionising radiation sources. The items can be packaged in airtight bags to ensure that they cannot be re-contaminated before use. The radiation will penetrate the packaging and destroy bacteria without damaging the item.

Some food products are treated in a similar way to make sure that they are free from any bacteria that will cause the food to rot or will cause food poisoning. The irradiation of food is an issue that causes concern amongst the public and is not a widely used procedure at the present time.

Irradiation will not destroy any poisons that bacteria may have already produced in the food before it is treated.
Irradiation does not destroy vitamins in the food like other means of killing bacteria, such as high-temperature treatment.

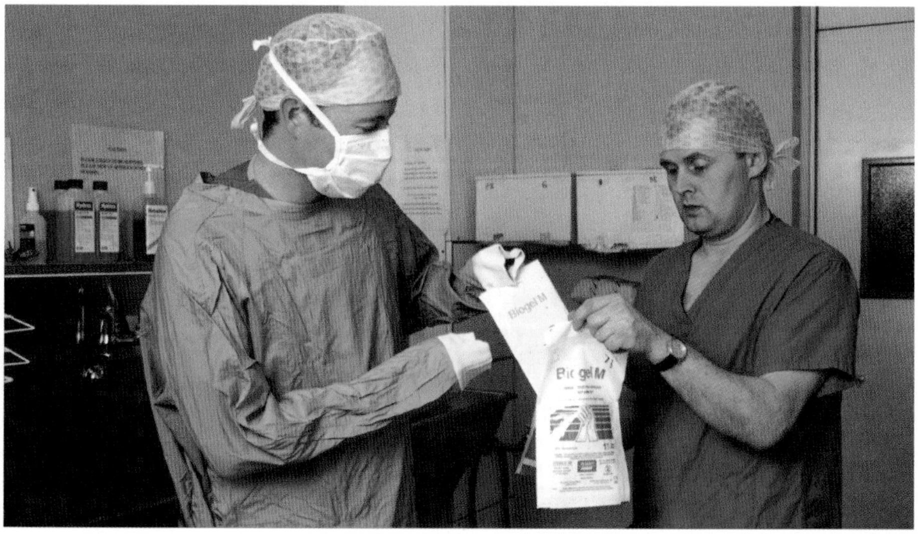

Figure 25.3 *Gamma radiation is used to sterilise medical equipment.*

The use of radioactivity in industry

Gamma radiography

A gamma ray camera is like the X-ray cameras used to examine the contents of your luggage at airports. A source of gamma radiation is placed on one side of the object to be scanned and a gamma camera is placed on the other. Gamma rays are more penetrating than X-rays. They can be used to check for imperfections in welded joints and for flaws in metal castings. Without this technique of gamma radiography, neither problem could be detected unless the welding or casting were cut through. An additional advantage of **gamma radiography** over the use of X-rays for this purpose is that gamma sources can be small and do not require a power source or large cumbersome equipment.

Gauging

In industrial processes, raw materials and fuel are stored in large tanks or hoppers. Figure 25.5 shows how radioactive isotopes are used to **gauge**, or measure, how much material there is in a storage vessel.

Figure 25.4 *A gamma camera image used to view inside a valve.*

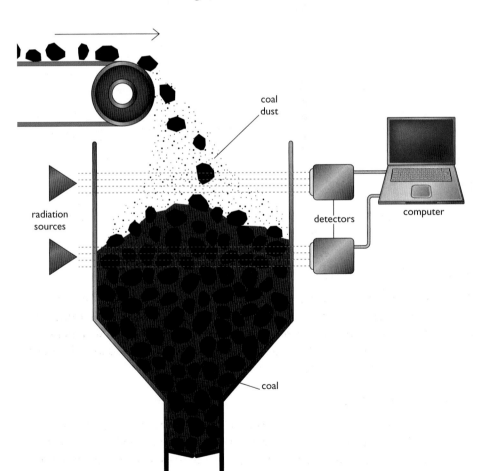

Figure 25.5 *The amount of coal in the hopper can be measured using gamma radiation.*

In Figure 25.5, the coal absorbs a large amount of the radiation so the reading on the lower detector will be small. As the upper part of the hopper is empty the upper detector will have a high reading.

This method of gauging has several advantages over other methods. There is no contact with the material being gauged. Also, coal dust might cause false readings with an optical gauging system (one using light beams). Coal dust is much less dense than coal so the gamma ray system still works properly.

Another example of gauging uses a similar process to monitor the thickness of plastic sheeting and film. The thicker the sheet, the greater the amount of radiation it absorbs. By monitoring the amount of radiation, the thickness of the sheeting can be closely controlled during manufacture.

Tracing and measuring the flow of liquids and gases

Radioisotopes are used to track the flow of liquids in industrial processes. Very tiny amounts of radiation can easily be detected. Complex piping systems, like heat exchangers in power stations, can be monitored for leaks. Radioactive tracers are even used to measure the rate of dispersal of sewage (Figure 25.6)!

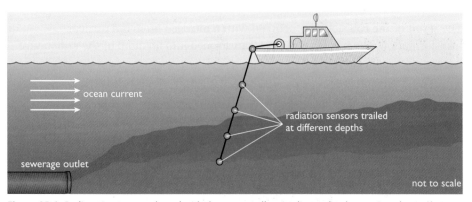

ocean current

radiation sensors trailed at different depths

sewerage outlet

not to scale

Figure 25.6 *Radioactive tracers released with the sewage allow its dispersal to be monitored to make sure the concentration does not reach harmful levels in any area.*

Radioactive dating

A variety of different methods involving radioisotopes are used to date minerals and organic matter. The most widely known method is **radiocarbon dating**. This is used to find the age of organic matter – for example, from trees and animals – that was once living. We shall also look at techniques that are used to find the age of inorganic material like rocks and minerals.

Radiocarbon dating

Radiocarbon dating measures the level of an isotope called carbon-14 (C-14). This is made in the atmosphere. Cosmic rays from space are continually raining down upon the Earth. These have a lot of energy. When they strike atoms of gas in the upper layers of the atmosphere, the nuclei of the atoms break apart. The parts fly off at high speed. If they strike other atoms they can cause nuclear transformations to take place. These transformations turn the elements in the air into different isotopes. One such collision involves a fast-moving neutron striking an atom of

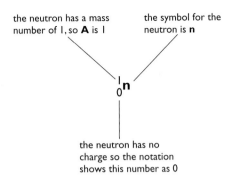

Figure 25.7 *The neutron.*

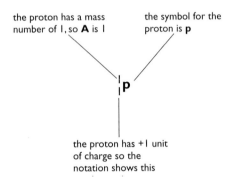

Figure 25.8 *The proton.*

nitrogen. (Nitrogen forms nearly 80% of our atmosphere.) The nuclear equation for this process is:

$$^{14}_{7}\text{N} + {}^{1}_{0}\text{n} \rightarrow {}^{14}_{6}\text{C} + {}^{1}_{1}\text{p}$$

Notice that, as in the other nuclear equations we have seen, the top numbers – which show the number of nucleons – add up to the same total on each side of the equation. This is because the mass number is conserved. The bottom numbers – which show the amount of charge on the particles – are also conserved.

In this equation, the neutron is represented by:

$${}^{1}_{0}\text{n}$$

Its notation is explained in Figure 25.7.

The proton formed as a result of the collision is represented by:

$${}^{1}_{1}\text{p}$$

The notation for this is explained in Figure 25.8.

The result of the collision of a neutron with a nitrogen atom is a nuclear transformation. The nitrogen atom is transformed into an atom of the radioactive isotope of carbon, carbon-14.

As we have already mentioned, isotopes of an element have the same chemical behaviour. This means that the carbon-14 atoms react with oxygen in our atmosphere to form carbon dioxide, just like the much more common and stable isotope, carbon-12. The carbon dioxide is then absorbed by plants in the process of photosynthesis. As a result, a proportion of the carbon that makes up any plant will be the radioactive form, carbon-14. Incorporated in plant material, the radioactive isotope carbon-14 enters the food chain, which means that animals and humans will also have a proportion of carbon-14 in their bodies. These carbon-14 atoms will decay but, in living plants and animals, they are continuously replaced by new ones.

When a living organism dies, the replacement process stops. As time passes, the radioactive carbon decays and the proportion of radioactive carbon in the remains of the plant or animal, compared with the stable carbon isotope, decreases.

The half-life for the decay of carbon-14 is approximately 5600 years. This means that every 5600 years the proportion of carbon-14 in dead plant and animal material will halve. The amount of carbon-14 present in a sample of dead plant or animal material is found by measuring the activity of the sample. This is compared with the amount of carbon-14 that would have been present when the sample was part of a living organism. From this, it is possible to estimate when the source of the sample died.

Example 1

120 g of living wood has a radioactive activity (corrected for background radiation) of 24 Bq. A 120 g sample of wood from an archaeological site is found to have an activity of 6 Bq. If the half-life of carbon-14 is 5600 years, estimate the age of the wood from the site.

$$6\,\text{Bq} = 24\,\text{Bq} \times \frac{1}{2} \times \frac{1}{2}$$

Since the activity of the sample has halved twice from that expected in living wood, two half-lives must have passed.

The age of the sample is therefore around 2×5600 years = 11 200 years.

There are limitations to the method of radiocarbon dating. It assumes the level of cosmic radiation reaching the Earth is constant, which is not necessarily an accurate assumption. Fortunately, the technique has been calibrated to take the variations of cosmic ray activity into account. This is done by testing samples of a known age, like material from the mummies of Egyptian Pharaohs and from very ancient living trees.

The radiocarbon method is not used to date samples older than 50 000–60 000 years because, after 10 half-lives, the amount of carbon-14 remaining in samples is too small to measure accurately.

Dating rocks

Inorganic, non-living matter does not absorb carbon-14, so different techniques must be used for finding out the age of rocks and minerals.

When a radioactive substance decays it transforms into a different isotope, sometimes of the same element, sometimes of a different element. The original radioisotope is called the **parent** nuclide (unstable nucleus) and the product is called the **daughter** nuclide. Many of the products of decay, the daughter isotopes, are also unstable and these too decay, in turn. This means that as the parent isotope decays it breeds a whole family of elements in what is called a **decay series**. The end of the decay series is a **stable** isotope – one that does not decay further.

The table shows some radioactive parent isotopes with the stable daughters formed at the end of their particular decay series. The half-life quoted is the time for half the original number of parent nuclei to decay to the stable daughter element.

Radioactive parent isotope	Stable daughter element	Half-life (years)
potassium-40	argon-40	1.25 billion
thorium-232	lead-208	14 billion
uranium-235	lead-207	704 billion
uranium-238	lead-206	4.47 billion
carbon-14	nitrogen-14	5568

For rocks containing such radioactive isotopes, the proportion of parent to stable daughter nuclide gives a measure of the age of the rock. Notice that the half-lives of most of the radioactive parent isotopes are extremely long, in some cases greater than the lifetime of the Earth.

The decay series of potassium-40 ends with argon gas. As potassium-40 decays in igneous rock, the argon produced remains trapped in the rock. Igneous rocks are formed when molten rock becomes solid. Igneous rocks are non-porous. The proportion of argon to potassium-40 again gives a measure of the age of the rock.

The health hazards of ionising radiation

Ionising radiation can damage the molecules that make up the cells of living tissue. Cells suffer this kind of damage all the time for many different reasons. Fortunately, cells can repair or replace themselves given time so, usually, no permanent damage results. However, if cells suffer repeated damage because of ionising radiation, the cell may be killed. Alternatively the cell may start to behave in an unexpected way because it has been damaged. We call this effect cell **mutation**. Some types of cancer happen because damaged cells start to divide uncontrollably.

Different types of ionising radiation present different risks. Alpha particles have the greatest ionising effect, but they have little penetrating power. This means that an alpha source presents little risk, as alpha particles do not penetrate the skin. The problem of alpha radiation is much greater if the source of alpha particles is taken into the body. Here the radiation will be very close to many different types of cells and they may be damaged if the exposure is prolonged. Alpha emitters can be breathed in or taken in through eating food. Radon gas is a decay product of radium and is an alpha emitter. It therefore presents a real risk to health. Smokers greatly increase their exposure to this kind of damage as they draw the radiation source right into their lungs (cigarette smoke contains radon).

Beta and gamma radiation do provide a serious health risk when outside the body. Both can penetrate skin and flesh and can cause cell damage by ionisation. Gamma radiation, as we have mentioned earlier, is the most penetrating. The damage caused by gamma rays will depend on how much of their energy is absorbed by ionising atoms along their path. Beta and gamma emitters that are absorbed by the body present less risk than alpha emitters, because of their lower ionising power.

In all cases, the longer the period of exposure to radiation the greater the risk of serious cell damage. Workers in the nuclear industry wear badges to indicate their level of exposure. Some are strips of photographic film that become increasingly "foggy" as the radiation exposure increases. Another type of badge uses a property called **thermoluminescence**. Thermoluminescence means that the exposed material will give out light when it is warmed. The radiation releases energy to make heat so the thermoluminescent badges give out more light when exposed to higher levels of radiation. Workers have their badges checked regularly and this gives a measure of their overall exposure to radiation.

Safe handling of radioactive materials

Samples of radioactive isotopes used in schools and colleges are very small. This is to limit the risk to users, particularly those who use them regularly – the teachers! Although the risk is small, certain precautions must be followed. The samples are stored in lead containers to block even the most penetrating form of radiation, gamma rays. The containers are clearly labelled as a radiation hazard and must be stored in a locked metal cabinet. The samples are handled using tongs and are kept as far from the body as possible.

Figure 25.9 *Radioactive samples are stored in lead-lined containers and are handled with tongs.*

In the nuclear industry and research laboratories, much larger amounts of radioactive material are used. These have to be handled with great care. Very energetic sources will be handled remotely by operators who are shielded by lead, concrete and thick glass viewing panels.

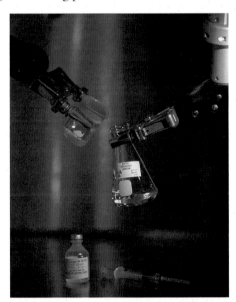

Figure 25.10 *Industrial sources of radioactivity must be handed with a lot of care.*

The major problem with nuclear materials is long-term storage. Some materials have extremely long half-lives so they remain active for thousands and sometimes tens of thousands of years. Nuclear waste must be stored in sealed containers that must be capable of containing the radioactivity for enormously long periods of time.

End of Chapter Checklist

You will need to be able to do the following:

✓ be aware of the various medical applications of radioactive isotopes

✓ recall that some isotopes are used in diagnosis, either by imaging particular parts of the body or by showing whether an organ is working properly by the rate at which it processes particular chemicals

✓ recall that some isotopes are used to destroy diseased cells in the treatment of illness

✓ be aware of the industrial uses of radioactive isotopes in tracing the movement of liquids and gases, identifying leaks and gauging

✓ understand the principles of dating organic materials and minerals using radioisotopes

✓ recall the health hazards presented by different types of radiation from radioisotopes and understand the need to monitor exposure

✓ appreciate the need for appropriate handling techniques and methods of disposal.

Questions

More questions on applications of radioactivity can be found at the end of Section G on page 232.

1 The most widely used isotope in medicine is technetium-99. It has a half-life of six hours and decays by the emission of low-energy gamma rays and beta particles.

a) Explain why the characteristics of technetium-99 make it suitable for diagnostic use in medicine.

b) Technetium-99 can be chemically attached to a wide variety of pharmaceutical products so that it can be targeted at particular tissues or organs. How can its progress through the body be measured and monitored?

2 Technetium-99 is produced from molybdenum-99 in a device called a technetium generator. Which decay process – α, β or γ – could cause molybdenum-99 to decay to technetium-99? Explain your answer. (Hint: Look at Chapter 23.)

3 A radioactive isotope of iodine is used in both the diagnosis and treatment of a condition of the thyroid gland. This gland naturally takes up ordinary iodine as part of its function. If a patient has an overactive thyroid it concentrates too much iodine in the gland and this has serious effects on the patient's health.

How might the radioisotope iodine-131 be used to:

a) identify an overactive thyroid gland

b) treat the overactive thyroid?

(Iodine-131 has a half-life of eight days and is a high-energy beta emitter.)

4 Explain the advantages of using ionising radiation for sterilising surgical equipment.

5 Paper is made in a variety of different "weights", with different thicknesses. How could ionising radiation be used to check the thickness of paper during production? You should consider the following:

● the type of radiation to be used

● how it will be used to measure the paper thickness

● what checks should be made to ensure that the measurements are accurate

● safety procedures.

6 Radiocarbon dating is used to estimate the age of organic (once-living) materials. It uses a radioisotope of carbon, carbon-14 (C-14).

a) How is carbon-14 formed?

b) Why does all living matter contain a proportion of C-14?

c) What happens to the proportion of C-14 in an organism once it has died?

d) What assumptions are made in the process of radiocarbon dating?

e) Why is this method unsuitable for accurately dating material that is more than 50 000 years old?

7 Most radioactive isotopes of elements have half-lives that are extremely short compared to the age of the Earth. The Earth is about 4.5 billion years old. Radium has a half-life of only about 1600 years.

a) How many half-lives of radium have there been since the Earth formed?

Student A says all the radium formed when the Earth condensed out of the Sun's atmosphere should have decayed away to an unmeasurably small amount by now.

Student B says that it depends on how much there was to start with.

Student C says that there is still a significant amount of radium on the Earth.

b) Discuss these statements. Who do you think is right?

c) What other information would you need to make a better decision?

8 An isotope that decays by alpha emission is relatively safe when outside the body but very dangerous if absorbed by the body, either through breathing or eating.

a) Explain why this is so.

b) Why is radon-220 a particularly dangerous isotope?

Chapter 26: Particles

Scientists have speculated about the nature of the atom for thousands of years, but it is only relatively recently that our current ideas were developed. In this chapter you will read about how our ideas about the structure of the atom have developed over the centuries and how we use nuclear energy to produce electricity.

Dalton's model

About 2500 years ago, a Greek philosopher called Democritus suggested the idea that matter is made up of tiny, indivisible particles. The name for these particles – **atoms** – comes from a Greek word meaning "cannot be cut or divided".

John Dalton (Figure 26.1) was a scientist who studied gases in the early part of the nineteenth century. He thought that Demokritos was right – that all matter is made up of atoms. He imagined these atoms to be tiny, hard spheres.

Dalton said that some substances were made up of identical atoms – these substances are called **elements**. An important discovery was that atoms of an element always had the same mass – different elements had atoms with different masses. Each different element has its own type of atom. Today we know of the existence of more than 110 different elements. About 90 of these occur naturally on the Earth.

Figure 26.1 *John Dalton (1766–1844) was a meteorologist who studied the properties of gases. He proposed his atomic theory in 1803. Though some of his ideas have since been discarded, his work marked the start of the development of modern atomic theory.*

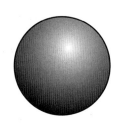

Figure 26.2 *Dalton's model of the atom as a solid sphere.*

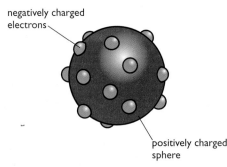

negatively charged electrons

positively charged sphere

Figure 26.3 *J. J. Thompson (1865–1940) thought that atoms were positively charged spheres with negatively charged electrons embedded in them.*

The plum pudding model

In 1897, J. J. Thomson discovered the electron while studying the properties of cathode rays. He found that the atom itself was made up of smaller particles that we now call sub-atomic particles. The electron was the first sub-atomic particle to be discovered. Thomson showed that it was a negatively charged particle of very light weight.

He thought that the atom was a ball of positive charge with electrons dotted through it, rather like currants in a bun or plums in a pudding. For this reason, Thomson's idea is called the plum pudding model of the atom.

J. J. Thomson (1856–1940), speaking of the electron in 1934 when he was 78 years old, said, "its mass is an insignificant fraction of the mass of a hydrogen atom ..."

Evidence for the existence of the nucleus

The Rutherford model of the atom

Ernest Rutherford (1871–1937) was a scientist who studied the atom at the start of the twentieth century. He worked with Hans Geiger, who is probably best known for developing the Geiger counter for measuring radiation. Geiger also worked with an undergraduate student called Ernest Marsden. Together they carried out a series of experiments that involved firing **alpha particles** at very thin gold foil. Alpha particles are positively charged particles given off by some radioactive substances. Geiger and Marsden's experiment is shown in Figure 26.4.

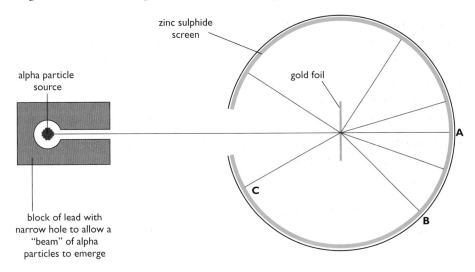

Figure 26.4 *Geiger and Marsden fired alpha particles at thin gold foil to see how they would be deflected.*

The zinc sulphide screen gives out tiny sparks of light, called **scintillations**, when hit by an alpha particle. Geiger and Marsden were able to see what happened to the alpha particles as they passed through the gold foil by noting where the sparks occurred on the screen.

Most of the alpha particles passed straight through the gold foil as if it wasn't there at all (A). Once in a while an alpha particle was knocked off course (B). A very small proportion (about 1 in 8000) actually seemed to bounce off the gold foil (C).

Rutherford studied these results. He realised that, as most of the alpha particles passed straight through the gold foil, most of each gold atom must be empty space. However, Rutherford knew that atoms *did* have mass, so they could not be *just* empty space. The rare event of a rebound meant that an alpha particle had run into something very massive. Rutherford realised that the mass must be concentrated in a very tiny volume at the centre of the atom, which he called the **nucleus** (the plural is **nuclei**). The deflections and rebounds were because the positive charges on the alpha particles were repelled by positive charges in the nuclei. The amount of deflection depends on a number of factors:

1 the *speed* of the alpha particle – the alpha particle is deflected less if it is travelling faster

2 the *nuclear charge* – if the nucleus is strongly positive, then the alpha particle will be more strongly repelled away from it.

3 *how close* the alpha particle gets to the positively charged nucleus (this is shown in Figure 26.5).

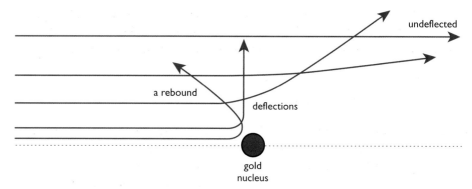

Figure 26.5 *Alpha particles passing very close to a gold atom nucleus are deflected more than those passing at a greater distance.*

Analysis of the results of Geiger and Marsden's experiment not only gave evidence for the existence of the nucleus but also allowed Rutherford to estimate the size of the nucleus (Figure 26.6).

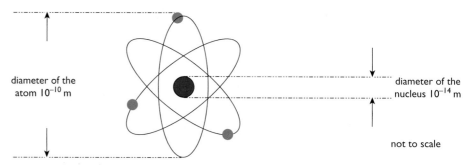

Figure 26.6 *Rutherford's model of the atom had a tiny, dense nucleus and electrons around the outside.*

Generating electricity using nuclear fuels

Uranium-235 is used as fuel in a nuclear reactor. It is used because its nuclei can be split by a neutron. The process of splitting an atom is called **fission**. Uranium-235 is called a **fissile** material because it goes through the splitting process easily. The fission process is shown in Figure 26.7.

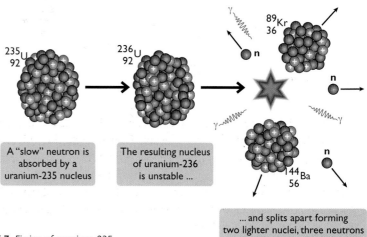

Figure 26.7 *Fission of uranium-235.*

In the fission reaction, a slow-moving neutron is absorbed by a nucleus of uranium-235.

The resulting nucleus of uranium-236 is unstable and splits apart. The fragments of this decay are the two **daughter** nuclei of barium-144 and krypton-89. The decay also produces gamma radiation and three more neutrons. The equation for this decay is:

$$^{236}_{92}U \rightarrow\ ^{144}_{56}Ba +\ ^{89}_{36}Kr + 3\ ^{1}_{0}n + \gamma\ radiation$$

The fission reaction produces a huge amount of energy. This is because some of the mass of the original uranium-236 nuclei is converted to energy. Most of the energy is carried away as the kinetic energy of the two lighter nuclei. Some is emitted as gamma radiation. The three neutrons produced by the fission may hit other nuclei of uranium-235, so causing the process to repeat, as shown in Figure 26.8. If one neutron from each fission causes one nearby uranium-235 to split, then the fission reaction will keep going. If more than one neutron from each fission causes fission in surrounding nuclei, then the reaction escalates – a bit like an avalanche.

A "slow" neutron is a low-energy neutron produced by a nuclear decay. Faster moving, more energetic neutrons do not cause fission.

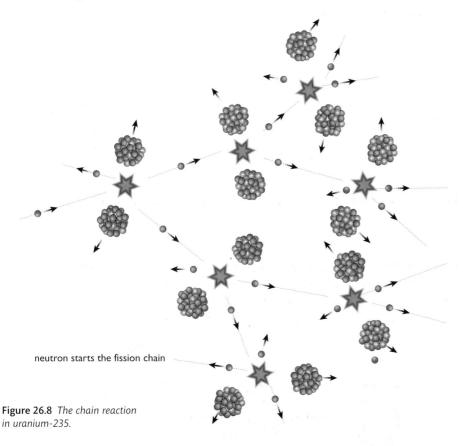

neutron starts the fission chain

Figure 26.8 *The chain reaction in uranium-235.*

This is called a **chain reaction**. If this reaction is allowed to take place in an uncontrolled way, the result is a nuclear explosion. This involves the sudden release of enormous amounts of heat energy and radiation. In a nuclear reactor the process is controlled so that the heat energy is released over a longer period of time. The heat produced in the **core** or heart of the reactor is used to heat water. The steam produced then drives turbines to turn generators. The basic parts of a nuclear reactor are shown in Figure 26.9.

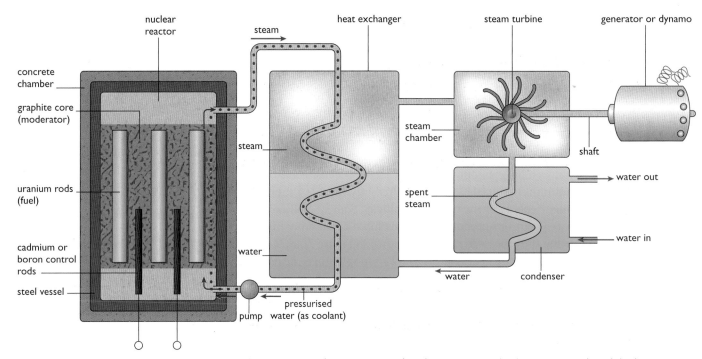

The following labels appear on the diagram:

nuclear reactor

heat exchanger

steam turbine

generator or dynamo

steam

concrete chamber

graphite core (moderator)

steam

steam chamber

shaft

uranium rods (fuel)

steam

spent steam

water out

cadmium or boron control rods

water

water in

steel vessel

water

condenser

pressurised water (as coolant)

pump

Figure 26.9 *A nuclear reactor controls a chain reaction so that heat energy is released slowly.*

The reactor core contains fuel rods of enriched uranium. Enriched uranium is uranium-238 with a higher proportion of uranium-235 than is found in natural reserves of uranium. Graphite is used as a moderator. The job of the **moderator** is to absorb some of the kinetic energy of the neutrons to slow them down. This is because slow neutrons are more easily absorbed by uranium-235. A neutron slowed in this way can start the fission process. In the nuclear reactor there are also **control rods**, made of boron or cadmium. These absorb the neutrons and take them out of the fission process completely. When the control rods are fully inserted into the core, the chain reaction is almost completely stopped and the rate of production of heat is low. As the control rods are withdrawn, the rate of fission increases producing heat at a greater rate.

The nuclear process in a reactor produces a variety of different types of radioactive material. Some have relatively short half-lives and decay rapidly. These soon become safe to handle and do not present problems of long-term storage. Other materials have extremely long half-lives. These will continue to produce dangerous levels of ionising radiation for thousands of years. These waste products present a serious problem for long-term storage. They are usually sealed in containers that are then buried deep underground. The sites for underground storage have to be carefully selected. The rock must be impermeable to water and the geology of the site must be stable – storing waste in earthquake zones or areas of volcanic activity would not be sensible.

Some reactors are designed to produce **plutonium**. Plutonium is a very radioactive artificial element. Small amounts of plutonium represent a serious health hazard. Plutonium is another fissile material. If a large enough mass of plutonium is brought together a chain reaction will start. Plutonium can be used in the production of nuclear weapons.

Nuclear power stations do not produce carbon dioxide or acidic gases as fossil fuel power stations do. This means that nuclear power does not contribute to global warming or acid rain. Only small amounts of uranium are needed for a chain reaction and the supply of nuclear fuel will last many hundreds of years – unlike some fossil fuels that could run out in the next fifty years.

You will need to be able to do the following:

✓ describe the results of Geiger and Marsden's experiments with gold foil and alpha particles

✓ describe Rutherford's model and how it can account for Geiger and Marsden's results

✓ describe the factors that affect the deflection of alpha particles by a nucleus

✓ describe how uranium-235 undergoes fission and how a chain reaction can occur

✓ explain what moderators and control rods are used for in nuclear power stations.

Questions

More questions on the structure of the atom can be found at the end of Section G on page 232.

1 Give one difference between Thomson's model of the atom and the Rutherford model.

2 *a)* Look at this diagram of Geiger and Marsden's apparatus. Write out the correct words for the labels A to E.

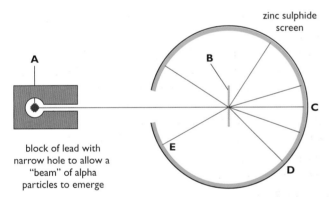

zinc sulphide
screen

A

block of lead with
narrow hole to allow a
"beam" of alpha
particles to emerge

B

C

E

D

b) What did the results of Geiger and Marsden's experiment reveal about the atom?

3 The diagram below shows the paths of several alpha particles travelling towards a gold nucleus.

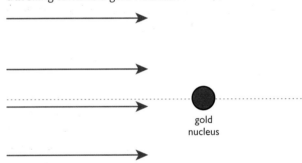

gold
nucleus

a) Copy and complete the diagram showing likely paths for the alpha particles as they continue towards the nucleus.

b) How would your diagram have differed if the particles had:

i) been travelling faster

ii) had only half as much electric charge?

4 *a)* Uranium-235 is a *fissile* material. What does this mean?

b) If there is a large enough mass of uranium-235, it may cause a chain reaction. (This is called the *critical mass* for the isotope.)

i) What is a chain reaction?

ii) Why does a chain reaction depend on how much of the fissile material there is in one piece?

5 List two advantages and two disadvantages of nuclear fission as a way of producing energy.

1 Copy and complete the following passage about the structure of the atom, filling in the spaces.

The atom is made up of three basic particles: _____ , which orbit the central core of the atom, and _____ and _____ , which together make up the central core. The central core is called the _____ of the atom, and the two types of particles in the central core are collectively called _____ .

The atom is electrically neutral because it has equal numbers of _____ and _____ .

Total 7 marks

2 Geiger and Marsden conducted an experiment that involved firing alpha particles at a thin sheet of gold foil.

a) What are alpha particles? *(2 marks)*

b) Describe, with the aid of a labelled diagram, the apparatus that Geiger and Marsden used in their experiment. *(4 marks)*

c) Describe the results that they obtained from their experiment and the conclusions that Rutherford drew from them. *(4 marks)*

d) Before this experiment, scientists had a different model of the atom. It was sometimes referred to as the "plum pudding" model. Describe this model. *(2 marks)*

Total 12 marks

3 Two students decide to use some six-sided dice to model radioactive decay. They throw the dice and remove all those that come up "6" after each throw.

(Assume that the dice are fair – that is, equally likely to come up with any number.)

a) One student decides to use 40 dice and the other uses 200. Which student is likely to produce the best model? Explain your answer. *(2 marks)*

b) What proportion of the dice are, on average, likely to be removed after each throw? *(1 mark)*

c) How could the model be altered to simulate a more rapid decay process? *(2 marks)*

Total 5 marks

4 The notation for the most abundant isotope of carbon is:

$^{12}_{6}C$

a) Explain what the numbers 12 and 6 in this notation mean. *(4 marks)*

b) Explain the term isotope. *(4 marks)*

c) Give an example of another isotope of carbon. You should write down the notation for the isotope and explain how it differs from the usual or most abundant isotope. *(4 marks)*

d) Explain the process of radiocarbon dating, used to estimate the age of organic material. *(4 marks)*

Total 16 marks

5 *a)* Describe how you would measure the half-life of a radioactive isotope, assuming the half-life can be measured in minutes (rather than hours or years, for example). You should mention the apparatus you would use, the measurements that you would need to take and any safety precautions you must follow. *(6 marks)*

b) The results of such an experiment are shown in the graph below.

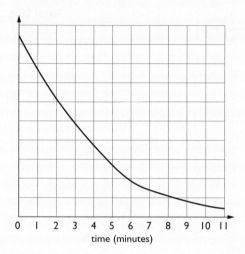

time (minutes)

i) What units should be marked on the vertical scale? *(1 mark)*

ii) Copy the graph, and show how you would use it to measure the half-life of the isotope. *(3 marks)*

iii) What is the half-life of the isotope in minutes? *(2 marks)*

c) In another experiment a student has a 200μg sample of a radioactive isotope that has a half-life of 10 minutes. How much of the sample will remain after half an hour? (Show how you calculated your answer.) *(3 marks)*

Total 15 marks

6 Radioactive isotopes are used in the treatment and diagnosis of certain illnesses. The type of isotope chosen will depend on whether the purpose is diagnosis or treatment of the illness. The atomic number of the isotope is also a factor that influences the choice.

  a) What type of isotope is likely to be used for treatment of a cancer? Give reasons for your answer. *(3 marks)*

  b) What type of isotope is likely to be chosen for diagnosis? Give reasons for your choice. *(4 marks)*

  c) A radioisotope of iodine is sometimes used in the treatment of thyroid cancer. Why is iodine used in preference to other isotopes with similar qualities? *(3 marks)*

  Total 10 marks

7 Copy and complete the following nuclear equations by filling in the boxes.

  a)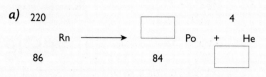

  $$^{220}_{86}\text{Rn} \longrightarrow \boxed{} \,^{}_{84}\text{Po} + \,^{4}\text{He}\,\boxed{}$$

  (2 marks)

  b)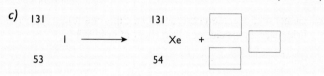

  $$\boxed{}\,^{}_{91}\text{Pa} \longrightarrow \,^{234}_{92}\text{U} + \,^{0}\text{e}\,\boxed{}$$

  (2 marks)

  c)

  $$^{131}_{53}\text{I} \longrightarrow \,^{131}_{54}\text{Xe} + \boxed{}\,\boxed{}$$

  (3 marks)

  d)

  $$^{228}_{90}\text{Th} \longrightarrow \boxed{}\,\text{Ra} + \boxed{}\,\text{He}$$

  (3 marks)

  Total 10 marks

Appendix A: Experimental and Investigative Skills

Your investigative skills will be tested by some of the questions in your examinations. This chapter summarises some of the skills you may be asked about.

The examination papers will test your ability to do some of these things:

- describe the method for an investigation
- take measurements
- record results in tables
- plot graphs to show results
- analyse results
- evaluate data.

You will learn these skills during practical work throughout your course. This Appendix provides some reminders of the kinds of skills you need. The main chapters in this book contain descriptions of various experiments and it might be helpful to look back at these as well.

Method

The **method** for a practical investigation is a list of instructions for carrying out the investigation. In an exam you may be given a list of apparatus and asked to describe how to use it to investigate a particular question. When you are writing a method, it is important to describe all the steps in the correct order. The person marking the exam paper cannot *watch* you doing the experiment – if you do not describe a step they will assume you have forgotten about it.

Reliable evidence

In many of the investigations you have carried out, you will have been asked to repeat readings and use a mean value when plotting a graph or writing your conclusion. By repeating results you can find out how reliable your evidence is (see more on this on page 240), and spot any mistakes. Your method should explain that you will repeat each measurement, and that you will discard any anomalous results (ones that do not fit the pattern) before finding a mean value. You should also explain why you would do this.

For some experiments you do not need to take repeat measurements of the same thing. For example, you might be finding out which type of insulation works best by measuring the temperature of hot water in insulated beakers. In this case, you can measure the temperature of the water every minute for 10 or 20 minutes, and plot a line graph of temperature against time. You will be able to spot any anomalous results because they will not lie on the line formed by most of your readings. You do not need to repeat the whole experiment several times. However you do need to explain this in your method – the person marking your paper will not just assume you understand why drawing a graph like this is useful.

Safety precautions

You may also be asked about safety precautions you would take when carrying out an investigation. The safety precautions depend on the type of investigation, but these are some of the things you should think about:

- if you are using weights, make sure they cannot fall and land on your feet
- make sure any clamp stands are fastened to the bench so they cannot overbalance
- if you are stretching wires or other objects that might break and spring back, wear eye protection
- if you are using electricity, make sure you are using a low-voltage source
- if you are using water, make sure that any spills are mopped up so you do not slip
- if you are projecting (firing) an object such as a ball bearing or an arrow make sure that no one is in the area and that an adequate absorbent target is in place
- if you are describing the use of radioactive materials make sure you know how they should be handled and stored safely
- if you are timing the descent of an object such as a model parachute make sure that any chairs or other furniture are out of the way.

Remember that most investigations and practicals are quite safe, and so **safety precautions** can also refer to care of the apparatus. For example:

- not stretching a spring too far so that it goes beyond its elastic limit
- if you are using electricity to heat something, such as fuse wire, use a heatproof mat to protect the bench and do not touch hot wires.

Measurements

Units

Measurements are a key part of investigations, but they do not mean anything unless you also give the units. A length of "15" could mean 15 mm, 15 cm, 15 m, or even 15 km!

Recording results

Results should always be recorded in a table. The factor that you change in an experiment usually goes in the first column.

This table shows the results for an experiment to investigate how the current changes when you change the length of a piece of wire in a circuit.

This is what you are changing in the experiment, so it goes in the first column.

This is what you will be measuring.

Always put the units in.

These are the lengths of wire you will be testing.

Use a ruler when you draw straight lines.

Length of wire (cm)	Current (A)
10	
20	
30	
40	
50	

Sometimes you need to record measurements in more than one situation. If you wanted to record current in a hot wire and a cold one, your results table might look like this:

This heading applies to both the columns underneath it.

Length of wire (cm)	Current (A)	
	Hot wire	Cold wire
10		
20		
30		
40		
50		

Graphs

Graphs are a very useful way of presenting results. A graph allows you to find patterns in results and also helps you to spot any results that may not fit the pattern. The graph below shows the results of an experiment to find the length of a spring with different weights on it.

Plot the points with small, neat crosses.

The numbers must be evenly spaced.

Graphs do not always start at zero.

Title

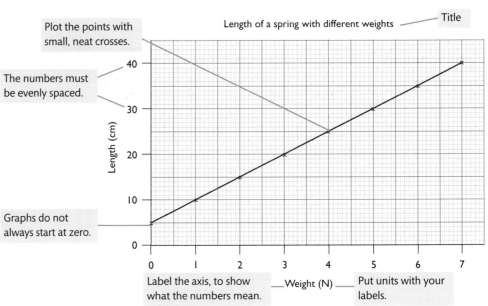

Length of a spring with different weights

Label the axis, to show what the numbers mean.

Weight (N)

Put units with your labels.

You should normally draw a straight line on a graph that goes through as many points as possible. This is called a line of best fit.

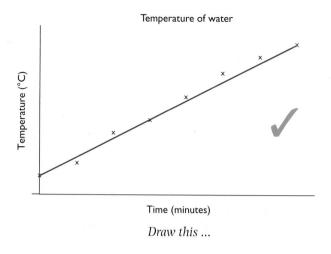

Draw this ...

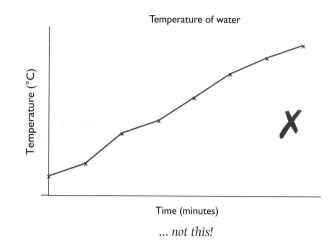

... not this!

However, a straight line is not always the best way of joining the points. You do need to think about what the results are showing you.

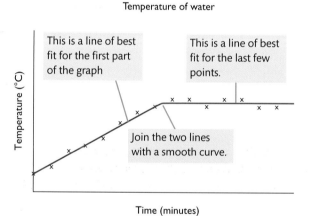

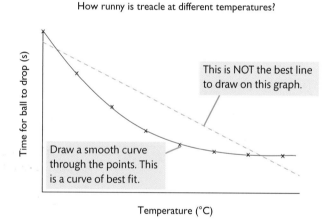

You can use a graph to spot mistakes – if all of your results except one lie close to either a straight line or a smooth curve, that result is likely to be wrong. You may have made a mistake when taking the measurement, or you may have written it down incorrectly or incorrectly calculated a derived quantity such as acceleration. You should try to work out why that result is wrong, so that you can suggest improvements to your method to improve the accuray of your results.

Sketch graphs

You may sometimes be asked to sketch a graph to show the results. A sketch graph shows the relationship between two variables without showing numbers. For example, you might be asked to sketch a graph to show what happens to the current in a wire when you increase the voltage. Your graph might look like the one below.

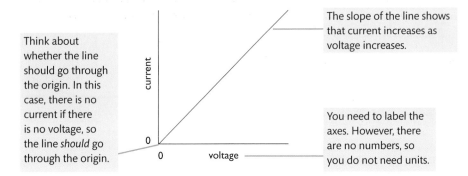

Think about whether the line should go through the origin. In this case, there is no current if there is no voltage, so the line *should* go through the origin.

The slope of the line shows that current increases as voltage increases.

You need to label the axes. However, there are no numbers, so you do not need units.

You may sometimes need to include units on a sketch graph, if more than one possible scale could be used. For example, if you were asked to sketch a graph to show how the pressure of a fixed volume of gas varies with temperature, either of these graphs would be correct.

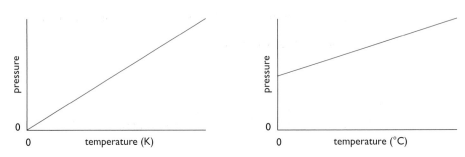

Analysing results

In some investigations you may have to carry out calculations on your results. For example, if you were investigating how the resistance of a wire depended on its length you would need to calculate the resistance from current and voltage measurements. When you show the results of your calculations, you should always give your result to an appropriate number of significant figures. The following examples should make this clear.

The current and voltage in the first table are both measured to two significant figures (2 sf). In this case, it means that the voltage is accurate to the nearest 0.1 V and the current is accurate to the nearest 0.01 A. When you divide the voltage by the current to get the resistance, you get numbers with lots of decimal places. If you just write down the whole answer as displayed on your calculator, this implies that the answer is more accurate than it is. For example, the last column in the table implies that the resistance value is accurate to the nearest 0.000 000 01 Ω – and this is obviously not the case!

Voltage (V)	Current (A)	Resistance (Ω)
2.0	0.24	8.33333333
4.0	0.51	7.84313725
6.0	0.85	7.05882353

The results of calculations should be given to the same number of significant figures as in the measurements used to calculate them. If your answer has more significant figures, then you need to round your answer. The table below is a better way of presenting these results.

Voltage (V)	Current (A)	Resistance (Ω)
2.0	0.24	8.3
4.0	0.51	7.8
6.0	0.85	7.1

Writing a conclusion

You may be asked to write a conclusion for a set of results, or to comment on a conclusion that is given.

For example, this graph shows the results of an experiment to test different insulating materials. The student covered two boiling tubes of water in different materials and measured the temperature every minute.

This is the conclusion the student wrote for the insulating materials investigation:

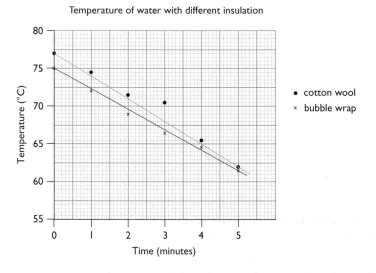

The water in the tube covered in cotton wool cooled from 77°C to 62°C, which is 15°C. The water in the tube covered in bubble wrap cooled from 75°C to 61.5°C, which is 13.5°C. The bubble wrap kept the water warmer, so it is the best insulator.

This conclusion is correct, but it is not the best conclusion that can be drawn from these results. The point about drawing a straight line through the points on a graph is that it evens out any errors in measurements. A better way to consider these results is to look at the lines on the graph – the line for cotton wool is steeper, showing that the water in this tube is cooling down faster than the water in the tube covered in bubble wrap.

You may also be asked to compare a conclusion with a prediction made before the investigation. Remember to read what the prediction said, and to clearly say whether or not you think the prediction has been shown to be correct. You should also explain *why* you think this.

Evaluation

Evaluation means deciding how accurate and reliable your results are. In the examination, you may be given a set of results and asked to comment on them.

You may be asked to identify any results that do not fit the overall pattern. In the example above, the result for cotton wool at three minutes is a significant distance from the line drawn through the other points, so it is possible that a mistake was made when reading this temperature.

You may be asked to comment on how precise or reliable the evidence is, or how to improve the accuracy or reliability of the results.

Precision

"Precise" means that things have been measured as accurately as possible. Particularly where the quantities being measured are small, the measurements should be taken with the most accurate equipment possible. For example, if the experiment described involved measuring very small currents, you might suggest that the results could have been more precise if a milliammeter had been used instead of an ammeter. Just saying something like "Take more care with the measurements" will *not* gain any marks!

The accuracy of measurements can be quite poor if human reaction times are involved. For example, if someone is timing how long it takes for a pendulum to complete one swing, they need to start and stop the stopclock as they see the pendulum passing a particular point on its swing. You could suggest two different ways to improve the accuracy of this measurement:

- use a light gate and datalogger to measure the time – this would remove any errors due to human reaction time
- measure the time it takes the pendulum to complete 10 swings, and then divide the total time by 10 to find the time for one swing. There may still be an error due to human reaction time here, but the error will be spread out over many swings, so the error on the time for one swing will be much smaller.

Reliability

"Reliable" results mean that if the measurements are repeated, the same result should be obtained. You can see how reliable a set of results are by comparing three or more measurements. If the results are close to each other, then the evidence is probably reliable.

The graph of the results of the insulation experiment shows a different way of checking reliability. In this investigation only one set of results was taken for the each type of insulation. However, because the results can be plotted on a line graph, you can use the closeness of the points to the line of best fit on the graph to judge the reliability. In this case, most of the results look reliable, because they are close to the lines of best fit. (Obviously, the point for the cotton wool insulation at 3 minutes is *not* a reliable result as it lies some way from the line.)

Maximising your success

The very best way of revising for the exam at the end of your course is to work through past papers set by your examiners – looking especially at the most recent ones. You need to check your answers against the published mark schemes and against the comments in the Examiners' Reports. The Examiners' Reports are particularly useful for these practically-based questions, as what they are looking for isn't always obvious.

This book was written for the new Edexcel IGCSE Physics specification (syllabus) to be examined for the first time in 2011, and so in the early stages there will be a shortage of past papers tied directly to the new specification. In that case, you will have to look instead at the questions set in similar exams in the past.

In the new specification, practically-based questions are mixed up with more theoretical ones in the same exam papers. Previously, there was a separate paper in which all the practical questions were found. You will find a set of these together with mark schemes and Examiners' Reports on the CD accompanying this book.

On the website accompanying this book, you will find advice about how to get hold of the same sort of material after May 2011 (the first exam for the new specification) as soon as it is available.

Appendix B: Electrical Circuit Symbols

Description	Symbol
conductors crossing with no connection	
junction of conductors	
open switch	
closed switch	
open push switch	
closed push switch	
cell	
battery of cells	
power supply	(dc) or (ac)
transformer	
ammeter	A
milliammeter	mA
voltmeter	V
fixed resistor	
variable resistor	

Description	Symbol
heater	
thermistor	
light-dependent resistor (LDR)	
relay	
diode	
light-emitting diode (LED)	
lamp	
loudspeaker	
microphone	
electric bell	
earth or ground	
motor	M
generator	G
fuse/circuit breaker	

Appendix C: Formulae and Relationships

The formulae and relationships listed below will not be provided for you in exams, so you will need to remember them. You may also need to rearrange some of these formulae in an exam.

1 The relationships between average speed, distance and time:

$$\text{average speed} = \frac{\text{distance}}{\text{time}}$$

2 The relationships between force, mass and acceleration and change in velocity:

$$\text{force} = \text{mass} \times \text{acceleration}$$

$$\text{acceleration} = \frac{\text{change in velocity}}{\text{time taken}}$$

3 The relationship between momentum, mass and velocity:

$$\text{momentum} = \text{mass} \times \text{velocity}$$

4 The relationship between density, mass and volume:

$$\text{density} = \frac{\text{mass}}{\text{volume}}$$

5 The relationship between energy transferred and efficiency:

$$\text{efficiency} = \frac{\text{useful energy output from the system}}{\text{total energy input to the system}} \times 100\%$$

6 The relationship between force, distance and work:

$$\text{work done} = \text{force} \times \text{distance moved in direction of force}$$

7 The energy relationships:

$$\text{energy transferred} = \text{work done}$$

$$\text{kinetic energy} = \tfrac{1}{2} \times \text{mass} \times \text{speed}^2$$

$$\begin{array}{c}\text{change in gravitational} \\ \text{potential energy}\end{array} = \text{mass} \times \begin{array}{c}\text{gravitational} \\ \text{field strength}\end{array} \times \begin{array}{c}\text{change} \\ \text{in height}\end{array}$$

8 The relationship between mass, weight and gravitational field strength:

$$\text{weight} = \text{mass} \times \text{gravitational field strength}$$

9 The relationship between an applied force, the area over which it acts and the resulting pressure:

$$\text{pressure} = \frac{\text{force}}{\text{area}}$$

10 The relationship between the moment of a force and its distance from the pivot:

moment = force × perpendicular distance from pivot

11 The relationships between charge, current, voltage, resistance and electrical power:

charge = current × time

voltage = current × resistance

electrical power = voltage × current

12 The relationship between wave speed, frequency and wavelength:

wave speed = frequency × wavelength

13 The relationship between the power put into a transformer and the power it produces:

input power = output power

14 The relationships between voltage, power and the turns ratio for a transformer:

$$\frac{\text{input (primary) voltage}}{\text{output (secondary) voltage}} = \frac{\text{primary turns}}{\text{secondary turns}}$$

$$\frac{V_p}{V_s} = \frac{n_p}{n_s}$$

15 The relationship between refractive index, angle of incidence and angle of refraction:

$$n = \frac{\sin i}{\sin r}$$

16 The relationship between refractive index and critical angle:

$$\sin c = \frac{1}{n}$$

17 The relationship for pressure difference:

pressure difference = height × density × g

$$p = h\rho g$$

Appendix D: Physical Quantities and Units

Fundamental physical quantities

Physical quantity	Unit(s)
length	metre (m)
	kilometre (km)
	centimetre (cm)
	millimetre (mm)
mass	kilogram (kg)
	gram (g)
	milligram (mg)
time	second (s)
	millisecond (ms)
temperature	degrees Celsius (°C)
	kelvin (K)
current	ampere or amp (A)
	milliampere or milliamp (mA)

Derived quantities and units

Physical quantity	Unit(s)
acceleration	m/s^2
area	cm^2
	m^2
density	kg/m^3
	g/cm^3
electrical charge	coulomb (C)
electrical current	ampere (A)
energy (work)	joule (J)
	kilojoule (kJ)
	megajoule (MJ)
frequency	hertz (Hz)
	kilohertz (kHz)
force	newton (N)
gravitational field strength	N/kg
moment of a force	Nm
	Ncm
momentum	kg m/s
potential difference (voltage)	volt (V)
	millivolt (mV)
power	watt (W)
	kilowatt (kW)
	megawatt (MW)
pressure	pascal (Pa or N/m^2)
	N/cm^2
radioactivity	becquerel (Bq)
resistance	ohm (Ω)
speed/velocity	m/s
	km/h
volume	cm^3
	m^3
	litre (l)
	millilitre (ml)

Index